# Drummers
# On
# Drumming

"[This Book] is an absolute gem—an easy-access resource of inspiration for both drummers and non-musicians alike. The depth here is next-level, pushing you to dive into each referenced record with fresh ears or a new perspective. Ben really hit it out of the park with this one."

— **Butch Vig**, iconic producer, drummer

"Reading the interviews in [*Drummers on Drumming*] makes a great case for the format of print vs. videos, podcasts, or blogs. It brings us back to carefully gathered, intimate insight and a deeper sense of connection that feels like sitting at a round table sharing stories with drumming colleagues. Well done, Ben!"

— **Jojo Mayer**, pioneering drummer, educator, band leader

"A beautiful tribute to the drumming community, this book showcases the many paths and stories that lead us to our shared love of drumming. Drummers, with their unique ability to unite and inspire, are truly remarkable."

— **Jared Falk**, founder of *Drumeo*, renowned educator

"*Drummers on Drumming* is a unique book that offers readers bite-sized inspiration through interviews with dozens of drummers, ranging from world-famous musicians to up-and-coming performers, industry experts, and teachers. Ben's eclectic mix of interview subjects, combined with his distinctive approach of breaking down each section into tracks that inspired each drummer, makes this book a fresh and engaging way to reignite your love for the instrument. It's a great book that you can open to any page and feel instantly inspired. Well done, Ben!"

— **Bart van der Zee**, host of *Drum History Podcast*

"If you are interested in where drummers draw inspiration from, as I am, Ben's book is chock full ideas from great players."

— **John Riley**, legendary drummer, educator, author of
*The Art of Bop Drumming, Beyond Bop Drumming,*
*The Jazz Drummer's Workshop, The Master Drummer DVD*

iii

"Ben Hilzinger did a fantastic job putting this book together. I had a ton of fun talking to him on the podcast and have thoroughly enjoyed going through such a wide array of drummers' experiences... Big Fat Snare Drum also makes excellent products, just saying..."

- **Ilan Rubin**, dynamic drummer, composer, band leader

"What a very cool and interesting concept for a book! It's so insightful to read about some of these great drummers' influences and discover the records that have inspired them and have helped them develop into the players they have become. I've even started making a playlist so I can dig in deeper and hear some of the music that I may have not been aware of previously... Congrats Ben and thank you for a fascinating and fantastic read!"

- **Stanton Moore**, groove-driven drummer, educator, founder of
*Stanton Moore Drum Academy*

"I'm so glad that Ben has reworked his incredible podcast into book form with *Drummers on Drumming*. I've discovered tons of new music (and drummers) to check out from these fun and insightful interviews. Honored to be a part of it!"

- **Mike Dawson**, articulate drummer, Chief Creative Officer for
*Drum Factory Direct*

"Great drummers are always drum nerds, always. Ask a drummer about their favorite drummers, and get ready to put the kettle on. This book is all that and more. How could anyone who plays the drums or is even vaguely interested in the art and science of drumming put it down? So much to learn, so much to argue about! "

- **Mike Edison**, drummer and author of
*Sympathy for the Drummer: Why Charlie Watts Matters*

"When Ben asked me to be a guest on the show and talk about 5 records that influenced me, I thought that was a great idea, but it was also extremely daunting! How was I going to pick only 5 albums? Well, I managed to figure it out, and so did all of these other great drummers and people. It's so important to know the lineage of influences when you want to be serious about art or music, and what an easy/fun way to do it!"

- **Dave Elitch**, revered drummer/educator

"...[This Book] is colloquial, engaging, yet quite comprehensive... One aspect of the book that I truly enjoyed was the brevity of many of the drummers' stories. I could read a drummer's words while waiting for my coffee to brew, for my clothes to come out of the dryer, or just before going to bed... There is a brotherhood/sisterhood among drummers and I felt this connection strongly while reading what they wanted me to know. A must read for those who love drums, drumming and drummers!

- **Bernie Schallehn**, drummer/percussionist,
Former columnist and contributing writer with
*Modern Drummer* magazine, author of *Mind Matters:
Overcoming Common Mental Barriers in Drumming*

"Ben has put to pen an extremely unique and fast reading compilation of responses from many of the drummers he's interviewed... Fascinating, and even inspirational, this book is a must in the library of any student or professional player interested in learning about experiences that influenced [these drummers] in their approach to playing the instrument. Once started, it's a hard book to put down."

- **Joel Rothman**, drummer author of almost
100 drum method books

# Drummers On Drumming

*The Stories and Records That
Shaped Their Sound*

# Ben Hilzinger

**in association with Big Fat Snare Drum**

# Acknowledgments

Thank you to all the incredible drummers who made this book a reality. A special shoutout to my partner-in-crime, Kris Mazzarisi of Big Fat Snare Drum, for his unwavering guidance, support, and inspiration. And, of course, a wry salute to my ever-present companions — crippling anxiety and existential dread — for keeping me motivated to see this through. Cheers

# Introduction

This book brings together highlights from my conversations with some of the world's top drummers.

Before we dive in, let me introduce myself. I'm Ben Hilzinger, the host of *Drummers on Drumming*, a podcast presented in association with Big Fat Snare Drum. In a segment called *Big Fat Five*, I talk with my favorite drummers about the five records or experiences that have profoundly shaped their approach to the instrument.

After hundreds of episodes and countless hours of conversations, I've gathered some of the most insightful responses and compiled them here. If any drummer's selections resonate with you, you can explore further by listening to their full podcast episode, which typically runs about an hour.

Lastly, this book isn't meant to be read in any particular order, though you're welcome to go chronologically if you prefer. Think of it as a wellspring of inspiration to revisit whenever you need a creative boost. By exploring the influences that shaped the musicians you admire, you'll find more clarity in discovering and refining your own unique style. Here's to your musical journey!

# Contents

# Jason McGerr

*"...embrace silence if it makes a song better."*

J ason McGerr is a highly regarded drummer, best known for his work with the acclaimed indie rock band, Death Cab for Cutie. Joining the band in 2003, McGerr's inventive drumming and innovative style have been integral to the band's sound, contributing to several critically acclaimed albums including *Plans* and *Narrow Stairs*. Here are Jason's choices…

---

### Talk Talk, *Laughing Stock* (1991), "Ascension Day"
### Drummer - Lee Harris

During my junior year of high school, I got a weekly gig at a small club with a group of musicians who were far more experienced than me. They introduced me to a ton of music I'd yet to discover, much of which was shared when we'd hang out. One day, the pianist put on some Talk Talk, but he didn't start with the hits; instead, he went straight to the last record they made, *Laughing Stock*. It was some of the most experimental and moody stuff I'd heard then. Only three of the six tracks had a traditional kit, but the second I heard drummer Lee Harris' hypnotic feel, sound, and phrasing on "Ascension Day," I freaked out and redirected my playing goals.

His washy ride, the room sound, a wide open, warm bass drum, and machine-like rim shot, or however he's getting the snare to ring out like that, is so rad. I'm guessing it's a thinner stick smacking an off-center rim shot, almost like a timbale with snare wires, occasionally with variation in the sound itself, then digging into the cymbals with the dynamic shifts in dissonant electric guitar. Everything about the track just grabbed me. I didn't notice the song was in 7/4 for months, or I didn't bother to overthink it. His placement of the backbeat, equally on "beat 3" and "& of 6," made it not feel like an odd meter! I was in love with the whole vibe of the record. It's a stunning and unconventional collection of songs that never gets old to me. Still, "Ascension Day" was undeniably one of the biggest and boldest arrows of direction for me to follow.

## CAN, *Tago Mago* [1971], "Mushroom"
**Drummer** - Jaki Liebezeit

When I first moved to Seattle, I started working in the drum shop at American Music, which is still there today. In between shop hours, I was taking on a few students, and one of the first was a drummer named Mike Williamson, who played in a Seattle band called Sage. He gave me a mix tape with several artists I'd never heard of. One band that particularly resonated with me was CAN, a '70s prog rock band from Germany whose records were still relatively obscure in the mid-90s. The first song on that mix tape was "Mushroom" from their album *Tago Mago*. Once more, I was struck by how infectious a drum sound could be, not to mention the attitude behind the kit. Jaki Liebezeit had such a sick feeling. You could always tell it was him. He had several different influences—a stew of European jazz and whatever music trickled in from overseas.

2

The most remarkable thing about Jaki's sound was that it seemed a bit broken and lo-fi. If you told me his ride cymbal was up for sale, I would pay almost anything for it, even if it was cracked (which I suspect). His kick and snare were both big and small sounding. It had as much to do with production as it did his approach or how he hit, tuned, or didn't tune, concert toms, the whole sha-bang. He and whoever engineered his drums knew what they were doing and were ahead of their time. Also..... Remember that I was 19 years old and working in a music store in Seattle in 1994. Think about that time and place and how much of the region's music sounded similar. I loved Nirvana, Pearl Jam, Soundgarden, and Mudhoney.... But CAN couldn't have been more cleansing and inspiring at that moment. I don't know if they would have meant as much if I'd heard their music five years before or five years later, but the right time and place means everything.

## Led Zeppelin, *Led Zeppelin IV* [1971], "Four Sticks"
### Drummer - John Bonham

John Bonham. Like, just put a period there.

When I was 14, in a tiny town with one FM radio station and two AM radio stations under the same roof, we had minimal access to any cool music that wasn't pre-programmed '80s pop already on said FM radio. So when I visited a friend with two older brothers who worked on their cars and trucks in a barn blasting Led Zeppelin, I entered the light. "Stairway to Heaven" might have been the first thing I recognized from some "Rock Block" on the radio, but the big brothers had the whole catalog on repeat, with *Zeppelin IV* on more than any other album.

For my next birthday, even without a car to work on, I also asked for the Zeppelin catalog and got it. There's enough Bonham curriculum to study for a lifetime. It takes time to pick a favorite or multiple. But the song "Four Sticks," with four sticks actually being played, two sticks per hand, audibly clicking, grooving in 5/4, out of the gates, seamlessly transitioning into 6/8 for the chorus and then back to 5/4, with that interplay between the toms and kick....???? I mean, who does that, or ever did that before?!?! I may be unaware if there is somebody John Bonham copied, but I'm guessing not. He left us the most extensive footprint in rock drumming history, and this song is a critical lesson on thinking outside the box. His sound is instantly known, and he has so many devout followers. Even I began with Ludwig and Paiste as my first two real endorsements...complete with a 26" bass drum.

---

### Soundgarden, *Badmotorfinger* [1991], "Jesus Christ Pose"
### **Drummer** - Matt Cameron

I mentioned Soundgarden because I love them, the whole band, and every record. *Badmotorfinger*, however, was played over and over again. Matt Cameron was my drum hero at a critical time of my life — when I had to decide what to do after graduating from high school because that's when I planned to move away from home and live on my own. The question was: Do I move to Seattle and make a go of this music thing? Matt Cameron is from Seattle; he can make a living playing drums there, so maybe I can, too?

Growing up 90 miles north of Seattle during the peak of the '90s grunge explosion made it seem possible to be in a band and get signed. I'd been playing long enough to know who the best bands and musicians were, including the parts they played. Soundgarden had the best

4

singer, the best drummer, the most angular and rocking guitar player, and a super-glue tough bass player to fill out the rhythm section. Even more, they all glued each other together and wrote amazing and often unpredictable songs with an incredible amount of hooks. "Jesus Christ Pose" is a peak example of all these elements working exceptionally well. Matt is full-throttle driving this song. There's so much command and intent in his sound and feel; everything is locked. I don't know whether Kim Thayil wrote the guitar riff first or if Matt started with the tom-fill groove, but it's nonstop rhythmic intoxication to get you pumped. The song would've never had the same magic if Matt had played a standard backbeat. He's brilliant, continually drawing lines through complicated arrangements, making them both accessible and inspiring.

Gregg Keplinger told me once, while he was teching for Matt, that a wall of sound comes from his kit if you're near it. Conceptually, I love that idea. And when certain songs call for that, I put on my best "Matt Hat."

## John Hopkins, *Immunity* [2013], "Abandon Window"

So many more songs, drummers, and genres have inspired me and helped shape my approach to composing parts. But my final, Big Fat Fifth song, is a bit of a curve ball. I've talked about some drumming heroes, but many of us holding sticks still need to remember to cultivate patience and choose not to play anything at all—to embrace silence if it makes a song better.

Not to get all Zen, but consider the idea of exhaustion. As in too much practice, too much playing. Everybody notices that if we rip out too many fills in a song, it's tiring to hear. There might be a point when you stop

5

making gains in your practice space, the point of diminishing returns, or when you need a break from a gig, touring, and the people you work with. I've found a lot of answers in not playing. Listening to music without drums is good for me, as it means not having to think about drums or rhythm. It's like unloading a weighted backpack or a brain full of ideas to relieve a mysterious headache. I begin to feel, hear, and see more of an open landscape of possibilities, which always leads to a fresh and inspired approach.

Jon Hopkins once considered a career as a classical pianist. Still, he gravitated towards electronic music, probably because he craved the freedom it offered, compared to the formality and pressure of classical performance. His songs are filled with thick synths, modulation, and programming in the spirit of IDM, glitch, and house. But he's also recorded some beautifully pastoral pieces that are equally arresting and thought-provoking. I've been listening to more music like this for the above reasons—songs that don't need drums, to help reset and wipe clean my catalog of rhythmic go-to patterns, and to quiet the constant noise of ideas. "Abandon Window" from Hopkins' *Immunity* album puts me in the room where Jon is playing piano. He's capable of playing more, but he chooses not to. He's patient and selective. I hear years of technical prowess held back, the resonant wood of the piano and the floor beneath it, memories, hardships, and accomplishments, emoted through his hands, feet, and body while growing ambiance and tension evolve into increasing dynamic and tonal range. Here, I am a listener, not a player, a drummer, or even a thinker.

*HONORABLE MENTION:*

Sonny Rollins, *East Broadway Rundown* [1966]

## "East Broadway Rundown"
## **Drummer** - Elvin Jones

Elvin Jones is/was one of the heaviest drummers on earth. Everything he's ever played is pure gold. His deep musical connection, wildly free approach, swing, and dynamic range left me numb and frozen the first and only time I saw him live. The man seemed to be sitting in outer space while reaching down to make his drums sound incredible. Regardless, he left his body and took me with him.

If I could only have one jazz record, it would be John Coltrane's *A Love Supreme*. But for Elvin fans looking beyond those golden Coltrane years, Sonny Rollins' *East Broadway Rundown* is my favorite, especially the title track. With one of the most compelling drum solos I've ever heard, followed by the warm wind of Jimmy Garrison's pulsing one-note on his upright bass and Elvin's interplay (that moment in the song at 10:40), the recording showcases what every rhythm section should aspire to be. This song reminds me to play in the same space as my bass player, with complete trust and appreciation for our instruments' connection.

# Butch Vig

*"I quickly realized I could not play like Keith Moon—no one could..."*

**B**utch Vig is universally acknowledged as one of the premier producers in rock history having worked on iconic albums like Nirvana's *Nevermind,* Smashing Pumpkins' *Gish* and *Siamese Dream,* and Sonic Youth's *Dirty.* Beyond his impressive production credits, Butch is an exceptional drummer, demonstrated through his work with Spooner, Fire Town, and Garbage. And be sure to check out his transatlantic musical alliance with UK DJ James Grillo and Bristol UK Producer Andy Jenks, called 5 Billion In Diamonds. Here are Butch's choices…

The Who, *Who's Next* [1971], "Behind Blue Eyes"
**Drummer** - Keith Moon

After seeing Keith Moon on a TV show, I quit piano in 6th grade and begged my parents for a drum set. They bought me a cheap Sears kit for Christmas, but I was lucky to eventually inherit my cousin Carl's "Ringo" Ludwig kit. I quickly realized I could not play like Keith Moon—no one could; he was a unique, wild beast behind the drums. I could, however, play like Ringo and Charlie Watts, the drummers I emulated early on.

## Roxy Music, *Country Life* [1974], "Out Of The Blue"
**Drummer** - Paul Thompson

I love all the Roxy Music albums. They are one of my fave bands, and I was the President of the Roxy Music Fan Club in Madison (we only had seven members). *Country Life* is my favorite album, as I love the songwriting and production. It continues to inspire me as a drummer and producer. Paul Thompson's drumming is a huge part of that album—powerful and tasteful; his performances fit into the arrangements perfectly.

## Ramones, *Ramones* [1976], "Beat On The Brat"
**Drummer** - Tommy Ramone

This is the best punk album ever! The Ramones greatly influenced the punk/new wave movement in the late '70s. It's all perfect, hooky two-minute pop songs that are tight as hell, and Tommy's drumming is as dead simple as you can get. FYI: check it out with headphones and pan from side to side; drums, bass, and guitar are all hard-panned; it's pretty awesome to listen to it with such wide stereo separation.

## Television, *Marquee Moon* [1977], "See No Evil"
**Drummer** - Billy Ficca

*Marquee Moon* is one of those albums that flew under mainstream radio but had huge underground critical acclaim. It's known as a "guitar album" as both Tom Verlaine and Richard Lloyd re-invented what you could do with six strings. But the rhythm section of Fred

Smith on bass and Billy Ficca on drums is brilliant. Smith keeps the pulse rolling along on each song, and Ficca plays some of the most tense, syncopated, jazzy rock grooves I've ever heard. A masterpiece!

## The Clash, *London Calling* [1979], "True In Vain"
## **Drummer** - Topper Headon

*London Calling* is in my Top Ten Albums of all time, usually hovering right near the #1 slot. The Clash were at the peak of their creativity when they recorded this, and they delivered a blistering 19-song double album manifesto. Stylistically, the band veers off on various tangents: pop, punk, jazz, funk, dub and rockabilly. Topper Headon effortlessly tackles each song with a crispness and extraordinary confidence, making him one of the best and most versatile drummers ever.

# Griffin Goldsmith

*"When I met Keltner, he said, 'You remind me of my old friend Jimmy.'"*

G riffin Goldsmith is a Los Angeles area-based drummer and songwriter celebrated for his work with indie folk-rockers, Dawes. His nuanced creativity and extensive knowledge of music history have been pivotal in shaping Dawes' acclaimed albums, including *North Hills, Nothing is Wrong,* and *All Your Favorite Bands.* Griffin's dynamic drumming style has earned him a reputation as an exceptional session musician, working with artists such as Jackson Browne, John Fogerty, Robbie Robertson, Jim Keltner, Elvis Costello, Sharon Van Etten, Angel Olsen, Jenny Lewis, Bahamas, and many others. Here are Griffin's choices…

---

### Carly Simon, *No Secrets* [1972], "You're So Vain"
### Drummer - Jim Gordon

Man…Jim Gordon is one of the best to do it. I doubt that's a controversial statement amongst drummers. He thrived in a unique time in the LA session scene. I've always thought he held the space after Hal Blaine and Earl Palmer but before the Jim Keltners and Jeff Porcaros had arrived. In terms of the timeline, I'm sure they all overlapped, but at least it seemed that way to me. When I met Keltner, he said, "You remind me of my old friend Jimmy." He was talking about Jim Gordon, of course. It goes without saying that that meant the world to me. Anyway... some drummers have a variety of sounds and rely on the different tones to inspire their parts or performances. And some drummers have their sound and are good enough to make that sound always work. Keltner is the king of the former style; this is an approach I take as well. It's fun because not only does it work for me, but it allows me to justify my bloated drum collection. I've wondered if this is the route I took to mask that I don't have chops. But the latter type of drummer would be Earl Palmer, Hal Blaine, Al Jackson, Jay Bellerose, and our boy Jim Gordon...among many others. Jim Gordon made his thing work in every context. It's like salt; it adds to any dish, and everyone has some in their cabinet. And if they don't, then they need some. Anyway, "You're So Vain" is a perfect drum track.

## James Brown & The Famous Flames, *Think!* [1960]

This was the first time I had ever heard a swing like this. I thought I understood the concept of playing straight or triplets, but this track demolished that; it's in that "in-between" space. I realized there is no end to the nuance within a swing.

## Little Milton, *Stax Profiles: Little Milton* [2006], "Let Me Down Easy"
### **Drummer** - Calep Emphrey Jr.

DYNAMICS!!! I was really taken aback by the drummer's dynamic range. Playing the verse at that volume really creates space for the drummer to say something by laying in. And the timekeeping is not metronomic; the tempo follows the energy.

## Attitudes, *Good News* [1977], "Drink My Water"
### Drummer - Jim Keltner

The feel and sounds on this one are impeccable. I love all of the overdubbed percussion. It really is a piece of the groove. I often wonder what I hear when I listen to Jim play.

## Bob Dylan, *Desire* [1976]
### Drummer - Howard Wyeth

This entire record is a master class. There's never been anything like it before or since. Everything about it is so unique, so right, and these are some of the coolest drum sounds there ever were. I've found several records that Howard Wyeth played on, but they're hard to come by. It's as if he just appeared, gave one of the greatest record performances ever, and then decided to retire on top. ;)

### HONORABLE MENTIONS:

**Earl Palmer** is a big one for me. They say he was the first drummer to put a backbeat on the 2 and 4. Has anyone changed music as much????

**Philly Joe Jones** – Nobody applied rudiments better than him.

**Pete La Roca** – He is often overlooked. His phrasing is brilliant. He's one of the most patient drummers. The way he solos has always thrilled me. Looooonnnnngggggg over the bar phrases.

13

**Art Blakey** – I love his playing, but what got me excited about him when I was a kid was how he led his band. You could feel the urgency.

**Andy Newmark** – "In Time" off the Sly and the Family Stone album *Fresh* could have easily made my list.

**Brian Blade** – He plays with such joy. It's especially enjoyable to watch. His happiness is infectious.

**Jon Christensen** – His playing with Keith Jarrett is all time.

**Joey Baron** – He is one of my favorite modern jazz drummers as a recording artist. He brings sounds into play that I would have never expected and that you don't hear often in a contemporary jazz setting.

**Jeff Porcaro** – All drummers love him, right? I took lessons with his father, Joe, for two years. It definitely gave me some insight into where his precision came from. Joe was very by the book. Very technical. He was an incredible teacher.

**Charlie Watts** – I suspect he wasn't as sloppy as he let on. He had the chops, but he was a genius and fit so well into that band that sometimes one could be fooled into thinking he was a bit sloppy.

**Keith Moon** – I loved it when I was a kid, and then, as I really began to study the drums, his wild style wasn't as interesting. My brain was trying to take things and break them down to make sense of them. After that phase passed and I found him again, his playing took on a new life for me; he's one of the coolest ever.

# Madden Klass

*"I had never heard of or experimented with the idea that a groove can be stretched and compressed all within one measure to create a push and pull."*

**M**adden Klass is a vibrant, multifaceted drummer whose recent collaborations include Boygenius, Big Wild, Matt Maltese, Watsky, Mike Doughty, and Wheatus. She thrives on challenging herself with diverse and progressive material, while her musical roots are deeply grounded in heavy rock, hip-hop, and pop. Since her time at Berklee College of Music, Madden has swiftly become one of the most sought-after drummers in the live music scene. Here are Madden's choices...

---

### Battles, *Gloss Drop* [2011], "Futura"
**Drummer** - John Stanier

John Stanier represents one-half of the band Battles. This band is an electronic and rock music hybrid featuring loads of looping and glitchy sounds. The drums play a vital role in developing these droning instrumentals, and it shows in John's approach to writing against these loops. Hearing John's playing was one of the first times I experienced a drummer acting as a true variable within a tune— completely commanding the feel and dynamics while the song

15

remained unchanged underneath. He successfully does this by adding melodies to his grooves through subdivision variations and accents. He changes the snare or hi-hat pattern in moments you wouldn't expect while respecting the backbeat. I admire how he takes a groove and proceeds to chop it up as if he were smashing the pads of a drum machine. The track "Futura" off of their sophomore album *Gloss Drop* is, in my opinion, the best example of this technique. What's so distinctive about this particular track is the static quality he implements on the hi-hat. It's almost as if he decided his parameters for the groove: no dynamics and all subdivision variation. I found this to be pretty atypical of anything I'd heard from a drummer before, especially in the rock world—although his approach does remind me of Stewart Copeland's quirky accents. John Stanier has inspired my writing on the kit immensely.

## Hiatus Kaiyote, *Live in Revolt EP* [2013], "Sphynx Gate" **Drummer** - Perrin Moss

I first came across Hiatus Kaiyote through Spotify's Discover Weekly when I was a junior in high school. His crispy and dry ride, sloshy hats, and the delicate ghost notes on his snare immediately drew me in. This band completely took over my world and introduced me to many artists who shaped their sound before their time. Perrin's grooves led me to discover a whole world of hip-hop and R&B that I was unfamiliar with then. I had never heard of or experimented with the idea that a groove can be stretched and compressed all within one measure to create a push and pull—a feel pulled from the legendary producer, J Dilla. The push and pull could stem from a quintuplet grid or be a calculated ebb and flow.

In addition to nailing and expanding upon this feel, he would experiment with textures and kit configurations that were unique to him—using all the bells and whistles to provide the most textural substance to a tune. Of course, from here on out, I had to gather all the knick-knacks for myself. I would find myself in trouble at sessions when I had tambourines or shells on top of cymbals, creating lots of unnecessary rattling. Despite the issues, I loved the unique sound it produced. On the live version of the track "Sphynx Gate," you'll hear how he takes a straight eighth groove and adds extra hat subdivisions that impact the grid, either before the downbeats or after, using triplets and sixteenths. It was such a simple addition that completely changed the flavor of the groove and opened my mind up to a whole new bag of tricks.

---

## The Aristocrats, *The Aristocrats* [2011], "Bad Asteroid"
### **Drummer** - Marco Minnemann

Marco Minnemann can showcase delicacy, tastefulness, dynamics, and flow all within a matter of seconds. These seconds I'm referring to can be heard on the "Bad Asteroid" track by The Aristocrats; his touch is masterful. I was introduced to his playing through Guthrie Govan's records. A great friend who plays guitar asked me and a few other musicians to learn Govan's "Erotic Cakes" for a competition at Berklee College of Music; this tune is bizarre. While Marco didn't play on this record, it was my gateway into his world. From then on, I dove into The Aristocrats and Steven Wilson, which feature Marco's drumming. I wanted to model my playing after him, especially when I was playing in my progressive rock groups. He has a way of taking sonic control of the pieces he records by adding loads of ornaments

17

with his cymbals and producing a super crisp studio drum sound. I admired his command over the kit and his capacity to execute fills and combinations I had yet to encounter. He was one of the best rock drummers I had experienced as I matured as a player and needed some guidance.

---

Ash Soan, *Ghostship Time-out* (YouTube video) [2020]
**Drummer** - Ash Soan

Watching Ash Soan is an instant inspiration. He's the epitome of drumming for me and many other musicians. I came across Ash when I was starting to build my home studio during quarantine. I looked towards him for gear guidance and configurations, as I thought he was producing the ideal studio sounds through his gear choices, mixing, and, most importantly, his playing. His drums come out sounding so punchy and isolated. His gear is so dialed in that he can record from his beautiful home Windmill Studio, and his touch is impeccable. His spacing is powerful, even regarding the smallest drag or ghost note. This example is apparent in one of his short videos on YouTube called *Ghostship Time-out*. I believe he writes these tracks after he's just done some free-form playing. You can feel how authentically he plays and reacts to his internal compass when watching his videos. He tends not to play something flashy for longer than half a measure, and I think he appreciates space just as much as playing a nasty fill. He treats the kit as a melodic instrument, achieving such a colorful sound with the fewest notes possible.

---

**Can you talk about Ilan Rubin's performance at the 2011 Guitar Center Drum Off and its impact on your playing?**

As a young Paramore fan, I consumed all of their records without

18

necessarily knowing who was behind the mastery. While I was aware of the core members, I didn't know of any of the session players that so massively contributed to Paramore's sound. This all changed a few years later when I attended my first proper music festival and was utterly astounded by the legendary playing of Ilan Rubin. Nine Inch Nails, whom I hadn't been interested in before that moment, was headlining this festival. I was casually resting on the hill at Randall's Island, observing the show, when "March of the Pigs" kicked in. I was immediately drawn into this fast-paced groove in seven, wondering who this person was behind the kit. People were losing their minds, and I was just getting started. I ended up watching the entire show and took a deep dive into Ilan's playing as soon as I got home. I quickly put it together that he had such an influence on me as a kid without even knowing it for so many years.

Naturally, I went to YouTube. One of the top videos was of his appearance at the 2011 Guitar Center Drum Off, where he ripped a solo. The precision, power, and musicality blew my mind. One of the elements of his solo that specifically caught my attention was his ability to write grooves on the spot, nonetheless, weave them into a solo. The beats he was coming up with could've transformed into full-fledged songs.

Additionally, I appreciated his development of new ideas by hitting the crash every four measures, followed by an embellishment to what was already being played or an entirely new section. I found this to be classic yet unconventional for today's approach to solos. He is full of material to pull from and has influenced much of my writing on the kit. From then on, I tried to mimic his off-kilter beats and commitment to powerful playing when supporting an artist, writing a part, or playing for myself. His playing even inspired me to play guitar and write more against the grooves I was coming up with.

# Adam Betts

*"The underlying thing here is that I love to dance. I'm not cool with it; it's full-on dad dancing, but I love a pulse that makes me bounce."*

A dam Betts is a drummer/teacher/producer/writer based in London, whose combination of boundary-setting hybrid drumming with bombastic, yet technically proficient playing has garnered a reputation around the world. Adam's list of collaborators includes Squarepusher, Three Trapped Tigers, Heritage Orchestra, Goldie, Jarvis Cocker, Pete Tong, and his solo project titled Colossal Squid. Here are Adam's choices...

Lightening Bolt, *Ride The Skies* [1999], "13 Monsters"
**Drummer** - Brian Chippendale

I think Brian's drumming was pretty much the freshest thing to happen to "heavy" drumming in years, and it still sounds that way. His phrasing, tone (that snare sound!), the "fuck it" messy sound, the energy at 1000%... It's incendiary and was utterly thrilling.

It is essentially getting rid of the backbeat. Now, I love a good backbeat; I'm not a weirdo. I love Phil Rudd. I love Al Jackson. I love Purdie. But to innovate away from it and, in doing so, give much more propulsion to the music, and basically put all the time onto the 8th-note kick and cymbals and then use the snare as a decorative device - it's magnificent and opened the door for me to explore grooves in a heavy context.

Honestly, this track probably isn't the best example of what I described — maybe something like the song "Assassins" does it better? But this was the first lightning bolt tune I heard, and as a 20-year-old, it flipped my existence. Add that to having just moved to London, meeting cool, weird art punk people, and having the rules of my drumming split open — I can't overstate the impact this time had on me. This also pertains to other incredible visionaries like Zach Hill and Greg Saunier.

## Squarepusher, *Big Loada* [1997]

I couldn't do this list without this tune. In some context, it's similar to *Lightning Bolt* — the backbeat has gone, there's a propulsive 8th note, and the snare is kind of decorative in (dare I say it) almost a jazz way.

Tom has one of the best ears for drum hooks, and his ability to transmute a break almost endlessly in the way a drummer would if they had the chops of, say, Mike Mitchell while having it still make sense is unmatched. He did this all on a hardware sampler and sequencer, with enough memory to do only 5 minutes. It's a staggering work of genius that technology has moved forward from, and it's hard to remember how insane what Tom did was. And he was like 20.

In addition, the tune is glorious. It's not DnB in any typical way — the diatonic glorious harmony, the waving from the top of the mountain element; it's its own thing, and it's wonderful for that.

21

## AFX, *Hangable Auto Bulb* [1995], "Every Day"

An argument could be made that AFX is my favorite artist, full stop. What do I need to say? He is enigmatic, artistically beyond compare, never sold out, always has the perfect mood of a rave at the heart of everything he writes, and has done multiple albums that are the absolute best of their respective genres.

"Every Day" has loads in common with the first two. It's massively propulsive but without the use of a backbeat. There's no use of a drum kit at all. I always loved the idea that you could push a track forward without a full drum beat—I'm curious where it might originate. "Wipeout"?! There's a jazz connotation—Tony Williams moving the band along with a massively broken ride cymbal feel. There's a found sound element to it, too. Very little in here sounds like a drum kit, but it plays the drummer's role. That's meaningful to me.

Autechre does this stuff to a genius level all the time, as have a whole load of amazing electronic artists since, but this song has its hooks in my heart.

## James Brown, *In The Jungle Groove* [1986], "Give It Up or Turnit A Loose"
**Drummer** - Clyde Stubblefield

True magic. This track is a tribute to many excellent funk drummers—Bernard Purdie, Idris Mohammed, Grady Tate, Jabo Starks, James Black, Al Jackson, and Crikey.

The underlying thing here is that I love to dance. I'm not cool with it; it's full-on dad dancing, but I love a pulse that makes me bounce. These guys have exemplified that ability to decorate the pulse while still expressing it in a way that will make a room full of 10,000 people stay stuck to the floor.

I think time is a subtle thing, especially in the quite proggy, technically challenging stuff I tend to play. I play everything like these guys would—as a funk beat. And I think connecting with an audience on a primal level is essential.

This break—its composition—is genius, too. Someone explained Stubblefield very well to me when they said it was the church expressed on the drum kit—the clapping and the tambourine are all in the hi-hat and the ghost notes. It's a beautiful thing.

## Remarc, *Champion Jungle Sound* [1995], "For Real"

This is another track that could have been a million others.

Jungle and DnB are those genres where so many people were getting stuck into the music—if you had a few bits of kit that didn't need much room, you could make tunes. It was beautiful, and so many songs were made; you can still discover seminal stuff today. This was quite a recent discovery for me, but it was such a banger; the break choices are exceptional. I probably should have done a Photek or Dillinja tune, but this one is so upbeat and banging and, like I say, fresh to me.

Also, I lived in Brockley in London for quite a few years, so it's nice to represent the local lad.

### HONORABLE MENTIONS:

**Vinnie Paul** – As a 13-year-old, his drumming helped me take a thing I enjoyed but did as a school band thing (playing "Match of the Day" at a Christmas concert, etc.) to owning it for myself. No adults

23

I knew liked Pantera, so it felt like my own thing, and his drumming was SO GOOD!—the ideas, groove, and sound. You can tie in a lot of '90s rock in that, e.g., *A Downward Spiral, Rage Against The Machine, Ænima, City* by Strapping Young Lad, and *Blood Sugar Sex Magik*, etc. As a 13-year-old, it felt like fantastic music was always coming out! It was exciting!

# Travis Orbin

*"He taught me to compose fearlessly... I sometimes miss him as if
I'd miss a family member or an old friend."*

T ravis Orbin is a powerful drummer known for his contributions
to the progressive metal genre. He gained fame as the drummer
for the band Periphery and has worked with artists such as Sky Eats
Airplane and Intervals. Orbin continues to display his exceptional
drumming and compositional skills through various projects and
session work, including his current band, Darkest Hour. Here are
Travis' choices...

Metallica, *...And Justice for All* [1988], "One," "The Frayed
Ends of Sanity"
**Drummer** - Lars Ulrich

I still vividly recall seeing the video for "Enter Sandman" on MTV
upon Metallica's self-titled/*Black Album* release. The unforgettable
density and swagger of those tunes were further impressed upon me
as I rode around with my dad in his humongous truck in the following
months. It was the loudest, heaviest music that had infiltrated my
8-year-old sensibilities. For whatever reason, the drums didn't strike
me or vie for my attention—all of the components seemed to be strictly
in service of the riffs and delivery of the vocals.

25

I saved up some money and explored the "M" aisle under cassettes at one of the stores in the mall. ...*And Justice For All*? Whoa, this looks rad. Although the "One" video either was—or eventually became—a staple of airplay on MTV, I can't recollect seeing it, so this was an impulse purchase.

I wish I could remember how I felt after my first full listen; all I'm left with is my impression. I'm not sure how many months that cassette took up residency in my boombox, but my junior-high friends and I destroyed several thousand brain cells head-banging to the sextuplet-climax riff in "One"; I'd furiously bang along on anything in sight.

Speaking of, this record is the sine qua non for my path to drumming. Never before had I articulated the motions of playing the drums sans kit—less (or more?) elegantly referred to as "air drumming"—until getting this masterpiece deeply under the skin. I had aimlessly beaten on various things and drummed on desks in grade school, but this transfigured a seemingly intrinsic drive, impelling a desire and passion that became all-consuming. I don't know what I'd be doing without it. It is my Favorite Heavy Metal Record.

---

*Serious Moves* VHS [1992], "Trim"
**Drummer** - Dennis Chambers

It's 1996, and I'd been playing for less than a year. I had some money burning a hole in my pocket and ventured to a local instrument store. I may have had an inkling that such a thing as instructional drum videos existed, as I frequently perused (read: ardently fantasized about owning every piece of gear) instrument catalogs, but it didn't exactly sink in until I was staring at a glass counter with an assemblage of 'em. On an absolute whim, I bought Dennis Chambers' *Serious Moves*, featuring most of the *Blue Matter/Loud Jazz/Pick Hits* band: John Scofield, Gary Grainger, and Jim Beard.

My parents were not enthusiasts of jazz, much less jazz-rock/jazz-fusion/electric jazz (pick your favorite sub-genre nomenclature), much less the freakish tornado that was John Scofield's band at that time. As a result, not having been exposed to such music, along with the sheer fact that it was astronomically above my head, you'd think there was a chance I'd be turned off. Primo negative.

Although touted as instructional, *Serious Moves* was mostly a performance video interpolated with an interview with Dennis, wherein he recounts stories and anecdotes of seeing other drummers live, tips and techniques, etc. There was another video available—*In the Pocket*—of which I've only seen portions featuring the same band (DCI probably booked a studio for a couple of days and shot a full set), but it didn't contain as adventurous material.

From the outset, "Trim" is performed. Angular yet flowing, Dennis deftly navigates the arrangement with undeniable brio. Towards the end, there's a drum solo over a vamp. Yes, tasty orchestrations and absurd chops abound, but in particular, there's this one groove he lands on—playing the ride—that is so gutbucket and GREASY it invariably induces stank-face. It's one of my all-time Favorite Drum Performances.

I suppose it's fair to say that there is a variety of drummers, including "super drummers"; Dennis was my first exposure to such an extraordinary breed of player. Coupled with the fantastic music and aid of a visual component, it rendered the VCR as a fixture in which only *Serious Moves* was to be played. I'd even make my friends sit through it!

## Tower of Power, *Soul Vaccination: Tower of Power Live* [1999], "Soul Vaccination," "So Very Hard to Go"
### Drummer - David Garibaldi

It was either 2000 or 2001 — I'm leaning towards the former — and audio-file sharing is widespread. Admittedly, my favorite platform was Audiogalaxy: cue up as many songs as you'd like (conveniently organized per genre), and the service did the work for you. I'd return later in the day and have a full record ready for recreational listening. This is an open admission, for I would subsequently purchase the CD if I enjoyed the material. This live Tower of Power record was one of those downloads/purchases.

By now, I had several years of practicing, reading, and general craft-honing under my belt. I was familiar with "funk drumming," but this record is another level. Garibaldi is a wizard and nonpareil. His blending of 16th-based funk playing and Afro-Cuban rhythms is unimpeachably delicious. The ghosting, the bouncy bow/bell ride patterns... Studying and playing along to Garibaldi imparted to me the importance of ghost notes and giving those morsels their proper subdivision worth rather than peppering them in with nonchalance. Okay, enough food references.

To boot, this record is superbly engineered and mixed. The performances of each track became so indelible that it was actually tough for me to retro-listen to the original, respective recordings and appreciate them.

Interesting footnote: many years later, I saw some footage of Chambers filling in for Garibaldi and had an epiphany. Of COURSE, he's a fan!

On The Virg, *Serious Young Insects* [1999], "Native Metal,"
"Alien Hip-Hop"
Planet X, *Universe* [2000], "Clonus"
**Drummer** - Virgil Donati

I was first subjected to Donati's inscrutable playing via the 1997 *Modern Drummer* Festival Highlights VHS. A friend and I would pop it in and marvel at guys like Tempesta, Royster (who was prepubescent and furious), et al. When Virg came on, it was as if a semi-opaque curtain dropped over the television; he induced much head-scratching, and we could barely understand what he was playing, let alone how he was executing it all—AND with traditional grip. This guy's a magician from another planet...probably another galaxy. But the protean adolescent mind took over, and I didn't do any further investigation.

Skipping ahead to around the same time as the live Tower of Power record, the memory becomes a tad hazy. I am trying to remember if I downloaded and/or bought one of the above. By then, I had become committed to going to the local FYE and special-ordering some of the more obscure records I was consuming or finding them on Audiophile Imports. But indeed, being exposed to one of the records mentioned above prompted me to purchase the other. It was simply in such quick succession that I found myself loving both concurrently, thus my dual pick.

I have retained two specific memories of each: I remember the sonic onslaught—superlatively transmitted through my PC's Klipsch speakers—of the *SYI* record, especially while cranking "Alien Hip-Hop." And I remember my tired commute from an old job, throwing on *Universe* for needed revitalization.

Although he became a firebrand in the drumming community after that *MD* Fest performance, I recall more press around him

29

then. I'd gobble up any interview or piece of media I could uncover and became — frankly — quite obsessed with the guy. He possessed a work ethic and an ascetic lifestyle that matched the one I had begun grooming myself, being a massive fan of Henry Rollins. But Henry wasn't a drummer. And if you've got even a kernel of that kind of passion looming inside, Virg will draw it out.

Another memory has presented itself: hearing Meshuggah's *Nothing* and thinking, "Oh, this is like what Donati's doing, except 'metal.'" Later, I'd do my homework, learn about them, and listen to more of their discography. Still, it's interesting that such sophisticated, rhythmically complex music that bore resemblances to each other was being produced simultaneously, and one form (read: enraptured) caught my attention before the other.

Anyway, I've done a lot of gushing about Virg, both online and in person, and there is still a lot of gushing to be done. The expressiveness and sheer grandeur of his playing can't be grasped within a couple of records or a handful of video clips; chances are you're seeing just one side or just one period of his growth, which is endless. He's my Favorite Drummer.

## Frank Zappa, *Joe's Garage* [1979], "Catholic Girls"
### Drummer - Vinnie Colaiuta

I can't imagine a more illustrious start to a career than this: Colaiuta's first big gig and only second (according to the discography on his website) record. But let's back up for a moment.

My father mostly listened to "classic" rock, i.e., the pop/rock music of his heyday. He had a couple of Zappa records, and I'd giggle along at the lyrics when he'd play them. He'd draw an arbitrary line in the sand at some point, though, commenting, "With some of his stuff, you need to be on acid or somethin'." In my early twenties, I took the plunge. I began buying up FZ's disco on my own—plucking anything that looked interesting (which proved, along with the number of available titles, to be formidable). *Joe's Garage* was a very early purchase, perhaps the first.

I fell deeply in love with the music: the songs, the playing, the story, everything. It's all still so intoxicating. I could've picked any track as the key track, but "Catholic Girls" merely jumped out because I think it'd appeal to a casual listener or someone new to FZ. Colaiuta is slinky and tasteful throughout, exhibiting the sort of aplomb only a seasoned vet could (remember, again: the second record in his career). His drum sound is particularly intriguing: fairly idiosyncratically devoid (maybe it's what Frank wanted) of his later tones, but rich, vibrant, and earthy.

Volumes have been written on the genius of Mr. Zappa, so I'll touch briefly on what he impressed upon me and my feelings. Frank taught me to compose fearlessly and to hold in esteem the dichotomy of not taking yourself seriously but doing what you do with utmost conviction. I sometimes miss him as if I'd miss a family member or an old friend. *Joe's Garage* is my you've-got-a-gun-to-your-head-and-you've-gotta-pick Favorite Zappa Record.

## Mr. Bungle, *California* [1999]
**Drummer** - Danny Heifetz

Something memorable from watching MTV as a child was the video for Faith No More's "Epic." I finally sated that intrigue in my twenties and bought all their records. It's some of my favorite alt/rock music, and I became a de facto fan of Mike Patton. His discography being a monolithic, prolific rabbit hole of amazingly unusual music, I'd occasionally peek inside that myriad and grab a few items of interest. In 2010, Mr. Bungle's records were pinpointed with said interest.

Just last year (at the time of writing this), I decided to roll the dice on YouTube's copyright rules and cover/re-interpret "Ars Moriendi" from *California*. So far, I'm winning. At the risk of being redundant, I'm closing with a quote from my video description. Thank you for reading.

"Mr. Bungle's *California* is one of my all-time favorite records. It's built atop the earmarks established in the two preceding records: an eclectic, assaulting mélange of genres (often in the same song), a penchant for film-score idolatry, and a lethal dose of humor while featuring a headier blend of world-music(s) influence—even employing session musicians in furtherance of authenticity—and an overall streamlined approach to the songwriting. The inscrutable, terrorizing nature of *Disco Volante* and the turpitude of the debut were dialed down, but it still caroms between experimental and radio-friendly until it's a kaleidoscopic smear of some of the weirdest rock music you're likely to hear—with some intensely gravid lyrics. This record blasts me off to the firmament. It's transcendent, atemporal; a collective triumph."

# Stella Mozgawa

*"He is the drummer I think about the most when coming up with ideas in the studio."*

Stella Mozgawa, renowned as an innovative drummer and producer, is a member of the critically acclaimed band Warpaint. Beyond her contributions to Warpaint, Mozgawa is one half of the electronica duo, Belief. She has also collaborated with artists such as Courtney Barnett, Kurt Vile, Flea, Adam Green, Regina Spektor, The xx, Sharon Van Etten, and many others. Here are Stella's choices...

## Tool, *Ænima* [1996], "Stinkfist"
### Drummer - Danny Carey

Listening to Tool was an enormous part of my musical education. I never had formal training outside of some very vital drum lessons as a teenager. However, I knew early on that listening was the most optimal form of learning for me. So, I absorbed a LOT of music at this age.

Learning Danny Carey's drum parts was a crash course in polyrhythm, meter, and the mathematical components of music. Most importantly, it was never too intellectual; there's always a soul and a groove that masks just how complex some of those patterns are—a huge inspiration.

## Steely Dan, *The Royal Scam* [1976], "Kid Charlemagne"
**Drummer** - Bernard Purdie

Purdie is the king! This album, but particularly this track, is seared into my mind. I didn't realize till years later how I had slowed the idea of the "Kid Charlemagne" beat down on Kurt Vile's "Pretty Pimpin." Bernard has a musical feel but with such an obvious awareness and reverence for the other parts. He dances around that piano but glues the whole song together—a work of genius!

## CAN, *Ege Bamyasi* [1972], "Spoon"
**Drummer** - Jaki Liebezeit

Jaki Liebezeit is the drummer I think about the most when coming up with ideas in the studio. He invented an approach rather than a specific beat and always served the song while endlessly elevating what was already there. I love how CAN incorporated early drum machines and loops, and Jaki sometimes sounded just like a drum machine, both in tone and feel. His groove is incomparable and unique, oft-imitated, never replicated.

## Bjork, *Homogenic* [1997], "Hunter"
**Drummer** - Mark Bell, Bjork

This is not a traditional drum performance, but Bjork's first 5 albums made such an indelible mark on my musical understanding and approach to drumming. I used to play my kit along to these crazy Mark Bell-programmed beats in my teenage bedroom, trying to figure out if they were even physically possible to execute outside of a drum machine sequence. Some were challenging, but they pushed me to see "acoustic" drumming from an entirely new perspective.

---

### Tony Allen, *Black Voices* [1999], "Asiko"
**Drummer** - Tony Allen

A true drumming pioneer, I love everything that Tony Allen ever touched. His ideas were utterly hypnotic, infectious, and effortless. It's like his feel was his speaking voice, his breath. As soon as you sit down and try to play one of these beats, you realize how complex that groove really is. Playing along to Tony Allen's tracks stretched my mind in a way I can't completely describe.

---

# Dom Famularo

*"...a person at peace with themselves is always living in the moment. That's where he resides."*

D om Famularo is a globally recognized drummer, educator, author, and motivational speaker known for his uplifting approach to drums and life. Referred to as "Drumming's Global Ambassador," Dom inspired drummers around the globe. Dom sadly passed away in the fall of 2023 before the publishing of this book, but chatting with him about his influences was an honor, and I feel so grateful to include him in this release. Here is some insight into what shaped Dom into the drummer we all knew and loved…

**How do you feel is the best way to digest your influences without becoming their carbon copy?**

I use the three-step process.

The first step is imitation.

There's nothing wrong with imitation. When I was younger, I tried to imitate and steal specific patterns from drummers like Buddy Rich, Steve Gadd, Tony Williams, and Max Roach. My success rate was never great because I still needed to gain the skills, but the imitation part was crucial. Imitation allows you to step into a different thought process.

The second step is assimilation.

Once you imitate it and start to take in that idea well, it becomes a way of life and a part of your playing. You're assimilating.

The third step is innovation.

Innovation is when you take that idea, break the rules of who you are, and uncover your unused creative potential.

And even to this day, after 56 years of playing professionally, I'll listen to and imitate a young drummer. To me, that is the journey of art. If you desire to be a constant student, you'll continue to grow, hopefully up until the day that you die.

---

## Paul Simon, *Still Crazy After All These Years* [1975], "50 Ways To Leave Your Lover"
### Drummer - Steve Gadd

Before Steve Gadd created the "50 Ways To Leave Your Lover" groove, he asked Paul Simon what the song meant. Paul said it was about experiencing the sadness of a relationship ending but clinging to hope and finally coming out the other side.

Hearing this, Steve visualized the beginning (sad) section as a funeral march in New Orleans. So, he played a drum cadence to put the listener in a somber, reflective state of mind. When these visualized funeral attendees realize they're going to celebrate life, they walk back from the grave site to a party and play happy music. At that point in the arrangement, Steve matches that emotion with a new groove showcasing life's joyous celebration.

Steve could have played a stock groove, but he stepped emotionally into his skills as an artist (not just as a drummer) to feel the bigger picture.

---

37

## Rickie Lee Jones, *Rickie Lee Jones* [1979], "Chuck E's in Love"
### Drummer - Steve Gadd

Steve Gadd was a complete disrupter. In tunes like "Chuck E's In Love," you specifically hear the interplay between the hi-hat and snare that had not been before. He always has a way of being so busy but not distracting. And he's still that way. I just heard him two weeks ago with James Taylor [in 2021]. It was a 13-piece band, and Steve found a way of playing the exact part inside the entire ensemble. Steve found the holes to fill in and other spots to leave alone. He accomplishes this by maintaining a presence in the now. A person with regrets is a person living in the past. A person who constantly worries or has anxiety is living in the future. They're worried about what might happen. But a person at peace with themselves is always living in the moment. That's where Steve Gadd resides.

## Buddy Rich, *Swingin' New Big Band* [1966], "West Side Story Medley"
### Drummer - Buddy Rich

I met Buddy in 1971. My drum teacher growing up was Al Miller. Al passed away in 2000, but he was THE teacher here on Long Island and became a mentor and a dear friend. One day, when I was 18, Al invited me to his house to meet his buddy friend. I come by to meet him, and there's Buddy Rich in his living room. Al and Buddy were in the Marines together and were both martial arts instructors. Being paired together for two years as friends made them very close. Whenever Buddy was in our area, he called Al, and we'd both see Buddy play. We would sit backstage and watch Buddy from behind the curtain; I remember every performance. It was so vividly clear how beautiful he played all the time and his dedication.

Leonard Bernstein wrote *West Side Story* for Broadway. The songs are classic American Standards. When Buddy had that arranged for his big band, he wanted the song to weave throughout the score. So, he would play all different types of feels and grooves, but when he gets to the drum solo, he creates the incredible feeling of the *West Side Story* battle. If you listen to this and your heart's not beating faster, you're freaking dead! I went to see Buddy well over 50 times with Al; of course, he played that song a lot. It was always a little different. It was always intense. And it always took you to exhilaration.

Buddy did not read music, but he could listen to an arrangement once and learn it. And I witnessed that as well.

## Toto, *Toto IV* [1982], "Rosanna"
### **Drummer** - Jeff Porcaro

I met Jeff in 1976. I had just moved to California and took a few lessons with Les Demerle. Les is a fantastic drummer who used to play with numerous great big bands, including Harry James and His Big Band. Les also had a teaching studio and a little theater called The Cellar. The Cellar only fit around 80 people, but he had all different bands there. One particular Monday night, I went there to hear Zappa play. After getting seated, only one spot was available, and it was next to me. Then, in comes Jeff Porcaro, and he sits right down. As the band played, Jeff kept reaching over and grabbing my arm; he didn't know who I was. Because of the intensity of the music going, we reacted in the same way. After the show, Jeff invited me out for a drink, and we hit it off. Witnessing Jeff's enthusiasm and zest for life was another incredible reward I've experienced. Jeff could sing, too! Any jazz album. He knew every melody and every solo. His knowledge of music history was excellent.

As far as the "Rosanna" groove goes, he wanted to create something unique. So, he pulled from Bernard Purdie's shuffle. The Purdie Shuffle has that unique, soft pocket and feel. Then, of course, you've got Bonham and "Fool in the Rain," a more rigid, edgier shuffle. Jeff realized that and kept working backward to gather information to produce something different. He imitated, assimilated, and then innovated by taking a bit of Bernard Purdie and a little of John Bonham, adding a Bo Diddly bass drum pattern. This groove is still revered many years after Jeff's death. He died in August 1992. And I remember the day vividly well. When that happened, the world got a little less fun.

## The Dave Brubeck Quartet, *Time Out* [1959], "Take Five"
## Drummer - Joe Morello

I met Joe in 1971. This man was not only a fantastic musician but a wonderful human being. Many people know him from The Dave Brubeck Quartet, specifically the song "Take Five," which is in 5/4. It's also arguably the most recognizable jazz song on this planet. It was incredible to hear a jazz song in odd time on the radio in the '60s, but the song also featured a drum solo! Joe studied with George Lawrence Stone (author of *Stick Control*) and quickly became his best student. Joe, being the overachiever he is, started adding his own accents into his *Stick Control* exercises to make them more challenging. When George saw this, he was inspired to write the book *Accents and Rebounds* and dedicated the first page to Joe Morello, citing him as an "outstanding perfectionist in modern drumming." Joe went on to write his own books, the first being *New Directions in Rhythm*, which included grooves in 3/4 and 5/4. It opened up a lot of drummers' minds. Other great books from Joe include *Off the Record, Rudimental Jazz,* and *Master Studies I & II*. I was lucky enough to study these books with Joe.

Eventually, I wrote my book, *It's Your Move*, which I partially dedicated to Joe. It was particularly sad when he passed away in 2011, but it's our responsibility to push this art form forward and keep Joe Morello's memory alive.

# Mark Guiliana

*"It felt rooted and dangerous and was the most embodied musical experience I've ever seen."*

Mark Guiliana is a visionary drummer whose eclectic style effortlessly bridges the gap between jazz, electronic, and experimental music. His acclaimed resume includes collaborations with David Bowie, Brad Mehldau, St. Vincent, and his own band, Beat Music, as well as numerous releases under his own name. Continuously pushing the boundaries of rhythm and sound, Mark's innovative approach to drumming has solidified his status as a trailblazer in contemporary music. Here are Mark's choices...

---

### Nirvana, *In Utero* [1993], "Scentless Apprentice"
**Drummer** - Dave Grohl

I love when you can identify a song by the drumbeat. And yes, this one starts with the drums, but even if it didn't, the beat is essentially the hook and it's played with such conviction. I hadn't started playing drums yet when this album came out (1993), but I immediately felt a strong connection to the music and specifically Dave's playing. When I started eventually sitting at the drums a couple years later, this is a good example of what I was playing. Within a year of beginning to play the drums, you could learn this beat and get through the song.

Although I was light years away from achieving this kind of energy (and still am!), it was so empowering as a teenager to put this record on and play along to it and think to myself, "Yeah… I'm in Nirvana right now." That being said, you could teach someone this beat, but they'll quickly realize that there's so much more that Dave embodies that gets it to the place that we're hearing. And that's the lifelong path.

---

**Was there a performance you either played or witnessed that altered your musical course?**

I've had the chance to visit Havana a couple times in the last ten years, and being down there, hearing the music, and meeting the musicians completely changed my musical life. In the US, music making can feel more formalized in that you're a musician when you step on stage, and when you get offstage, you're not. Down there, it felt like every moment of every day was an opportunity to make music and be creative. The second time I was down there, some friends brought me to hear Osain del Monte, and it was easily one of the best concerts I've ever seen. It felt rooted and dangerous and was the most embodied musical experience I've ever seen. It was truly connected to whatever there is to connect to.

---

John Coltrane Quartet, *Crescent* [1964], "The Drum Thing"
**Drummer** - Elvin Jones

There's drum set playing before Elvin and then drum set playing after Elvin. You'd be hard-pressed to find someone in the world today who wasn't influenced by Elvin. The records he made with John Coltrane are biblical, and I return to those very often because they still provide so many new surprises every listen. 1964 was a real sweet spot for Coltrane and his band. *Crescent* is the record before *A Love Supreme*, which most people have heard. If there's a record I love, I always investigate the timeline. What was the one just before it or just after it? Or what were they doing as a sideman in between? And especially in the jazz world, these guys were making so many records around that time that it's nice to dive into that and know who's on the records and who else they're playing with and try to wrap my head around those details.

## Squarepusher, *Feed Me Weird Things* [1996]

A friend gave me this album in college on a burned CD; I still remember his handwriting on the disc. When I first heard it, I didn't know what the f&*k was going on, but I knew in my gut that I needed to investigate this music. After wearing it out, I bought every Squarepusher record I could find and completely immersed myself. The artist's name is Tom Jenkinson; he's a bass player. There are some records where he plays drums, but it's usually more cut up and chopped up. Every record is masterful in its own way. Squarepusher made terrific rhythmic inventions and sonic choices, and although it isn't a drummer playing this stuff in real-time on the record, trying to pull it off and learn from it is enjoyable. Inevitably, you'll fail because you can't play it as you hear it, but you might land in a new, exciting place.

## Roy Haynes Quartet, *Out Of The Afternoon* [1962]
### Drummer - Roy Haynes

This album was tracked in the same room as the John Coltrane album above, Van Gelder Studios in New Jersey. Many of those classic Blue Note and Impulse! records that everybody knows were recorded there and it really shines in this album. Obviously, the room has some magic, and with the way it is recorded, you almost feel like you're in the room with the band as they're playing. For anyone who hasn't seen what that room looks like, I encourage you to close your eyes when you're listening and imagine the details of the space. And then, you can find some of the classic photographs taken in that room and check to see if your instincts are correct.

# Jojo Mayer

*"He barked at me: 'I'm not your f\*\*in' nanny - you got the best lesson there is already, do what I showed you.'"*

Jojo Mayer is a pioneering force in the world of drumming, celebrated for his groundbreaking techniques and innovative approach to rhythm. He seamlessly blends elements of drum and bass, jazz, and electronic music into his unique style. As the founder of the band Nerve and a sought-after educator, Jojo continues to inspire and influence drummers worldwide with his unmatched skill and boundless creativity. Please enjoy my chat with Jojo...

**Can you talk about your early lessons with Freddie Gruber and how he influenced your view on the physicality of drumming?**

I hung out a bunch of times with Freddie Gruber, but I only had two actual drum lessons with him. My first contact was a drum-lesson-meets-meta-smorgasbord, which could have made more sense. While I do appreciate the usefulness of a meta-discourse, it was BS. And Freddie knew it. When I paid him for the lesson, I assumed he got on a guilt trip and offered to treat me to dinner. Over dinner, we talked about music — jazz in particular. Freddie seemed surprised that I knew the Oscar Peterson, Basie, and Monk records he mentioned, as I didn't rock the typical NYC jazz-look. [On the contrary, I wore moto jackets with chains back then.] Eventually, he relaxed and warmed up. We went to the Village to hear some jazz afterward, and it was a fun hang.

When I took off, he said: "Hey man, I'm sorry this lesson was BS; let's do another one next time I'm in NYC." We reconnected at Drummers Collective for my second lesson a few months later. Freddie shot out to make a "quick" phone call as soon as I arrived. So, I sat down behind the kit and waited. 5... 10... 15... minutes. No Freddie. I started to play, as I thought I might as well. At 20 minutes to the hour, Freddie popped back into the room. I stopped playing, and he shouted: "No, no, continue..." I continued while Freddie paced around the kit like a cat, closing in on its prey. Finally, he signaled me to stop. "Ok, how can I help you?" This question almost sounded like a trick to me. A few weeks prior, Freddie had told me about his pet peeve being rock drummers who come merely for technical advice, being ignorant about the instrument's musical roots in jazz. I wouldn't classify myself as a rock, jazz, or whatever drummer, but I also came for technical advice. So to avoid triggering him, I carefully rephrased my question to address the musical fallout caused by my technical shortcomings. It was something like: "I feel the range of my low-end projection feels somewhat restricted and choked...etc." Freddie looked at me like a diver coming to the surface for air and pointed at me. "Aha! Now we're talking!" He completely transformed his manner, took a drum stool, and sat beside me.

I had never heard anyone talk about the technical and conceptual aspects of drumming with such clarity and depth. Freddie gave me multiple angles and approaches to solutions in those ten to fifteen minutes. He pointed out that, as an autodidact who started very early, I naturally acquired a great sense of technique that could be improved with a few conceptual components. Someone at the Collective later told me that Freddie was standing just outside the door listening to my playing for 20 minutes before he entered the room. I guess this was some audition.

However, the lesson was not over yet. After a few weeks, I came to a grinding halt with the constant release technique Freddie had shown me to balance myself behind the kit. I got lost and could neither play as I used to nor execute what Freddie had shown me. It was horrible, like standing in the middle of a six-lane highway trying not to get hit by a car. I called him up and begged for another lesson. He barked at me: "I'm not your f**in' nanny. You got the best lesson there is already, do what I showed you." So down the rabbit hole I went — for probably more than a year and a half. Suddenly, everything started to fall into place and make sense. I realized Freddie didn't give me any solutions. He gave me riddles to solve. Only when I solved them did I get the reward. It was not just my execution and projection on the kit that got more effortless. He essentially handed me down the blueprint for his understanding of the physics of drumming. A 360 way of thinking that shifts perspectives. He looked at a physical manifestation not as an isolated occurrence but interconnected with a conceptual and an emotional one.

Some of that also helped me to structure my *Secret Weapons for the Modern Drummer* video tutorials about drumming techniques.

What separated Freddie from other drum teachers is that he didn't have a "method" per se. His lessons were tailor-made. What he showed me might not have been suitable for someone else. And vice versa. He understood physics but never came across as dogmatic. This contradiction could be why he never published a book and was critical of former students teaching the "Freddie Gruber Method." Two years later, Freddie attended my soundcheck at the *Modern Drummer* Festival in 2005. He walked by, gave me a pat on the shoulder, and that "yeah baby" nod. Then he told me a story about him passing out in a bathtub with Allen Ginsberg. He was a devil yet a deep thinker who immensely helped me.

**Can you talk about the "Amen" break, Marque Gilmore, and the cassette he gave you?**

When I first came to NYC, I was amongst a rotating roster of drummers like Rodney Holmes, Steven Wolf, and Marque Gilmore, who played with an experimental funk band called Screaming Headless Torsos. In the early nineties, a significant and vibrant music community was around the East Village. At some point, I was roommates with Torsos' bandleader and guitarist, Dave "Fuze" Fiuzcynski. Eventually, I became a full-time band member, and we experimented with many new stylistic influences. I was interested in production techniques with samplers, DAWs, and drum machines. During the mid-'80s, I already started replicating old-school drum loops on the acoustic kit, like "Funky Drummer" or "Synthetic Substitution." When I moved to NYC in 1989, I had this down to a tee and brought that sensibility to the band.

One day, Fuze gave me a mixtape that Marque Gilmore had compiled from some very early UK jungle. Marque was ahead of the curve in experimenting with jungle in his projects Tender Matrix and Drum FM.

Initially, that mix tape didn't trigger too much of a reaction. I thought it was cool, but there was a lot of other innovative stuff happening around that time—grunge, neo-soul, black rock, M-Base, etc.

It wasn't until I found myself at a jungle / drum 'n' bass warehouse party seeing hundreds of kids dancing and going wild. Then, I realized the true force of it. It inspired me to pick up the thread of reverse engineering old skool hip-hop beats on the acoustic kit and expand that concept into sped-up and sliced-up "Amen" breaks. I went deep with it, and it took more than a year until I had a chance to unpack in front of a live audience. At that point, no one had seen a drummer recreating these beats like I did. I took a different approach that was purely acoustic, with no loops or electronic embellishments. When I finally did this at my Prohibited Beatz live drum 'n' bass parties, it spread around town like wildfire, and I understood I was onto something.

---

**Can you elaborate on how elimination and restriction can ignite creativity? During our initial conversation, you shared insights about how you came to understand this concept.**

Concepts of elimination and restriction are very powerful as limitation spurs resourcefulness. The first time I used this artistically was when I immersed myself in reverse engineering machine beats. At that time, I started to consciously restrict my access to the whole drum set by removing everything from the kit I didn't need. No toms, cymbals; I sometimes went with just snare and hat. Or kick and snare. Or kick, snare, hat. I spent weeks, perhaps months doing this. Initially, I ran out of ideas after a couple of hours. I initially operated more from a statistical angle when practicing beats, like sticking and coordination. But having only a snare drum and hats stretched my imagination and resourcefulness. I discovered these instruments have way more sounds than most people use. Could I create a hand-clap sound from a snare? A delay effect? A pitch bend? A reverse effect? I went to work. If you practice without a kick for five days, you will be amazed at what will happen when you add it back to the kit.

This practice expanded my technical and textural vocabulary and helped me with internal hearing, phrasing, and dynamics. In a nutshell, it became a gateway to my authentic sound. It made me a better improviser, producer, and a better musician. To this day, I embrace limitation and elimination when confronted with it, not just in music but in life in general. Understanding this brings freedom. Being able to create positive outcomes despite restriction will also increase your self-confidence, which is a prerequisite for making good decisions.

Don't get me wrong; I know I have plenty of facilities. But so do thousands of drummers. What's rarer is the ability to make good decisions with these facilities and own them technically, conceptually, and emotionally.

I encourage anyone to experiment with this and become creative with it. There are so many ways to do it. For instance, try to play a drum solo at 80 bpm. Try to void ratios faster than 8th notes and avoid putting a potential audience to sleep. Dig?

---

**Can you talk about how Tony Williams broke your heart when you were old enough to have it broken?**

Tony Williams. Yes, he broke my heart when I was old enough to have it broken. No other drummer has been as informative to my growth during my formative teenage years. I am fortunate enough to have grown up in a very musical household. Besides playing drums around the same time I started walking, I was exposed to various musical influences from the '60s — pop, jazz, rock, R&B, Latin, and classical...everything from Beatles to Aretha Franklin, Oscar Peterson, James Brown, Sinatra, Tito Puente and so on. In the early '70s, I developed a short-lived taste for the early prog rock bands [like Emerson, Lake, and Palmer or King Crimson] until fusion came with bands like Weather Report and Mahavishnu Orchestra with Billy Cobham. Cobham changed the game for every drummer who came after him, including myself. Around that time, I started transcribing and imitating his playing, which was a significant time for me.

At some point when I was a kid, a bass player friend of my dad named Peter Frei tutored me. He gave me Miles Davis' *Four and More*, with 18-year-old Tony Williams completely tearing it up. He said,

"Listen to this. That's where that fusion stuff started." I did listen—and I didn't get it at all! At the time, I could appreciate Tony's facility on the drums, but my tastes were more calibrated to the thunderous power of Cobham, Lenny White, or Alphonse Mouzon. So, I forgot about it. That is until Tony Williams played a club in Zürich in 1980 with his fusion trio featuring Zappa alumni Patrick O'Hearn on bass and Tom Grant on keys. My dad took me, and I sat about 4 feet before his yellow 24" bass drum. I was 17 and had no idea what would come at me. The band came out, and Tony opened the show by ripping into a drum solo. Within 20 seconds or less, my life was transformed. Never was I hit by something drumming-related that hard before. This performance was beyond chops or anything like that. It was like he explained something massive and complex to me with no words in a few seconds. He kicked a giant door open so I could see the scope of a universe I was unaware of. I remember remaining in my seat after the show, stunned and paralyzed. I watched his drum tech pack up his kit until the last vestige of yellow disappeared backstage.

Then, I went home and listened to *Four and More* again. It now sounded completely different. And perhaps the fact that I was the same age as Tony when he played with Miles catapulted me into a deep rabbit hole. I started transcribing every Tony recording I could get my hands on, and it turned out to be some of the best schooling ever.

A couple of years later, I had to consciously prohibit myself from exposure to Tony Williams as his gravitational field devoured my ability to develop any vocabulary. But today, I can listen to him and enjoy it. PS: You can find some live audio clips of that band I saw back then on YouTube, and they released a rather obscure and little-known record called *Play or Die*...in case you think I was hallucinating.

**Can you discuss your approach to tuning?**

Regarding tuning, my general approach is simple, regardless of style. I tune to the environment that the acoustics and the music provide or require. Generally, I go for a sound that works with the music but provides a sense of excitement that pops out. In that regard, I go for contrasting textures and character more than uniformity. I find interval-based tonal tuning boring. I can go with a dry "thud" from a floor tom next to a resonant "thang" from a rack tom.

As far as the influence of electronic music has had on my tuning approach, it is simple. I learned that anything can become a drum sound with the right attitude.

Depending on the context, even a sound perceived as "bad" could become a "great" sound. I experiment a lot by augmenting and preparing my acoustic drums with all sorts of stuff. Sometimes, a splash cymbal or an ashtray on a snare can be helpful. Other times, it gets messy, or I go into electronic solutions, as with my new generative project, Me/Machine. No matter what I might do for some time, I need to change things up occasionally to keep it interesting for myself.

I also like stuff such as the Big Fat Snare Drum heads, where I can drastically change the sound of my kit within seconds without creating a mess. That's really cool.

---

### HONORABLE MENTIONS:

**Ringo** – the first drummer I knew by name when I was 2.

**Charly Antolini** – my first drum hero at age 5. He is a Swiss jazz drummer and former bandmate of my dad. He's got serious chops and acquainted me with the whole Buddy, Bellson vocabulary before I knew who they were. He made some excellent-sounding records in the '60s and '70s that have reached cult status with some of today's DJs and producers.

53

**Zigaboo, Purdie, Stubblefield, Jabo Starks, Hal Blaine, Irv Cottler, Jo Jones, Blakey, Sonny Payne, Bobby Colomby, Bonzo,** and many more – the soundtrack of my childhood home. I knew these drum parts inside and out long before I cared to know who recorded them.

**Carl Palmer** – He impressed me with ELP in 1970 with odd meters and even more with his colossal drum kit. I was 7.

**Lenny White, Alphonse Mouzon, Mike Clark, Harvey Mason, Bozzio** – the funk-jazz-rock-fusion heroes who ruled my teenage world.

**Vinnie Colaiuta** – I remember seeing him on TV with Zappa around that time. Never forgot that. To me, he somehow incarnated Tony's atmosphere into a new realm.

**Omar Hakim** – I saw him live with Gil Evans for the first time and then again with Weather Report in '82. He slapped me out of my Tony Williams trance, and I fell in love with his super elegant yet slinky and punchy style that was full of surprises.

**Weather Report** - I'm a big Peter Erskine fan beyond his work with the band.

**Elvin Jones** – unprecedented, unfathomable, yet highly archaic. He was like an asteroid that crashed into the earth from outer space.

**Deantoni Parks** – So many drummers left an imprint on my playing, but to mention everyone would fill up this entire book. However, I need to shout out to my compatriot Deantoni Parks, who picked up on similar ideas circling electronic music around the same time as I did and never ceased to astound me with his fearless and radical approach.

Over the years, other musicians, singers, and bass players like **Jaco Pastorius, Ray Brown, Verdine White**, and **Louis Johnson** were

54

equally crucial.

At some point, my musical influences shifted to various composers and producers, ranging from **Steve Reich** to **Aphex Twin, Photek,** and **Squarepusher,** and those I had the pleasure to interact with personally, like **Roli Mosimann** or **Brian Eno.**

And the older I got, the more I started to draw from design, architecture, history, literature, philosophy, psychology, movies, and art. Beyond that, the most significant source of inspiration nowadays is exchanges with extraordinary people who share their generosity, wisdom, experiences, and viewpoints with me.

# Erin Tate

*"The way the beat drops was nothing short of life-changing for me. That one simple moment shaped how I thought about beat writing..."*

E rin Tate, a founding member of Seattle-based indie-rock band Minus the Bear, has showcased his talent with various notable bands throughout his career, including Kill Sadie from Minneapolis and Ghostwork. He also manages the Indie Drummer Collective. Loved for his adeptness in navigating odd time signatures and syncopated phrases, Erin demonstrates seamless ease and confidence in his drumming. Here are Erin's choices...

Guns N' Roses, *Appetite for Destruction* [1987], "Rocket Queen"
**Drummer** - Steven Adler

This album came out when I was 8 or 9. I had already been pretty into KISS by then, but this set a different tone for rock music in my tiny little head.

When the "Welcome To The Jungle" video hit MTV, I would imagine it was something like when kids heard Zeppelin for the first time. The "wait....... this is sooooo badass" feeling. They came to Minneapolis, opening for Alice Cooper right when the album came out, and my brother and I managed to talk my mom into taking us. Seeing them live was a life-changing experience, even more than the

KISS show I'd seen the year before.

This album became the soundtrack for my next few years; the drumming is nothing short of perfect for the tracks, and the song "Rocket Queen" placed last on the album (in a day and age where sequence meant something on a record) sums up all the grit and rock n' roll lifestyle perfectly.

---

### Genesis, *Invisible Touch* [1986], "Domino (Pt. 1&2)"
### **Drummer** - Phil Collins

In a time of hair metal and obsessing over making my clothing "cool," enters the video for "Land of Confusion." At eight years old, the puppet work in the video was an easy hook for a kid. I don't know if my brother got the cassette tape or I did, but Genesis broke through the Guns N' Roses and KISS obsession and showed me a different side of things in songwriting.

As I spent time learning the drums and realizing that actual songwriting and song structure are what made me so into music (not just being a badass), I got into "Domino (Parts 1 & 2)." The idea that you could have two songs and structurally turn them into one ten-minute "super song" was a mind-blowing concept that stayed in my songwriting process for years.

See the following songs from Minus The Bear:
- "Dr. L'ing / Part 2"
- "Into the Mirror / Animal Backwards"
- "Diamond Lighting / Toska"

Thanks, Phil!

---

## The Beatles, *Revolver* [1966], "Tomorrow Never Knows"
**Drummer** - Ringo Starr

I always knew of The Beatles and liked their songs, but around 18, I decided to learn more about the band. I bought every book I could, every movie, every album etc. It became quickly apparent to me that without this band, rock n' roll would be sooooooooooo different. They were the first to do many things and set a tone for what would come.

The ongoing early vs later Beatles debate is a damn fine one. While most folks do lean into the hip and cool, long-haired "care fucking free, stoned Beatles," I love and respect the early tunes as well.

*Revolver* is the perfect blend of everything that the band brought to the table. "Tomorrow Never Knows"'s driving beat is among the most inspiring things I've ever heard.

## A Tribe Called Quest, *The Low End Theory* [1991], "Excursions"

I hit a point in my rock/punk drumming in my teens where I just got unmotivated. I started hanging out with a group of people who were highly into graffiti, which led me into the heavy grooves of the wonderful world of '90s hip-hop.

When *The Low End Theory* dropped, I saw them perform "Scenario" on the Arsenio Hall show; everyone in my friend group rushed out to buy the CD. Throwing this record on for the first time and hearing the bass line of "Excursions" and the way the beat drops was nothing short of life-changing for me. That one simple moment shaped how I thought about beat writing from then on.

## Sunny Day Real Estate, *Diary* [1994], "Seven"
**Drummer** - William Goldsmith

In a time when I only listened to hip-hop and spent a couple of years shaping any drumming I did do around solid/simple "make ya move" kind of beats, I heard a weird ass song by this strange-voiced man named Jeremy Enigk called "Abegail Anne." Something about his voice and the structure of that song hit me so hard.

I began researching who the hell this guy was (yes, pre-internet style) and was told to check out Sunny Day Real Estate.

I randomly purchased the CD *Diary* because, back then, you bought an album without knowing it and hoped you liked it. I was hooked within the first 13 seconds when I heard William do the long snare roll on the song "Seven." I had never heard anything like this, and it set me on a path of returning to non-hip-hop music.

The then "Emo scene" of Sunny Day Real Estate, Promise Ring, Texas Is the Reason, Mineral, Braid, and Christie Front Drive became my stepping stone into playing rock music again—all thanks to William G.

# Andrew Marshall

*"Choosing the correct sounds and playing them with good feel is much more important than squeezing more notes in."*

Andrew Marshall is a Los Angeles-based drummer whose deep pocket and vast knowledge of augmented drum setups helped solidify his status as an elite modern drummer. Holding the throne for Billie Eilish and FINNEAS, Andrew has played the biggest stages in the world. He continues to be on the cutting edge of what you can accomplish with hybrid drumming and playback technology. Here are Andrew's choices...

Jaco Pastorius, *The Birthday Concert* [recorded in 1981], "Soul Intro / The Chicken"
**Drummer** - Peter Erskine

I am trying to remember who introduced this record to me, but I remember being a Jaco fan at a relatively early age. I played a lot of funk and R&B music in high school and sat in at jam sessions. "The Chicken" was a standard tune in that world, and I played it with different bands. The real cats were the ones who learned "Soul Intro" too!

That music and those grooves were incredibly influential to me. In the back of my mind, I'm always trying to make whatever I'm playing funky or give it the swagger I heard on this and other Jaco Pastorius recordings. Everything Jaco played was devastatingly hip, and his melodic and harmonic innovations were unparalleled (see: "Portrait of Tracy"). Still, his 16th-note funk feel was the thing that had the most impact on me. The Peter Erskine/Jaco Pastorius combo was a match made in heaven—on this tune, Peter's clean, funky, tight beat seamlessly interlocks with Jaco's bass line to create a masterclass in feel and groove.

Tower of Power, *Soul Vaccination: Tower of Power Live* [1999], "Soul Vaccination"
**Drummer** - David Garibaldi

Around the age of 12 or 13, I got into David Garibaldi because of my teachers, Jason Devlin and Charlie Lagond. Jason was taking me through Garibaldi's book, *The Funky Beat*, and I found it so satisfying to work up his iconic grooves from tunes like "Soul Vaccination," "The Oakland Stroke," and, of course, "What is Hip?." That study was so helpful in terms of learning that everything has to groove and fit in the pocket, no matter how complex it is. Also, it was huge to learn how to play linearly—even though I don't always play that way, it worked wonders for my time and ability to construct beats and fills. Charlie Lagond had a music school that I attended growing up where they assembled bands from middle and high school students, and they'd book gigs so we could get experience playing in real-world venues. Some of the groups I played in had 3- or 4-piece horn sections, and we'd cover songs by Tower of Power, Earth Wind & Fire, Maceo Parker, and other artists and bands in the funk and soul genre. Locking in with a great bass player in a large ensemble like that is a fantastic feeling and one I still chase.

This is an example of an absolutely airtight rhythm section. Seeing David Garibaldi and Rocco Prestia live was a force of nature. To this day, I want people in the audience to have the same feeling I had watching Tower of Power from the front row at B.B. King's in New York—to be blown away by the strength and funkiness of a group of musicians playing in lockstep. It really is a Tower of Power!

## Chick Corea Elektric Band, *To The Stars* [2004], "Mistress Luck - The Party"
### **Drummer** - Dave Weckl

The earliest jazz-oriented or semi-improvised music that caught my ear as a young drum nerd was fusion, especially Weather Report and the Chick Corea Elektric Band. I was lucky enough to see Dave Weckl play live several times with Chick Corea, as they would often come through NYC and play at the Blue Note. His fluidity, facility, lyrical expression, and sheer power on the instrument blew my mind. This song is an excellent example of Weckl in top form—a salsa-influenced, shreddy, up-tempo fusion party. To 13-year-old me, Dave Weckl's playing exemplified perfection, resulting from thousands of hours of practice and a Buddha-like level of drumming understanding that was light years beyond my teenage brain. I couldn't get enough. This record was one of the first ones I got of theirs, only because it was the most recent release when I saw them play in 2004, and it was for sale at the merch table. I later learned it was the first record after a hiatus and couldn't have come at a better time in my drumming development.

For a while, I tried to be Dave Weckl—I set my kit up like his (two up and two down with the second rack tom in what would typically be the first rack tom position with the smaller rack tom on a stand to its left for optimal traditional grip ergonomics), I played his signature sticks, and I practiced the hell out of my blushdas and songo grooves. That never really came to fruition, but I took a lot of fluidity, rhythmic and tonal clarity, and a slight underlying Latin influence from studying his playing during that period. And I still love blushdas!

---

## Say Anything, ...*Is A Real Boy* [2004], "Belt"
### **Drummer** - Coby Linder

In high school, I joined a pop-punk band with some friends who opened up my musical world. Until then, I never thought about song structure, specific kick drum patterns, playing the same fill into the chorus every time, accenting a vocal, crashing on the ride cymbal, or any other essential concepts in pop and rock music. We made a couple of albums and went to Bamboozle and Warped Tour during the summers. I started listening to bands like My Chemical Romance, Fall Out Boy, Paramore, Panic! At The Disco, and the like (pretty outside of what I had been into as a drum nerd who thought I was bound for jazz school!). Say Anything, and this record in particular, was a huge influence. I discovered them at Bamboozle when they were a surprise act playing at 11 am in the parking lot. My friends were excited—I had never heard of them, but they quickly became one of my favorite bands. I saw them live several times and loved their rawness paired with catchy songwriting and melodies. This song is an almost entirely through-composed drum part that supports the music and catches every tiny turn of phrase, guitar lick, and melody. It almost serves as another vocal, complementing and adding depth and texture to the melodic lines.

Nowadays, I call on this influence to channel some raw punk energy when it's called for while maintaining the thoughtfulness and musicality Coby Linder demonstrates on this track and album. I'm grateful for my experiences playing this type of music because it's helped me become a stronger foundation and presence onstage.

## James Blake, *The Bells Sketch* [2010], "Buzzard & Kestrel"

In college, I got very into electronic music. I listened to many producers, sifting through unknown artists on SoundCloud, and went to various electronica shows. James Blake burst onto the scene around 2011 with his self-titled debut album. Still, he put out some EPs before that, which were incredibly unique and fresh with minimal production, not much singing (and whatever singing there was was significantly effected to the point of being unrecognizable), and unconventional song structure. I loved how he carefully chose and highlighted sounds, giving different layers space to breathe. This song is an excellent example of that—most of the drum beat is just a stick-click sound on beat one, followed by some snare hits that change in velocity through the rest of the bar to create a slinky groove. It's understated but highly creative and exciting.

These days, I employ a less-is-more approach, especially when trying to recreate electronic beats for the stage or programming drums on records. What is the least I can get away with playing or programming while still getting the musical point across? This often works the best. More notes don't necessarily translate, especially through a big arena or festival PA system. Choosing the correct sounds and playing them with good feel is much more important than squeezing more notes in. Listening to minimal electronica was a considerable influence in helping me develop this side of my musical persona.

---

## D'Angelo, *Voodoo* [2000], "Untitled (How Does It Feel)"
### Drummer - Questlove

"Untitled (How Does It Feel)" by D'Angelo is an amazing lesson in minimalism, feel, and soul. The way bassist/producer Raphael Saadiq plays so far behind Questlove's simple but effective pocket makes the groove super wide and comfortable in its loping tilt. Masterful, deliberate, and sensitive playing with a complete focus on the feel. This record greatly influenced me in college as I listened to more jazz with hip-hop and electronic influences, and I played a minimal "boom-bap" two- or three-piece setup for a while, a configuration I still very much enjoy.

---

# Sarab Singh

*"...you could practice [this intro] on a loop, and it would be amazing for your facility and technique on the kit."*

S arab Singh, a Los Angeles-based drummer and music producer, is currently making waves with the band MUNA. With a career marked by versatility, Sarab has collaborated with a diverse range of artists, including Ingrid Michaelson, Charlie XCX, Joji, Harper Lynn, and his solo project called KLVR GRL, among others. Renowned for his exceptional musicality, technical prowess, and knowledge of drumming history, Sarab is the definition of a modern drummer. Here are Sarab's choices...

Tower of Power, *Back to Oakland* [1974], "Squib Cakes"
**Drummer** - David Garibaldi

My great drum set teacher, Bill Marconi, introduced this album to me in high school. It completely knocked my socks off and still does to this day. My main takeaway from it was David's 16th note-oriented feel, where his subdivisions give this constant motion to the music that feels so good and makes you want to bounce and move. Then, based around that, is his incredible linear approach and the fantastic patterns between his hands and feet, as you can hear in the intro to this track.

Those few bars where he plays that hand-foot pattern in the intro are something you could practice on a loop, and it would be amazing for your facility and technique on the kit. Everything that David plays always grooves so hard, even his fills, and there is so much to take away from that—to ensure that nothing ever takes you out of that motion and that groove.

## Wayne Shorter, *Night Dreamer* [1964], "Black Nile"
**Drummer** - Elvin Jones

This album and all of Wayne Shorter's other incredible albums as a leader were also introduced to me in high school. Every one of those albums is a great work, with an all-star lineup and beautiful compositions, and so much to learn from. This album and this track stuck out to me a lot because, first of all, Elvin is just on fire. He is so crisp and articulate sounding with his triplet comping, and the circular motion of his ideas is so mesmerizing to me.

The other reason I love this track is that I could always hear the song form really well, AABA, and it helped me understand how to play this type of jazz music with other people. Also, how Elvin plays around the figures and the sections always blew me away. It's some of the best triplet comping ever!

## Steely Dan, *The Royal Scam* [1976], "Kid Charlemagne"
**Drummer** - Bernard Purdie

I first heard this album in my friend's car while on break from college during the summer, and I couldn't believe just how incredible and deeeeep the pocket was. This track always blew me away because of how elastic it felt. I think it's the backbeat after the open hi-hat on the "+" of beats 1 and 3 in each bar; it's like a slingshot.

And then the way Bernard plays around the kit, even that is so funky. It's a bit like his "Rock Steady" groove, and it's so cool to see how you can apply the same feeling groove to different songs, and it works so well. I always also loved this guitar solo! But I still feel that if you can play a groove like this and make it feel good, someone out there will always want to hire you to play with them!!

## Brian Blade, *Perceptual* [2000], "Crooked Creek"
### Drummer - Brian Blade

This was another album that I discovered on summer break from college. I had been listening to so much Elvin; this album was the first time I heard Brian play. It was like the modern version of Elvin, with some of the same vocabulary, except it was taken to another place, as Brian is so otherworldly with the emotion that comes through his playing and the music itself that this particular band plays.

It's such a journey musically and just so beautiful and spiritual. Brian is a master of shading and dynamics, and the way he leads the band is something I am constantly trying to learn from. His playing is so open and expansive, with so much breath. He is a technical master, but I always feel his playing more in my heart than my head, which is pure magic.

## Fiona Apple, *When the Pawn...* [1999], "On the Bound"
### Drummer - Matt Chamberlain

I first heard this album when I was at music school at the University of Miami. I mainly listened to jazz, but I had a friend in the program who always listened to the most incredible stuff with the best songs. She played me this album, and I was amazed. I had heard Matt play before on the Macy Gray album, which came out around 1999 as well, and I recognized him immediately. This album was everything I wanted to hear because I could hear the Elvin/Garibaldi in Matt's playing, but it was music and songs that I wanted to listen to on a non-drummer level.

It was song-based music that I loved and wanted to listen to emotionally, but with playing that came from the same world I was coming from. Then, just the sounds of the drums and the whole recording were unique to me. Shout out, Jon Brion! Listening to this album taught me so much about playing with more singer-songwriter-based music, understanding what the song needs and how it always should feel, and also finding the places to be creative and signature wherever you can.

Miles Davis, *Seven Steps to Heaven* [1963], "Seven Steps to Heaven"
**Drummer** - Tony Williams

This is a perfect example of Tony Williams's up-tempo jazz approach. The blazing and blistering sound and feel of his ride cymbal and the crisp comping of the rest of his limbs on the kit are magical. It showed me how conversational you could be on the drum kit and how incredible jazz facility can be — also, such a beautifully composed drum solo in the middle of the tune.

## Shawn Colvin, *A Few Small Repairs* [1995] , "Sunny Came Home"
### **Drummer** - Shawn Pelton

I first heard "Sunny Came Home" in 1998, around when it came out, but I didn't come back to it until about 2005 when I moved to New York and used to go see Shawn Pelton play at the Living Room and other clubs in the lower east side. The pocket that Shawn has on this tune blows me away, as do the tiny things he does throughout the song. His fills groove as hard as the main beat, and it's a masterclass on how to play with feel, lilt, sensitivity, AND power!

## John Scofield, Pat Metheny, *I Can See Your House From Here* [1994], "The Red One"
### **Drummer** - Bill Stewart

Bill Stewart on "The Red One" is incredible. This album is a co-headline between John Scofield and Pat Metheny, which is already mind-blowing, but then add Bill in there, and holy smokes. Bill's playing here is funky and lyrical. As always, he is articulate and crisp in his ideas. I have always loved hearing him on this as it's not a swing feel on this tune but more like acid-jazz or funk. His sound on the kit is so beautiful, and his ride cymbal sound consistently has such a fantastic "stick" sound, which I think comes from how he holds the stick.

# Josh Dion

*"I tried to mimic his charisma and stage presence...It's almost hard to listen to now; the nostalgia might take me out."*

J osh Dion is a multi-talented musician known for his ability to play drums, keyboard, and sing simultaneously. He began his professional career at eight and has since collaborated with artists like John Scofield, Wayne Krantz, Jim Campilongo, Masters of the Telecaster, and many more. Currently, he's part of the duo paris_ monster with bandmate Geoff Kraly. Here are Josh's choices...

Full Moon, *Full Moon* [1972], "The Heavy Scuffles On"
**Drummer** - Phillip Wilson

To my knowledge, Full Moon was a band of fantastic studio musicians/musicians from other successful bands. They were short-lived, and this debut album from 1972 is the one I've heard people mention the most. They had played a local club in my hometown called The Shaboo. Local musicians, including my dad, always talked about Full Moon and how they were "ahead of their time" and an exciting fusion blend; there was a mystique around the record. I listened to it constantly and tried to play along. It was eclectic — with funk, gospel, blues, Latin, and jazz influences. I didn't know anything about the players. Now I know more about their history. I'm incredibly inspired

71

by how versatile Phillip Wilson was as a drummer. He connected Chicago blues, straight-ahead jazz, the AACM, R&B, and Woodstock—all in a unique, raw sound. I still listen to Full Moon often. Dave Holland, Randy Brecker, and other guests are on the album. I jump at any opportunity to get the word out.

---

## Earth, Wind and Fire, *Open Our Eyes* [1974], "Mighty Mighty"
**Drummers** - Maurice White, Ralph Johnson, Fred White

I chose this album because EWF [Earth, Wind and Fire] was a huge pivot point for me coming out of the church world into the secular world as a teen. I had heard them growing up, but I became immersed once I connected with their spiritual message. Once again, this album is incredibly eclectic. It's mad funky, but there are sambas and straight-ahead tunes. The title track is a gospel tune that has always spoken to me. And EWF features multiple singing drummers. Maurice White helped shape my singing style; his story of going from session drummer to frontman has always inspired me. These elements (pun) captured my spirit—a message I needed alongside fantastic musicianship. I repeatedly listened to "Mighty Mighty," trying to figure out how they sang that soulful. Verdine White's bass line is super awesome. And I loved how the soprano sax doubles with the synth to create the "horns." This was before they had Jerry Hey and those guys and right before their enormous success and pop stardom.

This album is all over the place and not commercial. But the groove is unified, and the writing is fantastic. I own every EWF album, and I'm a fan for life.

---

## John Scofield, *Loud Jazz* [1988], "Dirty Rice" (at 1:20)
### **Drummer** - Dennis Chambers

Like many, some of the only drum instructional videos I owned were *In The Pocket* and *Serious Moves* by Dennis Chambers, which featured Gary Grainger, John Scofield, and Jim Beard. Dennis was single-handedly responsible for opening up the funk floodgates in my life. I hadn't known The Meters, Parliament Funkadelic, James Brown, or Headhunters. I was 15, and suddenly, it shot me into an obsession that continues today — The Funk. It doesn't get any purer than Dennis and his influences. How he and Gary moved the beat changed me; I loved how the Scofield band played together. I immediately bought the three albums I could find with that quartet- *Pick Hits, Blue Matter*, and my all-time favorite, *Loud Jazz*. I randomly chose this track, "Dirty Rice," but I couldn't choose a track. George Duke guests on this album and plays synth solos (the one of this track KILLS). He's also one of my favorites and most significant influences on the synth. I've played with Sco for the past two years and even hung with Dennis and Gary a little. My mind often flashes back to that 15-year-old kid practicing in the corner of my bedroom. I love Sco's writing — his influence of gospel and how he modulates section to section is seamless. He's another one coming so deeply from blues and early rock. I love how their brand of "fusion" from the '80s redefined it… and brought SERIOUS funk to the table… and for many, through some DCI VHS tapes.

---

## Richard Smallwood Singers, *Testimony* [1992], "Wonderful Counselor"
### **Drummer** - Bill Maxwell

In my church phase, worship/contemporary Christian music came across as "communal" or "cheesy" and may not have aged well. But I still loved it because of its meaning. Music isn't about virtuosity as much as it is about emotion, intention, unity, and spirit. Richard Smallwood and company are absolute badasses in EVERY way. I wore this album out. I wished I could play the piano like this and sing like this. The message and the emotion lifted me and spoke to me. I later discovered that the drummer was Bill Maxwell, who I knew from the Christian fusion band Koinonia. Maxwell produced many albums in that genre and cross-pollinated with many artists. He's such a meat-and-potatoes type player. It reminded me of the way my Dad plays. I always remembered him and never realized he was on so many albums. I had *Testimony* on cassette. I remember listening on the school bus on my Walkman, feeling the spirit, and having the fire burning inside me at 8 a.m.; I was ready for church. The drumming on this album (as well as the arranging) is fantastic.

## Gene Krupa, *Compact Jazz* [1987], "Disc Jockey Jump" (at 1:22)
### Drummer - Gene Krupa

I probably watched *The Gene Krupa Story* (featuring Sal Mineo) way more than I ever listened to Gene. It may seem strange, but that was what I had then. Once I copped Benny Goodman's records, I was off. Gene was my gateway into big band drumming and, therefore, jazz drumming. I found whatever footage of him I could get my hands on. I memorized the licks, moves, stick twirls, etc. I tried to mimic his charisma and stage presence. My dad bought me this compilation cassette. It stopped playing after a while because I listened so much. It's almost hard to listen to now; the nostalgia might take me out.

I love Gene's swing. There's a beautiful simplicity to it. Most of all, it led me to King Oliver, Papa Jo Jones, Duke, Count, Fats, the Dorseys, Dave Tough, Jimmy Lunceford, Fletcher Henderson, Baby Dodds, etc. I used to photocopy photos and facts from the jazz encyclopedia, make laminated posters, and hang them in my room (memorizing the artist's names and band personnel). Gene was the spark for me. From what I could see, with all his success, Gene was humble and certainly gave it up for the other greats. The way he swung his single strokes was the heaviest thing I learned when I was young. All my early drum solos were copping Gene (and the great rock drummers). I played a drum solo on "Sing, Sing, Sing" in the 5th grade; it was a pinnacle moment for me as a performer, lol. I remember getting on the bus the next day, and everyone clapped. I got my initials painted on my bass drum in the same fashion as Gene and Buddy. I don't twirl my sticks much anymore, but Gene's showmanship and feel are engrained in me forever. Jazz geek forever!

# Rob "Beatdown" Brown

*"...[This Album] took everything I knew up to that point, and Hulk smashed it to pieces like Jenga; this stuff was crazy..."*

Rob "Beatdown" Brown, a prominent figure in the YouTube drumming scene, distinguishes himself not only through his stellar performances but also through his unique teaching style. Utilizing a blend of casual humor and clear instructional techniques, Brown engages viewers of all skill levels, making complex rhythms, perspectives and techniques accessible and enjoyable to learn. Here are Rob's choices...

The Police, *Ghost In The Machine* [1981], "One World (Not Three)"
**Drummer** - Stewart Copeland

There aren't many Police albums I didn't practice to constantly, but it was still easy to pick the standouts for some reason. There were certain things in certain songs that Stewart played that, to this day, stick in my head. He's pretty much why I picked up the sticks, and I'd consider him my first drum hero. *Ghost In The Machine* was the second Police album I picked up after hearing "Spirits In The Material World."

The whole album is a no-skip, but one song I used to play repeatedly was "One World (Not Three)."

Stuart is doing all kinds of cool improvisational stuff in that song, and it feels like it was just a straight plow from top to bottom when they recorded it: no cuts or punch-ins. That's what it sounds like to me—just tons of uninterrupted energy. But my favorite part is the halftime section at the end. He leads into it with this ferocious snare fill, then launches into this cool halftime groove. The whole tune is full of Stu'isms. And I've ripped off a bunch of them.

---

## Level 42, *World Machine* [1985], "Physical Presence"
### Drummer - Phil Gould

The first Level 42 song I remember hearing was called "Micro Kid" from the album *Standing In The Light*. That was probably my introduction to jazz-pop. After picking up that album, I became a big fan. During that time, I was really into keyboards, so my hero in the band was, at that point, Mike Lindup. I can't remember the lineage of which albums made it into the house after which, but I know we didn't buy them in order. Either way, by the time we got to *World Machine*, I was already pretty heavy into drums, and that's when I started paying attention to Phil Gould. That album is groove heaven for me. But the song that gets the biggest gold star out of all of them would be "Physical Presence."

Phil's 16th note grooves feel ridiculously good and rock solid. Even if you're not into drums, you'll be able to feel that when you listen to it. "Sleepwalkers" off the *Running In The Family* album is another one, but "Physical Presence" is probably the song I used to play along to the most; it taught me how to develop my right hand on the hi-hats. Phil was a big part of that band's sound, and although they are still plenty

77

good now, it wasn't the same once he left.

## Big Country, *Steeltown* [1984], "Steeltown"
**Drummer** - Mark Brzezicki

I don't have enough words for this album. The first time I saw the video for "In A Big Country," I became a big fan of Big Country. At that particular time, there were no bands that sounded like them. That was probably for many reasons, but one of the biggest reasons, at least for me, was Mark Brzezicki. Everyone who knows about Mark knows he is among the greatest and most underrated drummers. If you are as big a Big Country fan as I am, then you would probably agree that *Steeltown* is their best album; it's a drummer's record, as far as I'm concerned. It's littered with some of the most incredible drum parts and grooves you'll ever hear. But the TUNE "Steeltown" might be my favorite Big Country tune, period.

Mark is one of those drummers who doesn't simply play generic parts that get the job done. He creates these busy-but-somehow-not-busy compositions that are technical but groove hard simultaneously. He's got this fantastic, unique way of incorporating tom and cymbal patterns in his grooves that never get in the way. You might even wonder while listening, 'Is he playing all this at the same time?' I wore this particular tune out and practiced it until I learned every note. And I still keep a lot of the licks in my back pocket!

## Chick Corea Elektric Band, *Inside Out* [1990], "Tale Of Daring: Chapter 3"
**Drummer** - Dave Weckl

After my third year of playing all of this Police, Level 42, Big Country, and other pop/rock stuff, I discovered jazz fusion. I was pretty good at the time but was nowhere near as good as I could be after hearing this jazz fusion stuff. The late '80s and early '90s was a hugely significant time for me as a drummer learning because all of this wicked fusion stuff started spilling out simultaneously, and that's when I discovered EVERYBODY—Dennis Chambers, Peter Erskine, Steve Gadd, Vinnie Colaiuta, Will Kennedy, Steve Smith, all the Mount Rushmore guys—at the same time. But there was eventually a lot of Chick Corea Elektric Band in the house. I didn't realize what was possible on the drums until I heard all these guys I mentioned, but a significant one was Dave Weckl.

I had been practicing my favorite Elektric Band albums regularly when *Inside Out* came out, and I remember getting it immediately. Dave is doing some freaking stratospheric playing on that album. There's this one crazy 15-minute piece in four chapters on the record called "Tale Of Daring." "Chapter 3," in particular, is one I used to play repeatedly. There's this pretty amazing open conversation between Dave and Chick with just a million diamonds in it, and I tried my best to learn all of them. I'm glad I didn't record any of it because it'd probably be comically bad to listen to this many years later, but it did a serious number on my chops.

Steve Coleman & Five Elements, *Black Science* [1990], "Turbulence"
**Drummer** - Marvin 'Smitty' Smith

So, my jazz fusion phase was long, and I camped out on that stuff for a long time. At some point, my brother started listening to this sax player, Steve Coleman, who had a band called Five Elements. This music is hard to describe. It's structured and unstructured simultaneously, with time signatures up the wazoo far beyond 5 and 7. There's an album called *Black Science* that took everything I knew up to that point, and Hulk smashed it to pieces like Jenga; this stuff was crazy—probably what Mahavishnu or Zappa or Weather Report was to a first-time listener in the '70s. I'd never heard this type of music or heard of any of the musicians on that record before. And I'd certainly never heard musicianship on that level—the way those guys were all locked in incredibly complex stuff was something I wanted to learn.

That was my introduction to compound odd-time playing and my first time hearing Marvin 'Smitty' Smith. Practicing and playing this music helped me develop massive headroom for odd time signatures until 7/8 felt as comfortable as 4/4. These songs were cycling upwards of 13, 15, and 19, so your brain adjusts to hearing all kinds of pulses in different spots. But somehow, you're still easily nodding your head to all of it because of how hard the stuff grooves! Marvin plays the crap out of this whole record, just easily playing circles around these signatures, and "Turbulence" is one of the most remarkable examples of that. Marvin's playing did what Dave's playing with Chick did for me back when I discovered that music. It's always exciting when you accidentally find a new room in the building.

# Aaron Haggerty

*"The way he can make a quarter note swing...is an excellent example of how feel can be implied so effectively without having to play every note."*

Aaron Haggerty is a Los-Angeles based session drummer and producer known for his work with acclaimed artists like Al McKay, Kool & The Gang, Eric Gales, Willow, Gary Clark Jr., UB40, and Wicked Wisdom. Inspired by jazz, funk, R&B, house, techno, and world music, his drumming exhibits a wide-ranging skill set and dynamic approach. Here are Aaron's choices…

Buddy Rich Big Band (with various drummers), *Burning For Buddy - A Tribute To The Music of Buddy Rich* [1994], "Love For Sale"
**Drummer** - Steve Gadd

This record was huge for me as a youngster, hearing so many legendary drummers from different genres bring their own feel to these big band tunes. This track, in particular, stood out to me because of how Gadd swings on the ride cymbal. The way he can make a quarter note swing really stuck with me and is an excellent example of how feel can be implied so effectively without having to play every note.

## The New Tony Williams Lifetime, *Believe It* [1975], "Red Alert"
### Drummer - Tony Williams

This was another record that blew my mind when I discovered it. I had learned of Tony through Miles Davis records and was already a fan, but I knew of this record at a time when I was also getting into more progressive rock music, and it bridged this gap between the genres so perfectly.

The heavy riffs and blazing guitar solos, the dynamic arrangements, and Tony's explosive, virtuosic performances make this record one of the most important in my listening history.

## Tower of Power, *Back To Oakland* [1974], "Squib Cakes"
### Drummer - David Garibaldi

David Garibaldi is, without a doubt, one of my biggest influences. His busy, syncopated linear grooves and feel are synonymous with "funk" for me.

The drum intro on "Squib Cakes" is iconic. His feel and phrasing are just perfect. The interplay between the rhythm section is a masterclass in phrasing and syncopation throughout the tune and on any Tower tune.

## Tool, *Ænima* [1996], "Jimmy"
### Drummer - Danny Carey

Danny Carey was a massive influence on me as a teenager. I heard the single from this record on the radio and was blown away by the drum performance and drum sounds.

When I got the record, I spent many days after school playing along and breaking down Danny's cool polyrhythmic grooves and long rolling fills. This record still greatly influences my sensibilities toward playing heavy rock music.

## D'Angelo, *Voodoo* [2000], "Playa Playa"
**Drummer** - Questlove

When I discovered this record, it really blew my mind. The overall aesthetic was extraordinary and new to me. The feel that Questlove and Pino bring is so deep and relaxed.

This track, in particular, was so cool to me because of the interplay between the bass and kick drum. There's this continuous playful comping the entire way through. It gives it a live and improvised vibe, with superb phrasing throughout. There are fascinating tones on this record as well.

# Ash Soan

*"I owe him a massive amount for how I have progressed in music,
the advice, and the playing we have shared and still do."*

Ash Soan, a prominent figure in the British session and recording scene, rose to prominence in the 1990s with Del Amitri. He later contributed his talents to bands like Faithless and Squeeze. Since then, Ash has built a diverse career as a sought-after session player and clinician. His impressive resume includes collaborations with artists such as Marianne Faithfull, Boyzone, Cee Lo Green, Adele, and Dua Lipa. Here are Ash's choices…

Tower of Power, *Tower of Power* [1973], "What Is Hip?"
**Drummer** - David Garibaldi

David Garibaldi! I first heard him in 1989 while studying music in Manchester, England. A friend of mine, Neil Fairclough, was into two bands, Queen and Tower Of Power! Incredibly, Neil ended up playing bass in Queen, but that's a whole other inspirational story on its own… so….

Neil was always a great musician and wanted to play with a drummer who understood David Garibaldi's concept. When he played me "What is Hip?," that was it. I was hooked. Neil could play all the lines, and we spent many hours listening to and playing Tower of Power tracks.

## Toto, *Toto IV* [1982], "Rosanna"
### **Drummer** - Jeff Porcaro

I heard this track around the age of 14. Back then (1984), there was no easy way to find out how grooves were played notation-wise. When I heard the drum part, I asked my then-teacher, who said they didn't know what he was playing, so my journey began to find out for myself. I eventually found a transcription in *Modern Drummer*! The mist cleared! It's a groove I've loved and worked on ever since.

Jeff's simplistic approach to songs while keeping sophistication in his playing is something I have always aspired to.

---

**Can you discuss Steve Ferrone's influence on you?**

Ferrone!!! I first saw him with Eric (Clapton) at the Albert Hall, and I always dug his incredible groove with everyone from Chaka to Tom Petty.

The Average White Band was one of Steve's first big bands, and I'm very fortunate to play with Hamish Stuart, one of the founding members. I've known Hamish for about 30 years and, of course, came across Steve during that time. Since then, we have shared album credits with Rod Stewart and shared Hamish's solo gig. An absolute groove monster and, for me, one of the only independent British drummers to make a deep impression in the States. There are John Bonham, Ringo, etc., but they made it via bands; Steve made it via many different sessions. He is still, to this day, an absolute inspiration to me.

---

**Can you discuss Stewart Copeland's influence on you?**

Stewart!!!! As a teen, his energy blew my mind, as it still does. I worked in a music shop in 1987, and we would set splash cymbals up all over the shop and try and hit them in time with The Police tracks we had playing over the shop speakers.

I've always gravitated towards Stewart's love of reggae music, too. How he fused reggae, rock, punk, and pop has always been magical to me.

Fortunately, I have met and played with Stewart via my producer friend, Trevor Horn. Having spent time with Stewart, his music makes much more sense.

**Can you discuss Pino Pallidino's (bassist) influence on you?**

Pino!! I moved to London in 1991 and onto the same street as Pino. As a young musician, I would call his house, and we would hang out in his studio. I would bombard him with questions about music and the drummers he'd played with, and at that point, it was pretty much everyone.

I owe him a massive amount for how I have progressed in music, the advice, and the playing we have shared and still do. I saw him in LA recently when I was playing with Tori Amos. He is still the most musical and humble musician I've ever met.

### *HONORABLE MENTIONS:*

I should mention some other Brit drummers who deserve a name check: **Henry Spinetti** (Eric Clapton), **Dave Mattacks, Ian Thomas, Ralph Salmins,** and **Gavin Harrison**.

An honorary Brit who's worth a mention is the great **Andy Newmark**! He's lived in England for decades but hails from Bermuda. His playing with Lennon, Sly, and Roxy Music is just the tip of the iceberg. What a player!

# Richard Spaven

*"When you've learned a language, you can make your own authentic sentences and express yourself. Flow is crucial to my playing..."*

R ichard Spaven stands as one of the most coveted drummers in progressive and contemporary music. With collaborations spanning from Jose James to Flying Lotus, Gang Starr, Cinematic Orchestra, and Jameszoo, Richard has solidified his influence as a genre-defying musician. While his career as a sideman is undeniably impressive, it's his solo endeavors that truly highlight his distinctive artistic voice. Here are Richard's choices...

Meshell Ndegeocello feat. Herbie Hancock, *Stolen Moments: Red Hot + Cool* [1994], "Nocturnal Sunshine"
**Drummer** - Harvey Mason

This is an excellent example of when the groove is absolute pocket perfection, and then a fill comes along, introduces some flair and risk, and elevates. This is the ultimate embellishment from Harvey Mason.

I use the word embellishment a lot. It has long since occurred to me that our word "fills" implies "filling in" and putting the groove on hold as we deal with other matters — then getting right back to it as soon as we've finished. Embellishments, however, as the word suggests, will augment and add to what's already there. In drumming, we would choose relatable language—maintain the flow—and not interrupt the pocket while adding, varying, or expressing within what we already have established.

## Source Direct, "Secret Liaison" [1996]

I have probably taken inspiration from live music and programmed music in equal measure. Being from London, I have attended many club nights with fledgling genres in their early stages, with drum n bass, broken beat, and dubstep being prime examples. I remember hearing this track for the first time at Speed. It's a moody "Amen" break roller with a languid bass line and atmospheric piano sample. The drums are cut up and fired off with ferocious precision.

It wasn't until much later that I realized how much of an influence my clubbing days had on my drumming. I love to create effortless flow—at tempo—with precision. Understanding the language of drum n bass and respecting producers like Source Direct's manipulation of samples has taught me so much. When you've learned a language, you can make your own authentic sentences and express yourself. Flow is crucial to my playing, with many light ghost notes creating an undercurrent to maintain the momentum. I can directly relate this way of thinking back to a wide-eared Spaven soaking this inspiration in; at the time, I had no idea it would come in so handy.

## Meshell Ndegeocello, *Comfort Woman* [2003], "Come Smoke My Herb"
## **Drummer** - Chris Dave

88

I have been introduced to so many influential drummers through Meshell's music. Gene Lake is a spirited player with a filthy pocket and technical ability rolled tightly into one. That led me to a period of Steve Coleman records and got me into M-Base (it's all a journey, isn't it?). Sean Rickman is a remarkable drummer who can express himself within the most complicated parameters; he also played a lot of M-Base. We all know about Chris Dave, but I only discovered him when Meshell brought him to London as drummer in her band. It was the *Comfort Woman* tour, and it was special. He held it down so hard yet chose his moments to drop some utter outrageousness. Deantoni Parks is rare in that he has such a unique style all of his own.

That's a lot of remarkable drummers; combine those with my favorite bass player of all time, and that's it—musical bliss and endless inspiration.

## Burial, *Untrue* [2007], "Archangel"

If you know this record then you know. It's a moody, atmospheric, filmic masterpiece that hit me hard. It's an evocative listen, and this is something I relate to when it comes to making my records.

Making music means a lot to me. It's a deep process; there is emotional content and attachment. When I'm writing/producing, it's the feeling I have created that I want to translate effortlessly to the listener. The actual workings of the piece, such as chords and grooves, are vital elements but pale in significance when I think about transferring the mood onto the listener.

Burial's *Untrue* and my music are not directly comparable; however, if you mixed them up in a playlist, took a long journey, and stared out the window with your headphones cranked up, then I think you'd create and remain in your own world.

## David Axelrod, *Song of Innocence* [1968], "Holy Thursday" **Drummer** - Earl Palmer

Now, we are talking about tuning style and recording style.

My kit is essentially "jazz" sizes. I play an 18" bass drum, and my snares are pitched up (not cranked — just gotta have that crack). There's a motive here that relates to many of my influences.

First, there were drummers — and with drummers came breaks. Breaks are important because hip hop and drum n bass (my two biggest influences) would not have been invented without them. Breaks appeared on hip hop records and in drum n bass music — and for drummers like me, that's very influential indeed.

Now, let's talk about bass drum sound for a moment. Imagine the most famous of them all, "Funky Drummer" played by Clyde Stubblefield. Clyde didn't play a finger-tight 22" full of duvets with three mics and a sub. He played a higher-pitched kick with a tone and a resonance. Many of my favorite records use samples with higher-pitched bass drums — and air-shaking sub bass every time we hear a kick drum wouldn't compliment the music. So there it is — for my sound, I'm referencing the sound of the breaks era — and Earl Palmer was a master.

### HONORABLE MENTIONS:

Let's mention the unsung hero, **Gregory C. Coleman**, and a moment in time when he changed the course of music and created genres... all in a 6-second drum break.

Of course, I am talking about the "Amen" break, lifted from

the original "Amen Brother" by The Winstons and used in hip hop, hardcore, jungle, and jazz electronica. He is one of the most sampled drummers ever and the least credited. He didn't benefit financially as he should have, so thank you, and I tip my hat to GC Coleman.

---

# Aksel Coe

*"Playing along to this song...is a great relaxation exercise. I'd find that the more I tense up, the harder it would be to make it through the song."*

Aksel Coe, a platinum-certified session drummer from Nashville, TN, has collaborated with a wide range of artists such as Zach Bryan, Sierra Ferrell, K. Flay, Scarypoolparty, Cody Jinks, Pam Tillis, Sam Barber, Baerd, Jars of Clay, and others. Additionally, he's a member of the band Homes at Night. Renowned for infusing his unique style into every track, Aksel is rapidly establishing himself as a top choice in both Nashville and remote recording circles. Here are Aksel's choices...

Pat Metheny, *Bright Size Life* [1976], "Bright Size Life"
**Drummer** - Bob Moses

This record was introduced to me by my middle school band director. At the time, I couldn't comprehend exactly what was happening on the track. Bob Moses (the drummer) has an incredible ability to phrase melodically and often over the barline. I didn't fully understand this then, but I knew it was something I wanted to learn. Bob Moses, in my opinion, is one of the more underrated jazz drummers. He has an incredible amount of facility and ideas. This track opened my eyes to the importance of right-hand phrasing. My feel and identity as a player come from how I present my right hand. Most of the music I play and record these days is backbeat oriented, and while I'm not trying to access as much of the nuance as I would if I was playing with Pat Metheny, controlling my right hand has been an invaluable skill. Even something as simple as being aware of the cymbal volume in a pop-country session. This track started me on the journey of control.

Art Blakey & The Jazz Messengers, *Free for All* [1964], "Free For All"
**Drummer** - Art Blakey

Most of my early music education was done via YouTube. Every day when I would get home from middle school, I was allowed one hour of computer time, and I would spend this hour watching different jazz drummers on YouTube. One of my favorites to this day is Art Blakey. It was hard to pick a specific record because there were so many great ones. *Free for All* is such an astonishing Blakey record because he pushes the boundaries of what he usually does. To me, Art Blakey is known for specific licks that he plays during solos. He's also known for steady timekeeping and his Latin grooves on songs like "Night in Tunisia."

He usually keeps his hi-hat foot on 2&4 and plays straight time on the ride cymbal. However, he's approaching things differently on this track: hi-hat comping, straight 8th phrasing on the ride. He's using all his limbs to comp and push the soloist's energy and arrangement. He's also beating the shit out of the drums for the entire 11 minutes of the song. I remember hearing this for the first time and being so impressed with hearing a different side of one of my favorite drummers. Jazz education can be very stiff, especially for a young drummer. Hearing this record helped get me out of that mindset.

## Charles Wright & The Watts 103rd Street Rhythm Band, *You're So Beautiful* [1970], "What Can You Bring Me" **Drummer** - James Gadson

On YouTube, a video by a drummer named Mark Kuliini issued a fun challenge for drummers to try to play this entire song. Upon first listening, it's just a great funk song. However, upon trying to play along with the whole song, you realize how much technique and relaxation went into Gadson making the song feel so effortless. The tune is three minutes long, at around 104 bpm. James plays a right-hand 16th-note groove the entire song, not even breaking to play a fill or a crash! Playing along to this song became a regular part of my practice routine growing up for two reasons: 1. It's an entertaining way to work on right-hand stamina, and 2. It's a great relaxation exercise. I'd find that the more I tense up, the harder it would be to make it through the song.

This song was a springboard to get more into James Gadson's drumming. It also helped me have a distinct feel and pocket within my right hand. As I stated earlier, I think that a considerable part of every drummer's "sound" or "groove" comes from the way they approach and develop their "timekeeping" hand. For most drummers, this is their right hand; this applies to all tempos and styles of music. But if you can make this song feel good, it will undoubtedly increase your headroom and ability to play.

## Mutemath, *Mutemath* [2006], "Typical"
### **Drummer** - Darren King

I started listening to MuteMath a little later than some of my other picks. Near the end of high school, I began to discover that there were different genres than jazz. MuteMath and this record specifically played a significant impact on how I now think about the recording process. Darren King is an exciting drummer to watch live, but he has an insane ability to curate unique soundscapes and textures on a record. Until then, I considered drums an acoustic instrument to be practiced and played live. Darren King inspired me to want to record. He also played a massive part in the ultra low-pitched snare trend of the 2010s.

## Rocket Juice & The Moon, *Rocket Juice & The Moon* [2012], "Benko"
### **Drummer** - Tony Allen

I was introduced to Tony Allen by one of my drum teachers in high school in Portland, Oregon, Steve Nistor; Steve had a significant impact on my development as a young musician because he was actively playing and touring with so many of my favorite musicians at around the time I was getting lessons from him. He also constantly showed me drummers and artists that have become some of my main influences. One of those drummers is Tony Allen.

Steve was working with me on Gary Chafee's *Time Function* book. I had big dreams of being a session musician (haha) at the time, so we were working on the inner mechanics of playing some very basic grooves at slow tempos and low volumes. To offset some of this "monotony," Steve also showed me some of Tony's drumming; I was instantly hooked. My biggest takeaway from Tony's playing is how melodic he can be with a kick/snare/hat. He also plays many variations of the Afrobeat grooves that he invented and sounds fresh on so many different productions and styles of music. I love this *Rocket Juice & the Moon* record because it highlights Tony's playing so well.

# Nate Wood

*"If I had to pick an album of the greatest drumming ever, this would be it."*

N ate Wood stands out as a visionary musician, renowned for his role as a founding member of the cutting-edge jazz fusion trio, Kneebody. With his solo project, fOUR, he unveils his remarkable prowess as a drummer, bassist, and pianist, showcasing absolute mastery as a solo instrumentalist. Here are Nate's choices…

Miles Davis, *ESP* [1965], "ESP"
**Drummer** - Tony Williams

Tony is the only drummer I'm aware of who changed the instrument more than once. By *ESP*, he was already playing jazz music as no one had before. There is so much freedom, expression, and personality while still playing the role of the timekeeper perfectly. Honestly, instrumental jazz has not evolved much past this record.

The Tony Williams Lifetime, *Emergency!* [1969], "Emergency"
**Drummer** - Tony Williams

*Emergency!* was released BEFORE *Bitches Brew*. No one talks about this, but it may be the first fusion record? It's one of the first, if not the very first. Tony had abandoned jazz and was hitting so hard that the tape machine didn't know what to do with itself. This is the first record I'm aware of in terms of rock/jazz drumming (fusion) and the second time Tony definitely changed the instrument forever. Tony is still the most expressive and personal drummer in history and the closest to a John Coltrane the drum set has ever had. I like to play with a four-piece kit with two cymbals because that's what Tony was playing here. If I had to pick an album of the greatest drumming ever, this would be it.

## Astroid Power-up!, *Google Plex* [2005], "Tightrope"
### **Drummer** - Deantoni Parks

Deantoni was the first drummer I heard play flawless drum and bass at breakneck tempos with entirely his language! He wasn't just playing chopped-up James Brown beats (which is what most drummers and programmers do with drum and bass). All of the tracks on this record are just drum improvisations with music written to them, and the range and breadth of pure improvisation on every track are masterful. Deantoni is a high-level improviser who doesn't play from pre-learned patterns and phrases. I got ahold of this record in 2003, and it greatly influenced me. Deantoni is one of the most personal drummers out there.

## Wayne Krantz, *Greenwich Mean* [1999], "Greenwich Mean"
### **Drummer** - Keith Carlock

When I heard this record, I knew modern rock/jazz drumming had morphed into something else. Keith harkened back to Tony Williams, Zigaboo Modeliste, and Jack DeJohnette while sounding entirely like himself. The drum sound was more like Joey Baron's sound than fusion music, another indicator that things were changing.

Wayne Krantz should also get a huge shoutout. His music changed how drums are played, as Wayne informed his drummers how he wanted his music played. He plays guitar like a drummer and probably would have changed the drum set entirely if he had chosen that instrument instead of the guitar. Therefore, I have to cite Wayne Krantz as one of the most influential instrumentalists who changed the drum set.

## The Police, *Zenyatta Mondatta* [1980], "Shadows in the Rain"
### **Drummer** - Stewart Copeland

Stewart is a complete original with an unusual combination of elements, especially for a rock drummer! Drums went from bombastically low tuning to the highest tuning imaginable seemingly overnight because of Stewart. Cymbals got smaller, snare drums tighter, and the actual beat placement of pop music changed. He has such an intense sound that he can make any band sound like The Police. If you listen to the Klark Kent records (which are solo records recorded by Stewart in disguise), they sound identical to The Police. That was HIS band!

But what always really struck me about Stewart was his intelligence. There is a sharpness of wit to his playing that is very rare, especially in pop music. He could transform a rather trite pop progression into something captivating and creative, almost unpredictable. This track has so much shape and split-second decision-making, indicative of his influence, wit, ego, and fearlessness. Also, it has the best-missed rim shot of any recording ever. So much reverb on that rim hit!

---

## Wayne Krantz, *Two Drink Minimum* [1995], "Whipersnapper"
## **Drummer** - Zach Danziger

Zach was the first drummer to bring the intelligence I crave to modern improvisational drumming. Like Stewart, I could tell he had a fast and funny brain. When I met him, I was proven correct! This song changed what drumming was for me when I heard it (I was in high school!). It was a different kind of interaction than what I was used to with drummers of the time (more fearless and personal), with a seemingly faster interplay that reminded me more of the way Tony and Jack improvise but with modern language. Again, Wayne should get some credit for his writing and what he required of the drummer in his music.

---

## Keith Jarrett, *Keith Jarrett at the Blue Note* [1995], "Autumn Leaves"
## **Drummer** - Jack DeJohnette

Jack rides on the splash cymbal towards the end of this track for about 10 minutes. Need I say more? Jack is a perfect musician who always plays music with the correct state of mind. He is a vessel for music. He is the greatest living drummer currently.

---

# Blair Sinta

*"...the drum parts develop throughout the tune. I've always tried incorporating this idea into my playing, whether in a band or studio environment."*

B lair Sinta is a Los Angeles-based session and touring drummer. He has collaborated with numerous international artists, including Alanis Morissette, Ringo Starr, Gwen Stefani, Stevie Nicks, Chris Cornell, John Fogerty, and numerous others. He's currently busy playing with Fitz and the Tantrums and records daily in his studio, the "Donkey Den," for artists from all over the world. He also teaches drums and recording. Here are Blair's choices...

Van Halen, *1984* [1983], "Drop Dead Legs"
**Drummer** - Alex Van Halen

Alex Van Halen doesn't get his props. He has an incredible pocket, chops, and a unique snare sound—always experimenting with different sounds. He has a deep Bonham connection, feel wise, and has some fusion in him somewhere. As a kid, I was always trying to figure out the crash ride sound. It baffled me as to how he got that wash.

This tune, in particular, is just a fat groove. I love the ride cymbal bell overdub, but this entire record showcases that snare sound.

## Rush, *Hold Your Fire* [1987], "Turn The Page"
### Drummer - Neil Peart

My cousin turned me on to *Moving Pictures* right about when *Hold Your Fire* came out. So, this was one of my earliest exposures to Neil. My first rock concert was Rush touring this record, which is why this record holds a special place for me.

My biggest takeaway from Neil is his parts and song development. Of course, he has chops, fills, coordination, and all that stuff, but in every Rush song, the drum parts develop throughout the tune. I've always tried incorporating this idea into my playing, whether in a band or studio environment.

This particular song has so many coordination challenges I remember trying to get together. I love the brightness and the punch of the drums on this album.

## Miles Davis, *Four & More* [1966], "So What"
### Drummer - Tony Williams

Who doesn't think this album represents one of the most incredible jazz drum performances ever recorded? Innovation, swing, style, chops. All at 17 years old.

I went to school at the University Of North Texas. I was not a jazz drummer when I started there, and this cassette tape stayed in my Walkman for years. In retrospect, there were better records from which to try and learn how to play traditional jazz because of all the boundary-breaking going on. But, it is unparalleled today and just the beginning of the legend.

## James Brown, *In The Jungle Groove* [1986], "Talkin' Loud and Sayin' Nothing"
### Drummer - John "Jabo" Starks

To understand simplicity and feel, this record was my play-along. How light, funky, and popping Jabo and Clyde are still amazes me. No bullshit, all groove.

This tune's hi-hat/snare interplay is wild, and the recording has a slight distortion; it's simmering and incredible.

## Rage Against the Machine, *Evil Empire* [1996], "Bulls on Parade"
### Drummer - Brad Wilk

Brad Wilk...oooof. Power, laid back, massive sound, huge pocket. Whenever I listen to Rage Against The Machine, it feels so authentic and raw that I feel as though everything else is just candy.

Brad and Tim Commerford create the perfect blend of rock and hip-hop as the rhythm section—simplicity and to the point at its best.

# William Goldsmith

*"...[This Album] carried a deep level of emotional intelligence and sophistication behind the storytelling that hit me harder when I got older."*

W illiam Goldsmith, a highly revered drummer, co-founded two profoundly influential bands: Sunny Day Real Estate and Foo Fighters. Also associated with such acts as The Fire Theft and Assertion, William's emotive and dynamically powerful grooves have inspired an entire generation of drummers. Here are William's choices...

Chicago, *Chicago IX: Chicago's Greatest Hits* [1975], "25 or 6 to 4"

**Drummer** - Danny Seraphine

This particular Chicago record was one of the many soundtracks to my childhood. As I got older and revisited those songs and beyond, Chicago blew my mind even more. I had just revisited Chicago before our conversation, which is one of the reasons they came to mind.

Stevie Wonder, *Songs In The Key of Life* [1976], "Sir Duke"

**Drummers** - Stevie Wonder, Raymond Pounds, Greg Brown

104

While there is a playful aspect to "Sir Duke" that felt like it was meant for you to hear during childhood, it carried a deep level of emotional intelligence and sophistication behind the storytelling that hit me harder when I got older. It's fascinating to see how my kids react to it. However, my son Logan's favorite Stevie Wonder song is "All Day Sucker."

Rush, *Permanent Waves* [1980], "The Spirit of Radio"
**Drummer** - Neil Peart

When I was 13, my brother would invite me to his house and take me on musical journeys that changed my life forever. The moment "The Spirit of Radio" started playing for the first time is burned into my memory. I can still see my brother standing and playing air guitar in front of the turn table. It also greatly impacted me as a drummer for obvious reasons.

The Who, *Quadrophenia* [1973], "Is It In My Head?"
**Drummer** - Keith Moon

This album was another musical journey my brother took me on — telling me stories and legends about Keith Moon that had me on the edge of my seat. I had to pick this particular track out of a hat, but it is a peak moment of the story for me. This record was one of the main soundtracks from ages 13 to 18.

## Tubeway Army, Gary Numan, *Replicas* [1979], "Down in the Park"
### **Drummer** - Jess Lidyard

There is an interesting lifelong story connected to this one. When I was 5 or 6 years old, I saw Gary Numan perform on *Saturday Night Live*, and it both frightened and intrigued me (similar to how I felt seeing *Escape From New York* and *Blade Runner* for the first time). Fast forward to when I was 17, I rented *Urgh! A Music War* and included was a clip of Gary Numan performing "Down In The Park"; I fell in love with the song, and I was even more intrigued than frightened. Jeremy Enigk (Sunny Day Real Estate, The Fire Theft) also appreciates Gary Numan. Years later, when I was playing in the Foo Fighters, Dave (Grohl) stated that he wanted to do a cover and asked what it should be. I immediately yelled out "Down In The Park," and, coincidentally, Dave had always wanted to cover that one as well. We played it frequently on tour and recorded it for an *X-Files* soundtrack. Fast forward again to when I was playing in Sunny Day during the *How It Feels...* era, I was allowed to both see and meet Gary Numan. We talked for almost 3 hours, and he was profoundly kind, down-to-earth, and humble — interesting full circle, to say the least.

## NoMeansNo, *Wrong* [1989]
### **Drummer** - John Wright

*Wrong* by NoMeansNo is one of the greatest records of all time. I saw them live twice at the OK Hotel in Seattle. To this day, they are the greatest live band I have ever seen. I can still revisit their music, which blows me away like it did when I was 17. To quote my youngest daughter Mayura when she first heard them, "This is crazy." A few years ago, I began a dialogue and subsequent friendship with Andy Kerr from NoMeansNo. It was another experience meeting a musical hero and discovering them to be humble and down to earth. He was extremely patient while I was respect-struck and couldn't stay quiet. He mentioned that he and his son occasionally listened to Sunny Day Real Estate and The Fire Theft; I still have difficulty wrapping my head around that. I told him to tell his son that his father was responsible for the existence of those bands. Musically, it's wholly different and not even in the same league. Still, as far as inspiration goes, everyone I play with understands how vital that band is to us—another interesting full circle.

# Michael Benjamin Lerner

*"[This Album] is like a warm blanket; it's just comforting. It's the pinnacle for me. It can't get any better. All of them, together. It's a cosmic thing."*

Michael Benjamin Lerner is the multi-talented force behind Telekinesis, serving as the singer, songwriter, and drummer. Telekinesis is known for blending summery indie rock with buoyant power pop, creating a unique sound. Lerner, a prolific multi-instrumentalist, typically handles all instruments on Telekinesis recordings. Hailing from the Pacific Northwest music scene, he stands as a powerhouse, leaving his mark with a seemingly endless well of musical skills and distinctive sound. Here are Michael's choices…

The Kinks, *Lola Versus Powerman and the Moneygoround, Pt. 1* [1970], "Strangers"

**Drummer** - Mick Avory

Let me get this out of the way from the onset. Mick Avory is a highly underrated drummer. He doesn't get put in the pantheon of the Ringos, the Moons, or the Bonhams, but he deserves to be in that conversation. The Kinks themselves sort of fall into that category as a band; they were always the misfits of all the aforementioned peers of their time. But there are days when I feel like they were the best band on earth.

This song, in particular, is one that I adore tremendously. While I'm a student of the drums, I am also a student of the recording. And I often find myself returning to this song to remind myself that it's very easy to go down the rabbit hole of thinking you need a million dollars in equipment, top-of-the-line drums, etc. And when I feel myself starting down that rabbit hole, I'll put on this song and listen to the end where the tom toms have their moment, and you can literally hear how badly tuned they are, or probably what's most likely, how OLD the drum heads are. And I adore that they didn't fix it, or spend hours or money on getting new heads, or re-doing the take because the drums were making that bawwwwwmmmmm noise that we all seem to despise. Because ultimately, this song is unfuckwithable, and you couldn't ruin it if you tried.

---

## Neo, *Space Country* [2001], "Subterfuge"
### **Drummer** - Jason McGerr

I was fortunate to study drums with Jason as my teacher when I was a kid, and it was a massive factor in my musical development.

As an early teenager, I took lessons from Jason at the Seattle Drum School in Seattle, WA, for many years. While we would learn lots of the fundamentals, and while I would try my best to practice them to show off when the following week's lesson would arrive, we would spend our hour of allotted time together listening to and or discussing music. And I got as much out of that as I did the lessons.

So, during that time (I was around 15), Jason started playing with a new band, Neo. And I remember they were putting on a show at the drum school, which was for all ages, and that meant that I could see it (accompanied by my parents, of course). This was such a pivotal moment for me because I saw what greatness indeed was. It was an incredible moment to see my teacher and hero playing this great music, showing me what all this practice could eventually lead to in the world of being in a band.

The ending of this song gets me every single time. Seeing Jason play it live is something I won't ever forget. I've tried to play it many times, and it's deceptively tricky.

## Flin Flon, *A-Ok* [1998], "Ukraina"
### Drummer - Matt Datesman

This band was introduced to me by my record producer at the time, Chris Walla. And it changed the whole game for me. I was starting to learn the bass intently (this was around the time of my second record, *12 Desperate Straight Lines*), and this band changed my outlook on the relationship between the bass and guitar.

And that was pivotal for me as someone making music in the style of a one-person band (Telekinesis is a band, but I write, play, and record all the songs by myself).

I adore the interplay between the bass and drums on this particular song, and I also love the ethos of this band. Chris told me they had a Flin Flon rule where you couldn't hit a crash cymbal. And I believe it. I don't hear one. As a drummer, it's difficult because it's so ingrained in us to hit a crash on the one at SOME point in a song.

I read that this record was recorded onto analog tape, meaning the drums were recorded as you hear them, without fancy computer editing or quantization. And the drums sound robotic as heck, and that isn't easy to do without the magic of the computer.

---

## Radiohead, *Kid A* [2000], "Morning Bell"
## Drummer - Phil Selway

Radiohead is one of my favorite bands, so let's get that out of the way here. They can do no wrong for me, and Phil Selway is perfect for this band, like Ringo was perfect for the Beatles, always playing to the song. He's not the most technically proficient drummer, but the excellent drummer for this band.

Most of us know about the record *Kid A*, coming after *OK Computer*. But, as I listen to this record, the older I get, the more I deeply respect Phil Selway because of his unselfish ability to let Thom Yorke and company go down a path that didn't include drums in the traditional sense on most of the songs on this record. That must have been a tricky thing for Mr. Selway. They were coming off a massive *OK Computer* record/touring cycle (which was all drums all the time) into *Kid A*, where Thom Yorke was obsessing over electronic music, drum machines, and machine music in general. I don't know of many drummers who would be in one of the most successful bands of the time being able to say, "Okay, you know what, I'm okay with this." And that's enormous because it led to one of the best records ever. And I find it incredibly admirable.

But, when Phil Selway did have his moment to shine, he made it count. "Morning Bell" is one of those instantly identifiable drum beats. I play it at soundcheck almost daily, and someone always recognizes it. Even though his moments to shine on that record were few and far between, he made it count when it was his moment.

111

## The Beatles, *Revolver* [1966], "Tomorrow Never Knows"
## **Drummer** - Ringo Starr

Not much can be said about The Beatles at this point in history. And it seems cliche to include them on this list, but I mean it when I say I listen to The Beatles and all of the solo records weekly. It's like a warm blanket; it's just comforting. It's the pinnacle for me. It can't get any better. All of them, together. It's a cosmic thing.

And "Tomorrow Never Knows" is my absolute favorite Ringo. It's a song so ahead of its time, with a drum beat so ahead of its time—just perfection.

# Jerrod "J-rod" Sullivan

*"By studying this album, I understood the importance of POCKET, and how the rhythm section is supposed to lock."*

J errod "J-rod" Sullivan is an Atlanta-based drummer, producer, arranger, and programmer known for his expertise in gospel and R&B. He has collaborated with a host of notable artists, including The 4 Korners, Jeffrey Osborne, Avery Sunshine, Lalah Hathaway, Bebe Winans, Smokey Robinson, Stokley Williams, Eric Roberson, The Temptations, and many others. Here are J-rod's choices...

Hezekiah Walker, *Family Affair* [2000], "Wonderful Is Your Name"
**Drummer** - Jeff Lesley

This album was the first that I had ever owned. My dad bought me this CD for Christmas one year, along with a Walkman CD player. Hezekiah Walker is one of his favorite gospel artists, and since gospel music is my foundation, it only made sense for him to introduce me to this record first. I finally had the opportunity to listen and study a whole body of work independently. By studying this album, I understood the importance of POCKET and how the rhythm section is supposed to lock. You got Reggie Parker on bass and Jeff Lesley on drums. They made this music feel great, especially this particular song.

## John P. Kee, *Not Guilty* [2000], "Rain On Us"
### Drummer - Calvin Rodgers

This particular song introduced me to soloing within an entire composition. Calvin has always been among my favorite drummers, especially in gospel music. We all have specific influences that we sometimes channel when playing certain things. Whenever I play gospel music, I always think, "What would Calvin do?" He plays with so much authority and intentionality. Even when he solos, it's always musical.

"Rain on Us" is the anthem of gospel drumming, and it's all because of what Calvin played on this record. How he took the listener on a journey through his choices and built the solo was mind-blowing, especially for me as a kid. After hearing this record, I was inspired to transcribe his solo. It just didn't sound as good when I played it. Lol.

## Zapp & Roger, *All The Greatest Hits* [1993], "I Heard It Through the Grapevine"
### Drummer - Lester Troutman

I shout out to my mom for this one! She loves Zapp & Roger. She had this CD and would play it consistently whenever I was in the car with her. It taught me that you don't have to play much to make the music feel good and funky; less is more! This record is one that I referenced for feel and making the music sit in the pocket when producing. It will forever be a favorite of mine.

## Robert Glasper Experiment, *Black Radio* [2012], "Cherish The Day"
### Drummer - Chris "Daddy" Dave

This record is one of my all-time favorites. It was this record that helped me to understand the importance of dynamics. Coming from playing drums in the church behind a shield with no mics, I was told to play loud. Learning about Chris Dave and hearing him on this record helped me understand how using dynamics can make the music feel so much better! You'll notice how the music creeps in during the intro of this particular song. Chris is right there, matching the dynamics and mood of the section. Another inspiring thing about him is that he's unafraid to break the rules and play what he feels. I love that.

## Chick Corea Elektric Band, *Chick Corea Electrik Band* [1986], "Rumble"
### Drummer - Dave Weckl

This choice pertains to a pivotal moment in my career. I had just joined my band, The 4 Korners, and they introduced me to Chick Corea Elektric Band. Before joining 4K, I had never played jazz fusion, only R&B and gospel. Since they saw my potential, they decided to give me a chance and work with me.

Clarence "T-lee" Hill, the keyboardist in The 4K, gave me this album by Chick Corea Elektric Band and said, "Hey, study this album. This is our main influence as a band. Dave Weckl is on drums. Study his approach."

I began immersing myself in that music. After living with this album for about six months, I grasped Dave's approach. Clarence described it as him keeping a solid pocket but playing percussion around the groove.

115

That concept alone opened my mind. I began to evolve into my sound, blending my gospel and R&B background with the developing jazz fusion approach. Chick Corea Elektric Band and Dave Weckl have influenced me significantly.

*HONORABLE MENTIONS:*

Shout out to my parents for introducing me to great music. Had it not been for them sparking my interest, I may not be where I am today. Also, thanks to my mentors who took the time to teach me something, give advice, or encourage me. Most importantly, thank God for this gift of music! As musicians, we can inspire people through our instruments without saying a word, and that's beautiful. I'm grateful.

# Rajeev Maddela

*"I couldn't help but feel that the universe was intentionally shoving this recording in front of me."*

Rajeev Maddela, based in Brooklyn, NY, is a multi-talented musician known for his work as a drum set artist, electronic music composer, DJ, and rudimental percussion instructor. Operating under the name Maddela, he releases music spanning experimental drum and bass, future bass, and UK garage. One of his projects, CURRENCY AUDIO, explores improvisational performances across genres like jungle, IDM, UK garage, and dubstep. Here are Rajeev's choices…

---

*DCI 1993 | | Star Of Indiana* (YouTube video)

Around the years '94-'95 (and all the years since, to be honest), I was extremely obsessed with rudimental drumming, a gateway drug provided to me by my high school marching band program (Monsignor Farrell High School in Staten Island, NY). My best friend at the time, (now Maestro) James Gaffigan, was going to school in the city at LaGuardia High School—a school I was all signed up to attend; however, my parents were afraid I wouldn't focus on my other studies and decided to send me to this school that had, unbeknownst to them, one of the greatest rudimental percussion programs in New York City

117

(run by the great David Larsen). A jazz drummer friend of his (Harry?) gave him a bootleg drumline "parking lot" tape with some of the top DCI (Drum Corps International) from 1993—one of which was Star of Indiana. There was no way someone from that school could have more access to such "realness" than my rudimentally obsessed self (so I thought), so I was humbled to finally have a raw recording of the best drumlines in history on tape, and given to me by none other than a jazz drummer.

This line (and recording) had blindingly clean rolls with such exciting curves to their crescendos. At the time, I was more obsessed with flam-drags and hybrid rudiments, so hearing the effect of clean, thoroughly intentioned rolls and single taps got me to appreciate the power of a simple vocabulary, the satisfaction of synchronicity, and the dramatic effect of a "simple" double stroke roll.

Jamiroquai, *Travelling Without Moving* [1996], "Do You Know Where You're Coming From?"
**Drummer** - Derrick McKenzie

Around my senior year of high school, my friend at LaGuardia (with whom I shared a joint obsession with funk at the time) hipped me to this incredible band named Jamiroquai that sounded like the most real modern funk I'd ever heard—he showed me the album *Emergency on Planet Earth*. Of course, they hit it big just a few months later with their infectious and incredibly fresh single, "Virtual Insanity," and I immediately had to buy the album *Travelling Without Moving*.

The last track was "Do You Know Where You're Coming From?," and, unbeknownst to me, it was a bonus drum and bass track made in collaboration with a very hallowed UK jungle producer, M-Beat. At the time, however, I thought it was the drummer playing the entire rhythm track, leading me to questions like, "How is he making his drums sound like a box of change?." "Does he have multiple snare drums?." I knew I needed to up my game and come close to playing this style of beat.

Aside from the perceived dexterity of the drummer, I was instantly enamored with this new yet familiar feel — it felt like some new spin on fast funk that had a gliding quality but still had a very classic, nostalgic essence.

## Squarepusher, *Hard Normal Daddy* [1996], "Rustic Raver"

By the time I reached college (New York University in 1997 as a Biology Major), I was thoroughly obsessed with electronic music, with jungle/drum'n'bass being closer to my heart than any other genre. My friend had a copy of *URB* magazine, and there was a top ten list for "Best Drum and Bass albums"; #2 was *Hard Normal Daddy* by Squarepusher. The only record store carrying it was located right by my campus in Greenwich Village, the famed Other Music, and it was on sale for $26. I had never spent this much on a CD before. Still, after picking it up and putting it back on the CD rack during multiple visits, I pulled the trigger and finally bought it.

This track, in particular, sounded like drum corps drumline music from the future and still does to this day. Hearing such long, speech-like percussion phrases, the interplay between the breakbeat voices, the "advanced civilization" — like quality of the synth sounds, and the Leftfield sensibility of the melodies stimulated my mind in the freshest way possible but serendipitously felt like a natural extension of my obsession with rudimental drumming at that time.

## Herbie Hancock, *Future 2 Future* [2001], "The Essence"
### **Drummer** - Karsh Kale

By the time I discovered this record, after years of thinking there was no real point in being a drummer anymore since everyone was making such incredible music with samplers and computers, I finally decided to try to perform some of these jungle beats on the drum kit. Word hit the street that Herbie Hancock had come out with an electronic-influenced album, so I had to buy it.

One of the best tracks on the record, "The Essence," apparently had a live drummer named Karsh Kale (coincidentally, I would go on to be a long-time stage collaborator with him around seven years later). Since it was rare to hear any drummers play live drum'n'bass, I felt lucky to finally own an example I got to study and learn from thoroughly.

The biggest thing I learned from studying this record was how a large part of the effect of jungle rhythms is the consistency and repetition of "keystone" syncopations, which create both a trance-like and a "drums as melody" effect. Instead of always trying to replicate the complexity of the inner beats, being consistent with the accent patterns will create the signature attitude drum'n'bass is known for.

## Karsh Kale, "Saajana Live Version"
### **Drummer** - Jojo Mayer

After just graduating college, I was finally hip to this guy Jojo Mayer as arguably the "best" jungle/drum'n'bass drummer in NYC (and anywhere else, for that matter). Still, I had yet to see him live. A good friend of mine, Atul Ohri (who would perform as DJ Zakhm), was the DJ for Ajay Naidu's solo theater play *Darwaza*, where he played this live, unreleased version of Karsh Kale's track "Saajana" featuring Jojo Mayer on drums.

This recording served as a jungle vocabulary book for many years to come, as it was the cleanest example of the main figures I was used to hearing on jungle records, and still captured the inner beat complexity that I previously thought was only possible by placing both hands on the snare drum. Coincidentally, I had just discovered the Moeller Technique via Dom Famularo's *Wisdom Woodshed* video section on the *VicFirth.com* website—hearing Jojo's single-handed approach was the first real-world application of the Moeller Technique I had ever heard. I couldn't help but feel that the universe was intentionally shoving this recording in front of me.

# Dave Elitch

*"If you don't listen to heavy music, give them a chance. You may be surprised."*

D ave Elitch is a highly respected drummer and educator known for his emphasis on physical technique and biomechanics in drumming. With a career marked by collaborations with prominent artists such as The Mars Volta, Weezer, Miley Cyrus, and The 1975, Dave's versatile playing style and meticulous attention to detail have left an indelible mark on the music industry. His Zen-like approach to viewing drummers as athletes and listening to the body and how it relates to one's goals makes him one of the most sought-after teachers today. Here are Dave's choices…

Genesis, *The Platinum Collection*, "Jesus He Knows Me"
**Drummer** - Phil Collins

I got this cassette tape when I was young and, more importantly, before I played drums. I distinctly remember getting a spooky feeling of being transported into another era or creative field. I don't know; it's hard to describe. It's best compared to being engrossed in a good movie. Since this would've been in the early '90s, most of the music was contemporary, but it felt older for some reason.

Compilations are a great way to get to know an artist or band. You get a great cross-section of time periods. This does that well. There are so many hits from different albums, so having many of them in one place is nice.

I picked this tune because it's an excellent combination of everything that goes into a great song. I'm not one to listen to lyrics usually, but the lyrics in this tune are pretty damning and also relevant to what was happening at the time (televangelism scandals). The snare drum sound is Phil Collins' signature gated reverb vibe, but this one has so much attack! (I believe it was his N & C solid shell piccolo, but I'm not sure.) The ghost notes fill things out nicely. As always with Phil, it's a genius combination of tone, pocket, and compositional choices. Specifically, when the bridge drops into a reggae section, it's not expected at all, but it just works. He also has so much authority and aggression in his playing, which I don't think he gets enough credit for. He's so heavy, a true genius.

## Buddy Rich, *Very Live at Buddy's Place* [1974]
### Drummer - Buddy Rich

I wore this record out when I had just started playing. In retrospect, it was a strange era of Buddy to listen to! No one was doing big band stuff in the '70s, so this was an attempt to stay relevant. There's a percussionist (imagine being that guy!), a flutist, and a guitar with a wah pedal, sometimes giving it a different, almost funky sort of flavor. My dad played a lot of big band around the house, so I gravitated towards that when I started listening to jazz. Buddy's facility is just bonkers. His crisp and articulate snare sound had a significant impression on me. It's still essential that people can perceive what you're saying on the instrument, and if you're a busy player like he was, you need a drum that speaks clearly; that has always stayed with me. The band was medium-sized, so it also felt more contemporary. It was just different and weird, and that only became apparent to me as I got older and learned more about jazz. It's an odd-ball, lesser-known record that's a fun listen.

## Pantera, *Official Live: 101 Proof* [1997], "Becoming"
### **Drummer** - Vinnie Paul

This was the first Pantera record I ever got. I was 13 or 14 and listening to a bunch of really bad prog, so once I heard this, it blew my brain wide open. Where do I even start? Vinnie Paul essentially invented a tone out of nowhere—his tone. It's the clickiest bass drum sound of all time, with gigantic toms and a snare sound that was massive and fat but somehow cut through everything. He came up with such unique parts, compositionally speaking, to compliment (not just copy!) what Dimebag did on guitar. They had such a special relationship, being brothers and all. The thing that Vinnie needs to get more credit for is his pocket! Very few drummers or bands even know how to swing in heavy music. He swings his ass off; Pantera is funky as hell! Not to mention, the double-kick pattern on "Becoming" is still, to this day, one of the most unique and challenging patterns out there.

Everyone in this band was a genius. They're one of the few heavy bands with no weak links, and they wrote fantastic songs. The hooks are just earworms, and there are also a lot of curveballs hidden throughout their catalog—not on purpose, but just because they were such gifted musicians, they would think of really cool, novel ideas. Lastly, Phil's in-between-song banter is second to none!

If you don't listen to heavy music, give them a chance. You may be surprised.

**DAVE ELITCH**

## Meshuggah, *Chaosphere* [1998], "New Millennium Cyanide Christ"
**Drummer** - Tomas Haake

I distinctly remember the first time I heard this record, which was also the first time I heard Meshuggah. I was sitting in my friend Paul's truck outside my mom's house. He threw it on, and I can only describe the feeling as being hit by lightning and falling off a cliff simultaneously—just entirely disoriented! This was 1998, and it's a very different thing listening to Meshuggah then versus 2023 when you have a solid 15 years of rip-off bands copying them. It was still fresh and new! Also, *Chosphere* was a significant departure from *Destroy Erase Improve* (I would learn later).

"NMCC" has the signature Meshuggah cyclic, loping, revolving kicks/guitars/bass underneath the simple hand pattern. Like I discussed with Pantera, Meshuggah works because it's FUNKY! If it didn't feel good and make people involuntarily bob their heads, it wouldn't work. They're among the most important bands of all time, regardless of genre.

Haake's one of my all-time favorite drummers and most significant influences, and I'm proud to call him a good friend. Also, this record is one of the records that started me down to snare drum/gear rabbit hole. Listen to the snare sound on "The Mouth Licking What You've Bled." Cracking skulls!

## Brad Mehldau, *Largo* [2002], "Dusty McNugget"
**Drummers** - Matt Chamberlain (with Jim Keltner)

I sound like a broken record here (no pun intended), but I remember the first time I heard this album and had the same feeling I mentioned above. Time slows down, and you think, "What is THIS?!." I had listened to and played quite a bit of jazz up to this point, and I was also familiar with Matt's playing from the Tori stuff, but I had yet to go deep. I remember hearing "Dusty McNugget," which may have been the first time I had listened to a snare drum tuned down, muted, and fat. Everyone I had listened to up to that point had cranked snares. So the tonal aspect freaked me out, and then the playing. Oh man, the playing.

Matt's ghost notes are perfect. His choices (along with Keltner and Victor) are perfectly musical and supportive. This record had a huge impact when it came out because it was just so different. Get a bunch of pop/rock guys to play on a jazz piano player's record, and it works! If you're under 25, get this record now; you may have missed it.

# Rob Humphreys

*"His ability to create and release tension is unparalleled. For the first time, I felt a deep, emotional, and invaluable connection between the drums and music."*

R ob Humphreys, also known as Byrdie, is a Los Angeles-based session player. With an organic, classic-yet-hip playing style, his impressive list of credits includes collaborations with iconic artists such as Kacey Musgraves, Billy Ray Cyrus, Celine Dion, Nikka Costa, Leonard Cohen, Scary Pockets, and many others. Here are Rob's choices...

The Oneders (The Wonders), *That Thing You Do (Original Motion Picture Soundtrack)* [1996], "That Thing You Do"
**Drummers** - Guy Patterson (Kenny Aronoff, Adam Schlesinger)

I first saw *That Thing You Do* when it landed in the "New Releases" section of our local blockbuster (and let's be clear, we're talking about a MAJOR motion picture). I distinctly recall choosing the movie based solely on its VHS cover and pairing it with whatever questionable candy I was into in 3rd grade. The next day, I was creating drum sets from all the pots, pans, and kitchen utensils I could find, replaying each scene repeatedly, pretending to play along — this indeed marked the beginning for me.

The movie's music is phenomenal; it gave me a zeal that I still feel

30 years later about being a drummer in a band. Tom Hanks and Tom Everett Scott, you are, in your words, "my biggest fan." It stands as the most incredible music movie of my generation.

## Joshua Redman, *Elastic* [2002], "Molten Soul," "Still Pushin' That Rock"
**Drummer** - Brian Blade

BRIAN BLADE. After I heard this record, Blade quickly became my North Star (and still is to this day). WWBD? My older brother gifted me this CD while I was in high school around 2004 after he left our small town to go to music school (as a trombone player). I remember him saying, "You've got to check out this drummer."

This record was only my introduction to Blade. Soon after, I found Joni, Wayne Shorter, the Fellowship, and Black Dub—INSANE artists and records. His musicianship is genuinely universal; anyone, musician or not, can watch him play and be left speechless and inspired. You don't have to be "music smart" to understand what he does, yet there is no artistic sacrifice in his process. It is mysterious, joyous, and pure. His ability to create and release tension is unparalleled. I felt a deep, emotional, and invaluable connection between the drums and music for the first time. The calculated aspects of my playing started to matter much less than my sheer joy of making music.

## The Meters, *Rejuvenation* [1974], "People Say," "Just Kissed My Baby," "Jungle Man"
**Drummer** - Zigaboo Modeliste

Although I had some familiarity with The Meters, I wasn't "in the know" until I saw Zigaboo play at a club in LA around 2010. He was performing under his name, accompanied by members of the Kimmel band, whom I was honestly more familiar with than Zig himself. I was new to town and told I needed to catch this gig with no questions asked. When I arrived at the club, it was jam-packed, and I immediately noticed James Gadson (along with many other drumming legends) at the front of the stage, beaming with anticipation for the show to start.

The moment the show began, I was COMPLETELY changed. All of my practice—my cool licks, "perfect" subdivisions, my technique, and everything else I thought I knew about drums—went out the window. I had never heard or seen the drums played the way Zigaboo did. It felt like church. RLRL with no diddle or flamma jamma in sight. Gadson was singing every word and dancing harder than I knew anyone could. The groove and vibe were undeniably real, and I think I started to understand what that was for the first time.

---

Fiona Apple, *The Idler Wheel Is Wiser Than the Driver of the Screw and Whipping Cords Will Serve You More Than Ropes Will Ever Do* [2012], "Left Alone"
**Drummer** - Charlie Drayton

Aaron Redfield, one of my closest friends (and reDONKulous drummers), introduced me to this record. I was familiar with some of Fiona's music, especially knowing the crazy list of drummers that had been a part of it (Chamberlain, Questlove, Abe, etc....); however, the drum performance in this specific song, "Left Alone," hit me unlike anything before.

I had only heard of Charlie Drayton (who also produced the entire record) as the guy who would swap drum/bass roles with Steve Jordan in Keith Richards' band, The X-pensive Winos. As impressive as that was, the creativity of this recording was inspiring on a whole new level. I had no idea you could play a song or accompany a voice this way. The drum performance takes you on a journey, following Fiona through every lyric and feeling. Hearing Drayton play so fiercely and boldly in the context of this song became a lesson for me in being fearless (or at least trying to be!), especially in the recording process. We all have creativity inside us, but accessing it takes guts. Something changed for me after being exposed to this pick.

## Theo Katzman, *Be The Wheel* [2023], "She's In My Shoe"
**Drummer** - Jordan Rose

If anyone is unfamiliar with Theo Katzman or Jordan Rose, they are two of the greatest musicians on the planet. I had a great chat with Theo not too long after he recorded this album. We deeply talked about music careers, recording techniques, and all the insecurities that can come with being a musician. He made this whole record with everyone in the same room—drums, piano, acoustic guitar, vocals, etc.,...— every live sound bleeding into all the mics and being captured as one collective take. I had just ventured into recording drums remotely. I expressed my trials and insecurities, being alone in a room, trying too hard to make something sound hip or impress the artist I was recording for.

What became surprisingly profound to me in our conversation was that you can record something and be OK with it, regardless of a mistake or inconsistency(or what anyone else might think!). We are in the thick of a pop music era where everything is edited and perfected, and our ears have become very accustomed to that sound. Listening to yourself how you truly are can be very difficult, but when you edit to "fix" something, a real piece of you gets removed. This record is the unperfected, unedited, true self of Theo, Jordan, and the rest of the guys on the record. All the songs are listened to as whole takes, much like how we have to look at our whole selves in the mirror every day. It's a musician's practice of "self-love," and I've been continually inspired since Theo shared these sentiments.

## Rusty Bryant, *Fire Eater* [1971], "Fire Eater"
## Drummer - Idris Muhammad

This record inspired a lot of similar ideas that Zigaboo did but without the epic James Gadson singing/dancing imagery. There is something very contagious about the New Orleans influence; it's delightfully sloppy and crookedly swung with an energy that feels like a celebration. I've tried to let it seep into my playing as much as my New Mexico roots let it.

Speaking of "energy," my favorite part of this tune is the organ solo (played by Bill Mason); it's like a constantly-growing energy bubble on the verge of exploding for 4(ish) minutes, and Idris comps with "energy," not by any chops or ideas. I always associated more notes with more excitement, but that is not the case here. I'm sure it was a part of being entirely in the moment, but I also feel the NOLA spirit at large!

131

# Brendan Buckley

*"If he picked up a fork and a knife and dropped them on the dinner table, it would be the funkiest drop of cutlery in history."*

B rendan Buckley is a Los Angeles-based drummer, producer, and educator who's worked with Morrissey, Perry Farrell, Shakira, Tegan And Sara, Miley Cyrus, Damien Rice, Shelby Lynne, Daniel Powter, and many more. Brendan's knack for effortlessly traversing various musical genres and his commitment to educating others have garnered widespread recognition and esteem in the industry. Here are Brendan's choices...

## The Police, *Outlandos D'Amour* [1978], Can't Stand Losing You"
### Drummer - Stewart Copeland

Stewart Copeland is always included whenever I'm asked for a Top Five or Top Ten list of drummers. I loved Stewart Copeland's drumming when I was growing up, and I still do now; something about his style resonated with me. And as I grew older, I began to acknowledge the tremendous musical feat he accomplished. Throughout his five albums with The Police, every song in their catalog had its unique beat, which is incredibly difficult to do. And he did this while also being a Top 40 arena pop/rock band. His quirky, unusual drum parts still managed to get on the radio and never turned the band around (where is one?).

I chose this Police song because it comes from early in their career before Stewart got his full "signature sound" with his cranked-up rack toms, high-pitched snare drum, octobans, and splash cymbals. This song has his signature style and licks but on a lower-tuned, simpler drum set-up. And this song is fun because it has everything in one song: his big flams on beat four, his hi-hat work, his cross-stick reggae stuff, his punk 8th-note kick drum part, his beat on the verses is turned around (no beat one), and, towards the end during the fade-out, the toms double the kick drum on beat one. I am a bit of a Stewart Copeland fanatic. Enjoy!

---

## Kenny Garrett, *Triology* [1995], "Wayne's Thang"
### **Drummer** - Brian Blade

Brian Blade is incredible. If you ever see him live in one of his many projects, you will be spiritually moved by how he approaches the drum set. There is so much soul and joy in what he evokes out of the music he is making. Not only is he a great jazz drummer, he is a great musician. His "touch" on the drums is one of my all-time favorites. He gets terrific tones at such a whisper-quiet volume, and then it's slamming, and then it's back to whisper quiet again. His phrasing is beautiful. When he does fills, they come out on odd, unexpected beats. He has a fantastic swing, both up-tempo and super slow. He has that Louisiana upbringing. I first heard Brian play on the Joshua Redman album, *Mood Swings*. While studying at the University of Miami, I saw this quartet play live at a local theater. The show was so good that I was freaking out. After the performance, I jumped up on stage to say "hi" while he was packing up his drums. I've been a big Brian Blade fan ever since. He also has a cool solo project called The Fellowship. They have a very unique approach to instrumental jazz music. It doesn't sound like anything else out there.

This particular song is super funky. It's a little bit groove and a little bit jazz. It features a trio of alto sax, upright bass, and drums. It starts with the drums (which is perfect). I remember buying this album and liking it because it was "stripped down" (no piano, no guitar). There's so much space and freedom. Check it out.

## Living Colour, *Vivid* [1988], "Cult of Personality"
**Drummer** - Will Calhoun

This song came out in the late 1980s when I watched music videos on MTV daily. They had the *Headbanger's Ball* show, *120 Minutes*, etc. There were so many great bands and drummers to see. I was very into metal, punk rock, and alternative music then. I remember when this music video first came out, and I went, "WHOA!!!" That opening guitar riff and drum fill with the kick drum triplet is massive. There's a lot of great stuff in this song. There is an interplay between the ride cymbal and hi-hat on the choruses. There are the triplet fills around the toms, like John Bonham. He triggered electronic samples with a DrumKAT. At the song's end, it goes into a double-time section in 6/4. Then, the final unison riff of the song is in 5/8. As a young music nerd, I was like, "Wow!"

I saw Living Colour perform live several times. They were on the bill at the first Lollapalooza festival, and I believe they went on after Nine Inch Nails but before Jane's Addiction; it was incredible. And then, I saw Will perform a few years later in a random bar in Australia with a side project of his called Jungle Funk, which had the vocalist/percussionist Vinx and the Living Colour bassist Doug Wimbish. They had all of these electronic looping pedals hooked together. They were way ahead of their time! Whenever this song comes on the radio, I start air drumming. It reminds me of an era in which I listened to many bands with great drummers: Soundgarden (Matt Cameron), Jane's Addiction (Stephen Perkins), and more. This song is from an era of music that I love so much, and this song brings nostalgic joy out of me.

## Paul Simon, *One Trick Pony* [1980], "Late In The Evening" **Drummer** - Steve Gadd

Along with Stewart Copeland, Steve Gadd is always in my Top Five list of drummers (probably Top Three). His drumming means so much to me. I love his career, sound, pocket, musicality, and diversity. Everything about him speaks to me. Many fans would highlight his exceptional groove on "50 Ways To Leave Your Lover" or his drum solo on Steely Dan's "Aja." But I LOVE this song! I love the pattern he plays. He uses his classic Mozambique Latin rhythm on a ton of stuff, but he does it differently on this song; he uses a pair of sticks in each hand, with the right hand playing the Mozambique on the rim of the floor tom, and his left hand playing a melody on the toms. He plays quartet notes with his feet, sometimes splashing open hi-hats with his left foot. It's a fun, infectious beat to learn, play, hear, and jam. I play this beat whenever a front house engineer asks me to "play some drums" during soundcheck. There are some nice overdubs in here, too. You'll hear some cowbell and ride cymbal parts, and Steve adds super tasty fills to mark the end of each section. It's a bad-ass track that feels great!

I am a big fan of Steve's drumming. He played for a long time with Paul Simon, Eric Clapton (check out the *Live in Hyde Park* concert),

Chick Corea, Steely Dan, James Taylor, and many more. He's been super friendly to me every time I've met him. And he has my absolute favorite time feel. If Steve Gadd picked up a fork and a knife and dropped them on the dinner table, it would be the funkiest drop of cutlery in history. It would feel so good!

## Sérgio Mendes, *Brasileiro* [1992], "Magalenha"
**Drummer** - Carlinhos Brown

When I lived in Miami, I was surrounded by fantastic music—jazz, fusion, rock, and that heavy Latin scene; it's intrinsic to the city. There's all of the Cuban, Dominican, and Puerto Rican music. And also, there's all the South American influence: Colombian, Venezuelan, Brazilian, etc. Brazilian music is very different from other styles. They speak Portuguese, not Spanish. They have their rhythms: samba, bossa nova, baião. I had to learn all of these delineations in Miami because I learned rock, jazz, and "Latin music" growing up in New Jersey. But in Miami, I had to learn every subdivision of Latin music—where it came from and what separates each rhythm. It was an extensive education for me.

While I enjoyed learning all of these cultures and rhythms, the first style of Latin music that spoke to me was Brazilian. There's something about the joy, the groove, the swing, the funk, and the sounds. Everything about it lit a fire in me. I went down a rabbit hole of chasing these Brazilian artists and drummers. I remember a vocalist playing me this Sérgio Mendes album, and it blew me away. Carlinhos Brown is a famous percussionist/vocalist/artist from an area of Brazil called Bahia, known for its heavy percussion, and they have a lot of African influence in their music. Carlinhos was in a band called Tribalistas with

Marisa Monte and Arnaldo Antunes. The rhythm of this song is insane. Whenever you are in a club in Miami, and the DJ plays this song, the place goes berserk. There is something you can learn as a drummer by being in a dance club, watching DJs drop different tunes, and watching what captures people. This song always kills. It starts with only voice and triangle. And then it kicks in about halfway through; it's insane.

---

## James Taylor, *James Taylor Live* [1993], "Country Road"
## Drummer - Carlos Vega

Carlos Vega blew me away when I saw him live. He was part of that clique of LA drummers (Jeff Porcaro, Vinnie Colaiuta) who did many recording sessions but also had these hidden chops. I heard him on various recordings, but it was hard to tell what he could do because he played so simply and musically all the time. And I remember one year, James Taylor was on tour, and a couple of friends of mine said, "Hey, let's go see James Taylor live." And I thought, "Hmmm, it's kind of not my thing." It was too folksy for me at the time. I was more into Nine Inch Nails and stuff like that. But they said, "Trust us. His band is amazing!" So I went to see James Taylor live, and the show blew me away. The songs, the singing, and the band (Michael Landau, Jimmy Johnson, Don Grolnick, and Carlos Vega) were all perfect.

Carlos was the first guy I ever heard make those multi-rods sound good. Before that, drummers used rods when they were "too darn loud." Carlos had noticeably excellent dynamics. I remember he had a couple of congas set up to his left. And he had a WICKED feel; it was so laid back and musical. It impacted me. I stole so much from watching him play just once. I said to myself, "I want to approach music the way he is approaching music." It felt so good; it sounded so good. And I had to re-think what I was doing with the drums. Then, this live album came out from that tour. This song percolates and simmers all the way through, but at a midpoint, he does an 8-bar drum solo, and it's the best drum solo ever! It's just drums with vocals on top. It's crazy good. Super funky. It is fantastic! This solo means so much to me. People like to talk about "feel". Like, "I am trying to play behind the beat." Listen to this. This is how to play "laid back." Nothing is slowing down. It feels so big, and relaxed, and comfy. Masterful.

## The Cure, *Kiss Me Kiss Me Kiss Me* [1987], "Icing Sugar" **Drummer** - Boris Williams

I loved The Cure while growing up. I loved their drum parts. They've had several drummers: Lol Tolhurst, Andy Anderson, Jason Cooper, and Boris Williams. Boris had a fascinating style. He would develop 8-bar patterns and then play them for 13 minutes. These patterns would exist in their own world—crazy tom parts, wood blocks, clap sounds. And he would play them in an almost machine-like loop, like Jaki Liebezeit from CAN. They were mechanical, industrial-sounding loops. This approach spoke to me. He'd "create." He'd compose a drum part for the song. Sometimes, the part didn't even go with the rest of the music. Still, it all somehow worked. There are many ways to create drum parts. Some drummers free form and go with their gut, while others are very methodical, as though they sat down and "composed" their drum part from top to bottom; Boris does this. He played on The Cure albums *Head On The Door, Kiss Me Kiss Me Kiss Me, Disintegration*, and *Wish*. His parts and tones are killer.

138

# Aaron Gilbert Steele

*"I got married to the idea that an 8th-note pulse should be enough for any song to move. Ask anybody I was playing with then; I just wanted everything to truck along."*

A aron Gilbert Steele is a boundary-pushing drummer, songwriter, and producer. Having worked with artists such as Portugal. The Man, Hayley Williams, Leon Bridges, Jose James, Sam Dew, and Daniel Caesar, among others, Aaron has demonstrated a penchant for transcending musical genres. Here are Aaron's choices…

Death Cab For Cutie, *Transatlanticism* [2003],
"Transatlanticism"
**Drummer** - Jason McGerr

First, this album made me really think about lyrics and their relationship to the drums. Jason's playing on this record is simple yet inventive. He takes risks while still supporting the song. The parts are deliberate yet aren't so heady that the groove is lost. After hearing this album and the song "Transatlanticism" specifically, I got married to the idea that an 8th-note pulse should be enough for any song to move. Ask anybody I was playing with then; I just wanted everything to truck along. I still have to fight that urge often today.

## Wayne Shorter, *Beyond The Sound Barrier* [2005], "Over Shadow Hill Way"
### **Drummer** - Brian Blade

I briefly went to school for jazz performance, and during my time there, I got introduced to the pure genius of Brian Blade. Everyone on this album is next level (it wouldn't be a Wayne Shorter record if that weren't the case). Listening to everyone deconstruct the song, floating in and out of form like microorganisms splitting apart and becoming something new while still referencing where it began, showed me that almost anything is possible when you trust people in the musical process. On "Over Shadow Hill Way," the whole band is weaving in and out of insane pocket and having a free-form conversation with each other; it's transcendent for me. Also, there is a moment about 3 min in that Blade's pocket gets so deep that I fall in and get lost. I always get chills.

## Change, *Miracles* [1981], "Hold Tight"
### **Drummer** - Terry Silverlight

What is there to say about this tune? It's late disco era greatness. I was utterly obsessed with emulating this feel and pocket by Terry Silverlight on the drums for a good year or two. He was about 17 (I think, I may be very wrong) when he recorded this to tape in an era with no editing. Just perfect!

## Jameszoo, Metropole Orkest, Jules Buckley, *Melkweg* [2019], "(flake)"

This version of this song blows me away every time. It taught about the use of space, and the lack of drums on this super grooving tune is utterly insane. The orchestration by Jules is so beautiful I have no words for it. Again, I get chills every time I listen to it.

## Floating Points, *Crush* [2019], "Anasickmodular"

Floating Points is one of my favorite artists; he moves between DnB/EDM spaces, ambient soundscapes, orchestral arrangements, psych rock, and everything in between. In this tune, he uses a small high-pitch percussive sound to keep motion with slow-moving melodic content happening on top. He uses density with a choice of frequency range to propel the song forward. It is a tactic I've used in a very different musical context recently, and I know that this is where I'm hearing something like that; this song is patient zero for me.

# Sheridan Riley

*"The magical thing about these early rock drummers was that they weren't being rock musicians."*

S heridan Riley, a drummer and songwriter from Washington State, brings their unique style to the Grammy-nominated band Alvvays. Beyond their work with the band, Sheridan explores their creativity through personal projects like Peg and solo releases. Over the years, they've also collaborated with a wide range of artists, including Avi Buffalo, Hand Habits, Cassandra Jenkins, the John Mitchell Quartet, Time of Wolves, and Fort Wife, among others. Here are Sheridan's choices…

Led Zeppelin, *Early Days & Latter Days* [2002], "Since I've Been Lovin' You," "Babe I'm Gonna Leave You," "Ten Years Gone"
**Drummer** - John Bonham

It's not listed as one of my key tracks because I have grown tired of it, but the intro to "Rock and Roll" truly made me want to play drums. It's so distinct. It feels primordial. The impact of these drums forces the listener to pay attention, snatching them out of whatever state of mind they were in. The songs listed above, particularly "Since I've Been Lovin' You," captivated me because of how the drum part and feel served the song. Those kick hits felt so sneaky and reactionary in a way

I didn't think rock drums could be; my early "ensemble" ears were piqued. These songs caught my attention because it was a group of distinct instrumentalists making something together, and I particularly wanted to know what the drums were doing. That perspective, which is part-oriented AND group-oriented, is what I strive to have; it's what I am continually working towards as a drummer. "Rock and Roll" is certainly A PART, but it hit me before I could even conceive of it as that...if that makes sense. It just was DRUMS, and I wanted to have DRUMS in my life after that.

As obvious as Bonzo is as a rock Icon, he was a gateway into swing for me. The magical thing about these early rock drummers was that they weren't being rock musicians. Most started their drumming journey with swing music and/or drum corps. Bonham's approach feels inherently experimental to me. His triplets rubbing up against a straighter feel, his huge tones, and the way his playing felt unrelenting yet loose opened up what drums and being a drummer could be to my young ears.

---

### Deerhoof, *The Runners Four* [2005], "Twin Killers"
### **Drummer** - Greg Saunier

Greg and Deerhoof had a psychedelic effect on me, to be perfectly honest. It sounded familiar but then entirely alien; the one would shift mysteriously, yet I was still head-banging. Nothing landed where I thought it would, and that was very thrilling! Greg's relationship with time inspired my young ears; it felt tense yet melodic. His press rolls and the places he would choose to crash felt like guitar feedback to me — chaotic but also organized. Then I learned that he has a master's degree in composition, is a multi-instrumentalist and mastering engineer, and loves Charlie Watts. My life changed.

## The Meters, *Look-ka Py Py* [1969], "Look-ka Py Py"
**Drummer** - Zigaboo Modeliste

The space between every tastefully placed limb threw me through a loop. It still does. The vibe is so loose but also so tight. It has excellent drum parts and an amazing feel. I don't know what else to say; it's just another instance of something now seen as a classic example of its genre still feeling fresh, unique, and unclassifiable!

## John Coltrane, *A Love Supreme* [1965], "Part 1: Acknowledgment"
**Drummer** - Elvin Jones

He could sound like furniture falling down stairs but ALWAYS kept his left foot on the two and four. How?! His feel was so expressive; it could be so heavy yet nimble. His playing was immensely emotive, and it struck me as soon as the beat dropped in "Part 1," with the perfectly nice feel slowly eroded by thunderous floor tom and kick rolls. It's amazing. Also, I love his playing in Wayne Shorter's "Deluge"; it's very thick. The way he played, every hit was so intentional and a world of its own.

## Wilco, *A Ghost Is Born* [2004], "At Least That's What You Said"
**Drummer** - Glenn Kotche

Glenn's time feel and ear for tone is so adept. His playing feels familiar and welcoming but also odd and intercepted. When the drums come in on "At Least That's What You Said," I can still get emotional. They are so unabashed. His use of open hi-hat is melodic, and the fills at the end are gutting! He's matching the intensity of the guitars, and it doesn't feel excessive; it feels cathartic.

## Neil Young, *Harvest* [1972], "Words Between The Lines Of Age"
### **Drummer** - Kenny Buttrey

I love Neil Young. I love heavy-feeling music, and Kenny Buttrey's playing (as well as Ralph Molina of Crazy Horse) lend themselves to heft. They are two very different drummers, recorded and produced very differently, but both access emotive heft from Neil's music. "Words Between The Lines Of Age" felt like droney prog with its alternating 5/4 and 6/4 measures. His kick and snare placement keeps the feeling open and angsty.

## The Band, *The Band* [1969], "The Night They Drove Old Dixie Down," "King Harvest"
### **Drummer** - Levon Helm

Levon had a fantastic feel. The press roll in "The Night They Drove Old Dixie Down" took my breath away when I first heard it. It left me hanging as a listener; I felt mournful from it. There's also a video of "King Harvest" from the *Big Pink* sessions that I have watched hundreds of times. His groove locked with Rick, and his cymbal flourishes as he's singing struck me. Also, he is holding a cigarette in his left, traditional grip hand, and you don't see that very often

# Stanton Moore

*"...this record is a go-to goldmine of snare drum street beats that I have borrowed, stolen and drawn influence from countless times!"*

S tanton Moore is a Grammy Award-winning drummer, educator, and performer born and raised in New Orleans. Over his 25-year career, Stanton has collaborated with a diverse range of artists including Galactic, Maceo Parker, Joss Stone, Irma Thomas, Corrosion of Conformity, Donald Harrison Jr., and many others, showcasing his unique blend of jazz, funk, and rock-style drumming. To deepen his connection with students and continue sharing his passion for teaching, he recently launched his own online drum academy at stantonmooredrumacademy.com.

---

John Coltrane, *Live at Birdland* [1963], "Afro Blue"
**Drummer** - Elvin Jones

---

This was the first record where I really heard Elvin. I listened to it for the first time when I was about 17 years old. I was at a party, and a friend who was a few years older played me this record. It blew me away. At the time, I was playing more rock and classic rock, so Elvin's playing resonated with me because of his intense energy and raw emotional power. It was the first time I realized how powerful jazz drumming could be.

---

## James Brown, *20 All-Time Greatest Hits!* [1991]
**Drummers** - Melvin Parker, Jabo Starks, Clyde Stubblefield

I love playing funk and make my living playing funk. This record is an absolute go-to because it features 20 of James Brown's most important songs. Melvin Parker, Jabo Starks, and Clyde Stubblefield are the architects of funk, and I have gone to them for inspiration countless times over the years. If you want to learn something, it's best to go to the source, and this collection of songs is the source for funk.

## The Meters, *Look-Ka Py Py* [1970]
**Drummer** - Zigaboo Modeliste

Being a drummer from New Orleans, The Meters is my favorite band. The music they created in the late '60s and early '70s wrote the playbook for New Orleans funk. In my opinion, Zigaboo Modeliste is one of, if not the most funkiest drummer of all time. You cannot be from New Orleans and not be influenced and impacted by Zig's playing. Zig has been a significant influence on my playing, and I have come up with countless grooves that draw directly from the inspiration I've gotten from him.

## Led Zeppelin, *Physical Graffiti* [1975]
**Drummer** - John Bonham

John Bonham is one of my favorite drummers of all time, and I'm sure he is for many people reading this. His power, groove, creativity, and identifiable sound all combine to make him one of the most influential drummers of all time. I picked this record because I spent a lot of time playing along to it when I was younger. There is such a vast range of different styles and genres on this double record that really show the gamut of what Bonham was capable of.

## Professor Longhair, *Crawfish Fiesta* [1980]
### **Drummer** - Johnny Vidacovich

Professor Longhair is considered one of the early architects of rock 'n' roll and New Orleans funk. His records were often put-together sessions, but this particular record utilized his touring band with Johnny Vidacovich on drums. Johnny was one of my main teachers and his playing on this record is incredibly creative and as greasy as it gets. It features some fantastic snare drum street beats, and JV taught me some of them personally. Johnny has had a huge influence on me and my playing, and I've used what I learned from this record countless times in my career.

## John Mooney, *Testimony* [2015]
### **Drummer** - Johnny Vidacovich

The John Mooney record, *Testimony,* has Johnny Vidacovich on drums as well. It also features George Porter Jr. of The Meters on bass. Talk about a stellar rhythm section! Like Professor Longhair's *Crawfish Fiesta*, this record is also a go-to goldmine of snare drum street beats that I have borrowed, stolen and drawn influence from countless times!

# Ilan Rubin

*"Every fill and transition from section to section seems perfectly written and executed, but it's not. It's just a drummer in the zone playing at his peak."*

I lan Rubin is a multifaceted musician recognized for his roles as a drummer, producer, composer, artist, songwriter, and band leader. He is best known for drumming with prominent acts such as Nine Inch Nails, Paramore, Angels & Airwaves, and Danny Elfman. Notably, in 2020, Ilan was inducted into the Rock and Roll Hall of Fame as a member of Nine Inch Nails, earning distinction as the youngest living inductee in its history. Check out Ilan's band, The New Regime, and other releases under his name. Here are Ilan's choices...

Led Zeppelin, *Houses Of The Holy* [1973],
"The Song Remains The Same"
**Drummer** - John Bonham

To begin with, this is my favorite album of all time by my favorite band of all time, and it has an incredible opener. This song has a signature up-tempo galloping feel that I can listen to Bonham play all day long. I also love playing it myself while messing around at the drums. Another standout thing to me is the sound of his drums because they have this natural ambiance as if you're in the room listening. In the middle section, where everything slows down, there's a moment where Bonham gets centerstage for a very reserved fill, which shows his taste and lets the listener appreciate how beautifully he tunes his drums. There are other excellent fills in the song and one of the best-sounding ride cymbals I've ever heard. When he moves to the ride, you get another sense of his dynamic touch, enough to give the song an airy lift. I can't get enough!

## Led Zeppelin, *The Song Remains The Same* [1976], "Celebration Day"
### Drummer - John Bonham

Surprise, surprise, more Bonham. This live album was essential to my drumming upbringing, and I still frequently enjoy it today. This rendition of "Celebration Day" is a masterclass in the interlocking between bass player and drummer. The upbeats on the bass locking in with the bass drum propel this song forward in a way that gives it even more swagger than the album version. There are also some great locked bass and drum fills during the solo, which shows you how in tune the rhythm section of Bonham and Jones were, especially while laying down the foundation under a fantastic guitar solo. This tour contributed to the lasting popularity of Vistalites, and I can't help but picture them every time I listen.

## The Police, *Zenyatta Mondatta* [1980], "Driven To Tears"
### Drummer - Stewart Copeland

It's hard to pinpoint a Stewart Copeland track that does a decent job of summing up the signature aspects of his playing. "Driven To Tears" highlights his feel, his hi-hat work, and his ride work and immediately gives you a picture of his setup with a great tom fill before the first verse. While this song is generally up-tempo, the choruses cut to halftime, and another aspect of Copeland's playing shines. I spent so much time between the ages of 12-14 going through every bit of Police material I could get my hands on, and it'll always be a part of my playing. He's also the only player who made me think three rack toms weren't a bad idea.

## The Police, *The Police Live!* [1995], "Message In A Bottle" (Disc 2 from 1983)
### Drummer - Stewart Copeland

This "Message In A Bottle" performance has to be one of the tightest live performances by any band ever, and there's nothing reserved about Copeland's playing on it. From the outset, you are getting fill after fill that are busy, tasteful, and pure precision. Every fill and transition from section to section seems perfectly written and executed, but it's not. It's just a drummer in the zone playing at his peak. Something that struck me about Copeland at this time setup-wise was how juxtaposed his cymbal choices seemed to be. At the same time, he had 13" hi-hats with a tight, crisp sound and a bunch of Paiste RUDE cymbals, which I believe were used more by metal drummers than anything. But he made it work in a way that helped define his unmistakable sound.

## The Dave Brubeck Quartet, *Dave Brubeck Live At Carnegie Hall* [1963], "Castilian Drums"
### Drummer - Joe Morello

While this track might seem like the odd-man out, it exemplifies Joe Morello's drumming on an album I learned much from when I was younger. What struck me about this piece was the signature finesse of Morello's playing and his ability to solo and improvise in 5/4 (as well as other time signatures). He made it sound so easy because of how smoothly he played, but most would agree it isn't. As a drummer, I prefer drums to sound more open instead of punchier and tighter. This recording at Carnegie Hall captured the instruments beautifully, and his standard to small-sized kit could sound intricate or explosive depending on his choice of dynamics.

# Chris Marshak

*"He seems never to play the same thing twice. Someone once said
that he never plays the same thing 'once.'"*

C hris Marshak, a Long Island-based session drummer,
percussionist, and solo artist, is celebrated for his distinctive
groove and feel. With a career rooted in collaborations with renowned
singer-songwriters, Chris has worked with iconic artists like Steve
Linwood, Marc Cohn, Ricardo Arjona, and Amy Helm, carving out a
niche with his singular musical voice. Here are Chris' choices...

### Dr. John, *Gumbo* [1972], "Junko-Partner"
### **Drummer** - Freddy Staehle

Freddy Staehle's playing on this is fantastic! It starts with the
drums playing a second line feel that is so greasy and bouncy. The
first time I heard this, I was tapping my feet before the rest of the
band came in. Freddie Staehle makes something that is not easy to
play sound so effortless. His use of buzz rolls creates tension in the
phrasing and widens the beat in an exceptional way. The drumming
dances with the sax on the solo, and the way the groove interacts
with Dr. John's vocals is so musical. The variations he plays at the
end of the phrases open things up in such a way that keeps things
interesting from the beginning to the end of the song. It sounds so

free, almost like he never plays the same thing twice.

## John Hiatt, *Bring The Family* [1987], "Memphis In The Mean-time"
### Drummer - Jim Keltner

Jim Keltner's playing has always resonated with me, and his greasiness on this record is off the charts. One of the things I love about his playing on this is the snare crack on beat 2 with no snare on 4; it opens up the phrasing excellently, creating sonic room for the vocal. The interplay between the drums and guitars is masterful, and sonically, it is so interesting. Keltner always leaves me wondering, "What the hell is he playing?." There are these triangle or finger cymbal sounds(?) he occasionally injects that play a sort of musical peek-a-boo; just when you notice them, they are gone. Keltner seems never to play the same thing twice. Someone once said that Keltner never plays the same thing "once."

## Coleman Hawkins and Ben Webster, *Coleman Hawkins Encounters Ben Webster* [1959], "Rosita"
### Drummer - Alvin Stoller

The rumba-esque percussion at the top sets the tone. The sweetness of the sax melody is gorgeous, and when both saxes come in with the melody together the 2nd time through the form, it is heavenly. This song, as well as the others on the album, is soulful and understated; the breathiness of the saxes gets me every time. Alvin Stoller plays precisely what is needed. When it goes to the swing section and in the first 8 bars, Stoller drops a bass drum on beat 4 of the 7th bar. It is just

154

so incredibly musical and exciting. There are no "look at me" moments on this record. Not to mention Oscar Peterson on piano — unbelievable!

---

### James Taylor, *James Taylor Live* [1993], "Country Road"
### **Drummer** - Carlos Vega

The beauty of Carlos Vega's open, spacious, and deliberate fills is breathtaking; he plays the figures in this song with a relaxed and assertive energy. The sound of his toms is so low and earthy, and his pocket is so undeniably deep. I'm a big fan of all the drummers who have played with James Taylor, but Carlos Vega might be my favorite. The drum and vocal breakdown on this recording is so powerful, and how Carlos' drumming interacts with the vocal gives me the chills. In my opinion, this is as good as drumming gets. Also, what I love about this song and record is that the live tempos are slower than the original recordings. It is such a rare thing, and I think it gives these hit songs a space that allows James' voice to be heard in a new way.

---

### Los Lobos, *Kiko* [1992], "Wake Up Delores"
### **Drummer** - Gary Mallaber

The shuffly swagger of this song is so hypnotic; the drums make me want to move, and I love the way the drums interact with the horns and electric guitars as they make their way across the landscape of the track. The stomp of the feel works so well with the vocal phrasing, and the drums interact with the song in such a peripheral yet powerful way. Another drummer may have wanted to accent the horn and guitar hits, but the way the drums don't react and play through things is so tasteful.

---

# Connor Denis

*"To this day, his drumming inspires me...I am still finding more intricacies in his drum parts, even after hearing them hundreds of times."*

H ailing from South Florida, Connor Denis is a standout touring and session drummer lauded for his powerful playing style. With influences spanning from pop to metal, he's particularly renowned for his role as the touring drummer for the alternative rock band Beartooth. Here are Connor's choices...

## Smashing Pumpkins, *Siamese Dream* [1993], "Silverfuck"
**Drummer** - Jimmy Chamberlin

Smashing Pumpkins are the first band I ever remember hearing. I vividly remember being a little kid and hearing the beautiful melodies, loud guitars, and complex drum parts featured on *Siamese Dream*. Of course, I didn't know what I was hearing or understand it in a musical context, but I knew I wanted to keep listening. Smashing Pumpkins played an integral role in me discovering my love for music.

When I first started playing drums, I wanted to play along to my favorite records, including many Smashing Pumpkins songs. As time passed and I improved as a drummer, many of those records became easier to break down and play along to...except Smashing Pumpkins.

I started to realize how unique Jimmy Chamberlin's drumming was. While there were many similarities in the drum parts in the other music I was jamming to, Jimmy's drum parts were different, like nothing else I had ever heard. The way that he combined his jazz background with a powerhouse rock approach was beyond me. I was enamored with his playing and incredibly eager to dive deeper into his drum parts, hoping to play like him one day. To this day, his drumming still inspires me as much as it ever did, and I am still finding more intricacies in his drum parts, even after hearing them hundreds of times.

---

## Underoath, *Lost in the Sound of Separation* [2008], "Breathing In a New Mentality"
### **Drummer** - Aaron Gillespie

When I first heard about Underoath, everyone always seemed to talk about Aaron Gillespie, even the casual listener who didn't play drums. I was introduced to Underoath's music right before *Lost in the Sound of Separation* came out, and I instantly became a fan. Naturally, I was anticipating the release of this album. When I heard the opening track, "Breathing in a New Mentality," I was floored. There was an energy and intensity to the drums that only Aaron could bring, along with creative parts I wasn't used to hearing in heavier music. All I wanted to do was hit my drums as hard as I could and attempt to get that same incredible sound captured on the entire record.

This album greatly impacted me, as it helped me find my voice on the drums. I played along and immediately knew I wanted to perform on stage someday with the same energy as Aaron. I had never heard or seen someone play the drums with as much emotion and passion as Aaron seemed to, and something about his approach resonated with me and felt very relatable. Once I started playing shows, I channeled that same energy on stage, which became my playing style's foundation. Listening to this album as a young and aspiring drummer had a lasting impact on me that I am incredibly grateful for.

## Nirvana, *Nevermind* [1991], "Breed"
**Drummer** - Dave Grohl

There was a lot of grunge music playing in my household growing up, and Nirvana was no exception. I always loved the *Nevermind* album, but the drumming only stood out to me later in my life. As a younger drummer, I focused on playing as fast as possible, hitting hard, and learning impressive chops; eventually, that changed. I remember being in high school listening to *Nevermind*, and it felt like something clicked; I finally understood why many of my favorite drummers listed Dave Grohl as one of their biggest influences.

When listening to this record, I repeatedly returned to the song "Breed," falling in love with the simple yet impactful drum parts. The long snare roll at the beginning of the track felt so intentional to me, and I started to realize how powerful simplicity can be. Dave is a master at writing drum parts that serve the song; his parts on this record taught me that sometimes less is more. As a young drummer, I found it difficult to see the value in slowing down and playing less, but listening to *Nevermind* completely opened my eyes to just how valuable that can be.

## Led Zeppelin, *The Song Remains the Same* [1976], "Rock and Roll"
**Drummer** - John Bonham

*The Song Remains the Same* was my first deep dive into John Bonham's drumming. I had heard Led Zeppelin records growing up, and once I started to play drums, people always told me how great Bonham was. But it was when I watched *The Song Remains the Same* that I understood the hype. Of course, Bonham's playing on Zeppelin's studio albums is incredible, but seeing and hearing how he played those songs live made me fall in love with his drumming.

Bonham brought so much to the table with his incredible feel and time, incomparable power, and complete individuality on the drums. As soon as he starts playing, you know it's him. I find that especially true when listening to him play live, so this album is my favorite example of his playing. I had never seen a drummer play with so much energy and hit so hard while moving fluidly around the kit. Listening to this album, it feels like there is nothing that Bonham can't do on a drum set. His playing inspired me to branch out and be a more versatile player, all while sticking to my roots of hard-hitting rock drumming.

## Foo Fighters, *Wasting Light* [2011], "Rope"
### **Drummer** - Taylor Hawkins

Taylor Hawkins has always been one of my favorite drummers. While many of my favorite players were legends before I even started to play drums, I always felt like I got to watch Taylor become one of the all-time greats as it was happening.

When I first heard *Wasting Light*, many small nuances in the drum parts stood out. Taylor's drumming greatly impacts all these songs, but "Rope" is my favorite. From the ghost notes to the accent on the hi-hat in the verse that makes every drummer in the room start air drumming, everything Taylor played in this song was perfect. In

*Wasting Light,* the drum parts feel classic while pushing the boundaries and bringing entirely new ideas to rock drumming. You can hear so much of Taylor's personality as a drummer on these songs, and it is incredibly inspiring; his ability to serve the songs while completely being himself behind the drums is truly unique.

---

# Philo Tsoungui

*"This record was a perfect link, coming from classical percussion
and redirecting me towards pop music and jazz."*

P hilo Tsoungui is an experimental, avant-garde, hip-hop
(adjacent?) German drummer currently playing with The Mars
Volta. Previous collaborations include Chefket, Robert Glasper, Mine,
Fatoni, Mal Eleve, Elif, and Lxandra; Philo will surely be a tastemaker
for many years to come. Here are Philo's choices…

Keziah Jones, *Black Orpheus* [2003],
"Afrosurrealismfortheladies"
**Drummers** - Joshua McKenzie, Jose Joyette

I randomly picked this record in our local library, and this track
opens the album. How it begins very mellow and soft before introducing
the drums makes it one of the most exciting album openers I've ever
heard. Also, it might have been the first time I noticed the concept of
linear drumming as the hi-hat, kick, and snare interact in a new way.
The dynamics in the hi-hat are next level; to this day, I play along to
this tune and try to perfect the feel of it.

## Robert Glasper, *Black Radio* [2012], "Black Radio"
**Drummer** - Chris "Daddy" Dave

I was introduced to Chris Dave through Robert Glasper's first *Black Radio* album and could not stop listening. Chris Dave's drumming is unmatched, and the sound of the drums was eye-opening to me. How he altered his drum and cymbal sounds by putting stuff on top of them became such a thing back then. I found so much joy and excitement in similar experimentation. This record was a perfect link, coming from classical percussion and redirecting me towards pop music and jazz. The title track, "Black Radio," is something that still has me mesmerized.

## Omar Rodriguez Lopez Group, *Omar Rodriguez Lopez Group: Live Los Angeles on Sept 14th, 2010* (video) [2010]
**Drummer** - Deantoni Parks

This must have been my most-watched YouTube video back in the day. I love these performances so much, and Deantoni's drumming is exciting, new, dynamic, precise, chunky, and soft, all at the same time. I'd never heard rim clicks played with such dynamic range and speed, either. So I started practicing rim clicks, something people notoriously underestimated, which opened a new sonic and dynamic horizon for me.

*HONORABLE MENTIONS:*

I need to mention **Chyke Madu**, drummer of the legendary Nigerian Afro-psych rock band the Funkees and, though not a drummer, the

162

guitarist of the Cameroonian bikutsi band Les Têtes brûlées "Zanzibar" who transformed Cameroonian pop culture and the sound of bikutsi and who left this earth way too early. They influenced me way before I could even form my own words, let alone bring musical ideas to life.

# Ben Barter

*"I try to inject just the right amount of 'shittiness' into my drumming...*
*embracing some imperfection to add personality and character.""*

B en Barter is a New Zealand drummer based in Los Angeles, CA, and is widely recognized as Lorde's touring drummer. His versatile skills and knowledge of hybrid drumming have also led him to perform with artists like Broods, Jarryd James, and Passion Pit. Notably, Barter has lent his talent as a session drummer to Grammy Award-winning producer Joel Little on several recordings. Here are Ben's choices...

---

### The Rolling Stones, *Live at the Max* [1991], "Start Me Up"
### **Drummer** - Charlie Watts

To me, Charlie Watts was excellent at playing perfectly imperfect. His drumming possessed a loose yet rich quality that pushed and pulled the tempo, giving The Rolling Stones a raw, exciting energy. His background in jazz played a role in his unique feel, infusing a jazz informed language into a rock setting, resulting in a style of playing only he could pull off. His love of jazz also taught him to intuitively react to the music, resulting in a natural performance that didn't seem overthought.

The raw, intuitive aspect of his playing resonates with me. I try to inject just the right amount of "shittiness" into my drumming, and by shittiness, I mean embracing some imperfection to add personality and character. Depending on the context, this touch of grit or controlled sloppiness brings a human element to the part and makes it more interesting. During performances or recording sessions, I often get into a character or persona (in my head) to get myself into the vibe and maintain the song's theme. While I'll never replicate Charlie Watts' playing style, he remains a constant source of inspiration.

## Usher, 2006 *Modern Drummer Festival DVD*, "Caught Up"
### **Drummer** - Aaron Spears

I forget how old I was when I saw this, but I remember I hadn't seen anything like it before. I replayed that one fill in the "Caught Up" performance Aaron Spears did for an entire afternoon at 0.25x playback speed, and I still couldn't work out what was going on. I eventually found a transcription that someone had posted online and learned it, but I could never get it to sound as good as Aaron did.

Besides having exceptional feel and timing, what I love about Aaron's playing is the power and intention with which he plays. He uniquely puts inflections in really odd parts of a fill that completely flip the feel for a second. A drummer has not impressed me more in 2 seconds than Aaron did with that fill.

## Oasis, *Live at V Festival* [2005], "Lyla"
### **Drummer** - Zak Starkey

I've been lucky to see Zak Starkey perform twice with The Who.

I was impressed with how he moved around the kit with a beautiful fluidity despite the complexity of Keith Moon's parts. His playing during this performance with Oasis showcases his confidence and power but with an effortless, laid-back feel. It's a somewhat simple drum part yet still captivating and brings so much energy to the crowd while he seemingly remains so calm on stage.

Knowing his background adds to the intrigue while watching him, and it must give him some inner confidence that shines through his playing, I'd imagine. I met him once in San Fran when Lorde played before The Who; he was so sweet and cool. We talked about ButtKickers.

## Patrick Cowley, *Afternooners* [1982], "Big Shot"

I had just started playing around with synths when I was introduced to Patrick Cowley's *Afternooners* album, and it's one album that got me into my love of electronic music. I love the simplicity of his drumming and how it seamlessly integrates with the synth parts. I'm a big fan of a no-nonsense, no-frills groove, but one that still makes you want to dance. The parts are effective and tasteful but subtle and simple, a hallmark of successful dance music.

The drums on this record sound so full and punchy. The tone and energy of the drums make me think his earlier drumming in bands had some punk tendencies, or at least I've read he had been introduced to bands like Devo and the Talking Heads around that time, which may have influenced his drum sound. He was also a successful disco producer, with his most notable song being "You Make Me Feel (Mighty Real)" by Sylvester. These two worlds combine so well, producing raw, straight-ahead, but very danceable music.

## Incredible Bongo Band, *Bongo Rock* [1973], "Apache"
## Drummer – Jim Gordon

There is a 50% chance that Jim Gordon is the drummer for the Incredible Bongo Band's notorious "Apache" break; it may have been a Canadian drummer, Kat Hendrikse, who also recorded on the same album, but for this book's sake, my money is on Jim Gordon. The whole story behind the album recording is great; whether he played that infamous break or not, the rest of his discography is one of the longest and greatest. He had a golden touch and managed to play exactly what the song needed every time. Like Charlie Watts, his parts seem so effortless and exactly what needed to be played to make it a successful song.

To have drummed on a break like "Apache", Clyde Stubblefield's "Funky Drummer" break, or Gregory Sylvester Coleman on the "Amen" break is one of the greatest achievements. To influence multiple generations and spark new genres through a snippet of playing what comes naturally to you is the kind of drumming that inspires me. Jim Gordon had a tragic and sad story and recently passed away, but I got to play one of Jim Gordon's kits in a session a few years ago at a studio called Electrovox in LA. It sounded incredible; they also had Hal Blaine's concert toms, one of the more memorable sessions I've been lucky to have participated in.

# Ian Froman

*"His progression from the mid-'60s to the '90s was more inventive for a more extended period than anyone. Period!"*

Ian Froman is an jazz drummer and educator based in New York City. With a rich teaching background at institutions like Berklee College of Music, Drummers Collective, New School University, and City College of New York, he's imparted his expertise through both group classes and private lessons. Ian's touring résumé reads like a who's who of jazz, having shared stages worldwide with luminaries such as John Abercrombie, Dave Holland, Michael Brecker, Gary Burton, and Matthew Garrison. Here are Ian's choices…

John Coltrane, *A Love Supreme* [1965], "Resolution"
**Drummer** - Elvin Jones

Having studied with Elvin and getting the opportunity to practice on the *A Love Supreme* cymbals, this recording means so much to me. The tune "Resolution" has the deepest piano solo build-up that Elvin joins when McCoy plays chords over the bar line. Elvin alters the ride cymbal pattern to accommodate the chords as he crashes the ride with the rhythms he hears around him.

I asked him about this: did you and McCoy plan on hitting the chords together? Was it discussed in advance or planned? His response was: "We were just playing." LOL!!!!! WOW!!!!!!!

---

### Chick Corea, *Now He Sings, Now He Sobs* [1968], "Steps"
**Drummer** - Roy Haynes

McCoy heavily influences Chick on this recording. Roy created a language and vocabulary with this style of playing by using a flat ride for the first time and alternating the ride pattern as an improvisation. The snare drum, bass drum, and hi-hat are used as equal comping voices! Snap, crackle, and pop! Sublime!

---

### Keith Jarrett, *Still Live* [1986]
**Drummer** - Jack DeJohnette

I have seen this group many times. Jack is incredible. Period. The most supportive in a trio setting. Loose, open, and modern. From delicate to heavy duty! Jack is the culmination of Tony, Elvin, and Roy — the best.

---

### Michael Brecker, *Michael Brecker* [1987], "Syzygy"
**Drummer** - Jack DeJohnette

Jack is at it again, starting the tune in duo with Mike. The straight 8th linear vocabulary in the context of a medium up-tempo is extremely modern, and he took everyone farther. His progression from the mid-'60s to the '90s was more inventive for a more extended period than anyone. Period!

---

169

## Jan Garbarek, *Paths Prints* [1982]
## **Drummer** - Jon Christensen

Jon went from a straight-ahead European drummer backing up American artists to being influenced by mid-'60s Tony Williams to being at the forefront of creating the ECM music scene. He was a brilliant artist, musician, and drummer. I am honored to have called him a friend and miss him - as he passed away too soon.

---

### *HONORABLE MENTION:*

TONY, TONY, TONY.

How could I not have mentioned him!?

He was simply incredible. Mid-'60s with Miles, of course, but the big yellow Gretsch era showcased brilliant technical prowess playing jazz. It's a shame that he passed away suddenly ... and too soon.

---

# Eric Slick

*"He said, 'Everything you need to know about perfect technique and expression is in this video.'"*

E ric Slick is an American singer, songwriter, and drummer best recognized for his contributions to the indie rock band Dr. Dog. However, he has also collaborated with a diverse range of artists including Adrian Belew, Kevin Morby, Daniel Rossen, Natalie Prass, Nels Cline, Ween, and others. In addition to his work with Dr. Dog, Slick has released several solo albums and operates his vinyl label, Least Records. Here are Eric's choices…

## George Harrison, *Cloud Nine* [1987], "When We Was Fab"
**Drummer** - Ringo Starr

This choice is etched into my memory because it was one of the first music videos I saw on MTV. My parents didn't have cable, so we only watched MTV on vacation in Ocean City, NJ. I saw this video and "Shock The Monkey" by Peter Gabriel. Our musical DNA is formed early, which sums up my current personality well. "When We Was Fab" is the perfect song for a kid who doesn't quite understand music yet. The lyrics are simple and easy to understand. The video had lots of visual stimulation with hands coming out of the sky strumming Rickenbackers and hands hitting drums that are clearly blue-screened.

I remember seeing Ringo in this video and thinking he was so cool. Then I saw him on *Shining Time Station* (aka *Thomas The Tank Engine*) as the train conductor and thought he was even cooler. Finally, I saw him on a worn VHS copy of The Beatles' *Ready Steady Go!* that my dad had lying around. Ringo had this effervescence on the kit. I loved how he played the drums; that was the moment I was hooked. I begged my parents for a drum kit.

Ringo often smiled and shook his mop of hair, especially in the early Beatles days. He was a caricature of someone who was born to do it. Again, this is perfect kid stuff. I didn't resonate with the dark and moody personas of Ginger Baker or Bill Ward yet. It all came full circle when my band Dr. Dog eventually did *Yo Gabba Gabba!* for Nickelodeon. The producers instructed me to smile and shake my head like Ringo because kids would pay more attention if I did that. I wondered if any kid would see me playing a gigantic drum kit made out of pumpkins with sticks made of carrots. Who knows, maybe that would influence them in the same way!

*Bruford & the Beat* (Instructional Video) [1982]
**Drummer** - Bill Bruford

After years of obsessing over Ringo in elementary school and then John Bonham in middle school, I was introduced to Yes by my parents in 8th grade. The drumming sounded alien to me. I had no clue what the drummer was doing. It was a flurry of notes that felt like they were dangling in mid-air like I could grab them for only a second, and then they'd fly away. My dad told me the drummer was Bill Bruford, the best in the world. We had just gotten the internet, and I would research what Bill Bruford was up to every day. Maybe he was on tour, and I'd get to see him play one day. Unfortunately, that day never came.

In 10th grade, I started getting the *Interstate Music* catalog, and they had a slew of VHS instructional videos and some DVDs for sale. I saw *Bruford and The Beat* and gasped. I had no idea that he made a video. My birthday was coming up, so I asked my parents for it. That was all I wanted. This is before YouTube, everyone. I would sit for weeks, waiting for a VHS tape to arrive at my house like a clown.

The tape arrived, and I must've watched that thing over 300 times. I had a 12" color VHS/TV in my bedroom, and I'd put it on before walking to school. I'd come home and watch it after school. I wanted his setup so badly: a Ludwig Supraphonic snare, Tama octobans, Simmons drums...I researched it and eventually bought a Simmons kit off of eBay with some money I saved up working as a busboy at a pizzeria. The tape ended with a performance by the 1980's incarnation of King Crimson. The rhythm guitarist struck me, and I discovered his name was Adrian Belew. It is still mind-blowing that Adrian would ask me to join his band a few years later, and I'd eventually meet all these people. I finally met Bill Bruford in 2016, and I completely blacked out as we talked. He was so kind and even complimented my playing. What a mensch.

## Frank Zappa, *A Token of His Extreme* [2013] (recorded in 1974), "Inca Roads"
### Drummer - Chester Thompson

Bill Bruford was my gateway into prog rock. I got heavily into Frank Zappa around the same time. In 10th grade, I listened to Zappa's *One Size Fits All* on my Discman daily during lunch. The drummer on that record is Chester Thompson. He played in many odd time signatures, but everything had an incredible pocket. I loved how much the weird shit would groove. The opening track is an 8-minute behemoth called "Inca Roads." If you haven't heard it, stop what you're doing right now and put it on. I'm assuming Thundercat loves this song too.

In the early days of the 'net, there was a program called Limewire. You could download albums, but also videos. Proto-YouTube, I guess. Someone ripped a warbled copy of a filmed 1974 Zappa performance from KCET Los Angeles, and I later found out that it was the basis for some of the tracks on *One Size Fits All*. I could now see what Chester Thompson was doing on the drums. I'm a visual learner, so this development was crucial for me. I am still trying to figure out what Chester is doing on this song. The opening groove is so slinky and expertly executed. The rest of the song is absolutely bonkers.

I eventually got to play with most of Zappa's alums, and it's been one of the great honors of my life. I learn something from every one of them. Their dedication to excellence has been crucial to my progress on the kit. They kicked my ass into shape, too.

---

### Captain Beefheart & His Magic Band, *Trout Mask Replica* [1969], "Ella Guru"
**Drummer** - John "Drumbo" French

When I was 17, I got into all kinds of weird shit. My prog rock days were coming to a close, and I was enrolled in jazz school at University of the Arts. I went on my first real tour that year. We passed through Fort Collins, Colorado, and I stopped at a CD shop. I'd heard about Captain Beefheart for a while and how it was right up my alley. I bought his album *Trout Mask Replica*. Frank Zappa produced it, so surely I'd love it. I'll never forget hearing the opening track, "Frownland." What the fuck was this music? Are they joking? Everyone is playing in a different time signature, in a different key. I listened through the whole thing, and my mind was blown. Every note was intentional, and it wasn't just free improv. It was densely composed over a long period and played with the reckless abandon of a punk band.

The drummer, of course, is John "Drumbo" French. He's one of my all-time favorites; he has such a unique style and is a real hodge-podge of Joe Morello, Denardo Coleman, and Ed Blackwell. I learned that he was the one transcribing Beefheart's piano meandering that got decoded into guitar parts for the record. I started transcribing all of the material. John showed me that you could be a drummer and also a composer. His parts on TMR could be isolated and listened to as pieces of music.

I joined a Captain Beefheart cover band in 2005 and got to play the with a bunch of my friends. There's always something to learn from it.

---

*Tony Williams Drum Clinic @ Zildjian Day* [1985]
**Drummer** - Tony Williams

I started touring with Adrian Belew in 2006. To be honest, I was never happy with my playing. I was touring a lot on the side with the Ween guys in various projects. I told Dave Dreiwitz, their bass player, that I was struggling with my technique. He insisted I go to Boston and study with Kenwood Dennard, Jaco Pastorius' drummer. I started taking the bus up to Boston once a month from Philly.

Kenwood kicked my ass and got my hands and feet into shape. He showed me how to play along with a metronome. We studied from the Alan Dawson book, and there was a lot of talk about Alan's protege, Tony Williams. It dawned on me that I should check him out. I went to

Tower Records every week with what little money I had and purchased a CD with Tony on it every week. I was lucky many of those records were in the $7 bin. I stumbled upon Eric Dolphy's *Out To Lunch*, and I was hooked. I could see Eric Dolphy's and Captain Beefheart's lineage, and it thrilled me.

Kenwood showed me a tape of Tony Williams playing at the Zildjian Day Clinic in 1985 during one of our lessons. He said, "Everything you need to know about perfect technique and expression is in this video." I would watch that video every night before playing, rewind, and fast forward. Tony's hands were impeccable. I would sit in front of the mirror at the venue with my practice pad and agonize over every stroke. It was my Zen practice, and it prepared me for every performance. It did teach me so much about what I was missing in my playing, and I can't overstate the importance of Tony's influence.

# Petar Janjic

*"...it is a perfect example of musical drumming—hitting all the hits but not making it a huge event."*

P etar Janjic, originally from Serbia but now based in Nashville, Tennessee, via Minneapolis, Minnesota, is known for his incredibly funky grooves. He serves as the drummer for the highly acclaimed guitarist and bandleader Cory Wong, showcasing his exceptional skills in contemporary funk music. Even the legendary Prince recognized Petar's talent, inviting Petar to play on one of his records before his passing. Petar is also involved in various musical endeavors, including his projects named Uncle Bronco and Heavy Chevy. Here are Petar's choices...

James Brown, *Star Time* [1991], "Get It Together," "Funky Drummer"
**Drummers** - John "Jabo" Starks, Clyde Stubblefield

This is a fun one. It was sometime in November of 2012. I remember picking up Michael Bland for his house gig in Minneapolis and giving him a ride every Monday for a few months. He always brought CDs to listen to in the car to help me improve my playing. He brought *Star Time* that day and immediately hit track 10. Honestly, after the first bar, the rest was history. Funk drumming made so much sense regarding feel, groove, and attitude. The tune "Get it Together" perfectly exemplifies how it's done.

## Prince, *[Love Symbol]* [1992], "Sexy MF"
**Drummer** - Michael Bland

This is another example of funk at its finest. Michael Bland is such a machine and musical drummer. Every single hit, crash, and fill serves the song. Not to mention, "Sexy MF" was recorded without a click. These cats are locked; the time is not moving, and Michael is driving the bus. From the first hit into the verse to the sax solo outro, where he switches to the ride bell, this groove is driving and not slowing down. It's so funky!!!!

## Toto, *Toto* [1978], "Georgy Porgy"
**Drummer** - Jeff Porcaro

One of my all-time favorites is the legendary Jeff Porcaro. His approach to the single-hand 16th-note grooves on the hi-hat greatly impacted my drumming. While plenty of Jeff grooves and tunes are out there, this one is quite special. You can hear how the feel is so smooth from the fade-in; the groove floats, and it's so relaxed — truly a signature Jeff groove and feel.

## Weather Report, *Weather Report Live in Tokyo 1984* (Video)
## "D Flat Waltz"
**Drummer** - Omar Hakim

I saw a VHS of *Weather Report 1984 Live in Tokyo* when I was six; the entire show was fire. The rhythm section then was a young Omar Hakim and Victor Baily, and God, were they tight! They were ferocious, hungry, son-locked, and full of energy. "D Flat Waltz" is a perfect example of musical drumming—hitting all the hits but not making it a huge event. It is extremely tasty and subtle playing.

---

David Garfield, Larry Carlton, *Tribute to Jeff* [2005], "Jeff's Strut"
**Drummer** - Steve Gadd

GADD IS KING. THIS IS MY ALL-TIME FAVORITE DRUM SOLO. GADD IS KING :)

---

179

# Dan Bailey

*"...[his drumming] is a perfect foundation for these bone-dry songs
of despair: the sounds, the performances, the restraint: all impeccable."*

D an Bailey is a musician, music director, and drum engineer
located in Southern California. He has served as Father John
Misty's drummer since 2014 and assumed the role of music director in
2017. Balancing his time between touring and remote recording from
his studio, Trackland 2, Dan has collaborated with a diverse array
of artists. His credits include Aaron Lee Tasjan, Johnathan Wilson,
Everest, Mating Ritual, First Aid Kit, Reignwolf, Elephant Castle,
OneRepublic, and many more. Here are Dan's choices…

Radiohead, *Amnesiac* [2001], "Dollars and Cents"
**Drummer** - Phil Selway

I had barely recovered from *Kid A* blowing my 19-year-old mind
apart the year before, so when *Amnesiac* came out, it was even stranger,
and the instrumentation was even less cohesive; it completely
contrasted against the wave of dominant corporate rock at the time.

My first reaction to hearing "Dollars and Cents" was confusion.
Phil is hitting the "snare" on the downbeat and doubling the bass part
on the toms. Why would you do that? That's like a drum part a singer
would come up with.

It was one of the first times I remembered hearing the drums do something other than provide the song's momentum; Phil was setting the whole sonic texture while Colin provided the necessary inertia from the bass. This tune flipped the switch that drums don't need to provide a backbeat. I'd never considered that before.

## Tears for Fears, *The Seeds of Love* [1989], "Woman in Chains"
### Drummer - Phil Collins

It's easy to look at Phil Collins from our current perspective and see him as the movie soundtrack dad-rock guy, but Phil is one of the most criminally underrated drummers ever. Just listen to Genesis. He's my pick for the best prog drummer of all time; certainly my favorite and as musical as they came.

In this track, he's at the peak of his pop-star powers and playing these incredible, song-serving, considerate drums. He weaves in and around the sequencer and percussion elements, and there are three to four fills that couldn't be anybody else; it's a masterclass in how to fit something so signature into a musical context and not have it feel forced at all—an incredible drum track.

## Daniel Lanois, *Shine* [2003], "Power of One"
### Drummer - Brian Blade

This could be any song that Lanois, Blade, and Daryl Johnson have played together, but there's a playfulness and improvisation on this cut that's particularly stellar. Blade is joyful and creates these little moments out of seemingly nothing while Daryl is the stabilizer.

It's just musicianship on the highest level. I don't know what else to say about the track, but the way it feels is something I've been chasing most of my career. Brian Blade would be my pick for the drummer with the best combination of ability and taste we've heard, so it's no surprise that a track like this would be the bar to strive for.

## Jeff Buckley, *Grace* [1994], "Dream Brother"
### **Drummer** - Matt Johnson

I spent a lot of time early in my years on the instrument, concerned about my note-throwing ability. How fast could I play? How many notes could I cram in a given space? How do I make things harder to play? — that kind of college nonsense.

Then I went through this period of attempting to turn all that off because it wasn't serving me in the music I was trying to make.

This entire album, in general, but "Dream Brother" specifically, showed musical ways to use your ability on the kit. It doesn't have to be busy, annoying, and self-important. Matt Johnson utilizes a tremendous bag of tricks in ways that sound interesting and help give the songs a swagger and confidence that a player of lesser ability wouldn't have.

## Beck, *Sea Change* [2002], "The Golden Age"
### **Drummer** - Joey Waronker

This one goes hand in hand with the earlier Phil Selway track from *Amnesiac*. Both were in heavy rotation for me around the same time.

Whereas the Phil Selway track turned me on to thinking about non-traditional parts, Joey Waronker shows you that sometimes kick/snare/hat is all you need.

It's just a perfect foundation for these bone-dry songs of despair: the sounds, the performances, the restraint: all impeccable.

## John Lennon, *Plastic Ono Band* [1970], "God"
## Drummer - Ringo Starr

My favorite song and drum performance of all time is Ringo on "God" from *Plastic Ono Band*. It's Ringo at the absolute peak of his powers. The musicality and lyricism of the fills still get to me as much as the first time I heard them.

By the bridge, Lennon is reading off this list of grievances, many of them very public things about his life and beliefs, and Ringo backdrops them each with a response. I've heard the song a hundred times, and I'm still surprised by some of the fills: they give me a sense that Ringo is making the argument for the things Lennon is saying with the drums. It's almost as if John is tossing these things aside that don't serve him anymore, while Ringo uses a fill to throw a shovel full of dirt on each one.

It documented one of our greatest songwriters being supported by one of our greatest musicians.

# Jonathan Pinson

*"...he is an excellent example of a masterful drummer consistently doing masterful things, and this song is so good it's laughable."*

Jonathan Pinson is an award-winning drummer and accomplished band leader. He has shared the stage with luminaries such as Herbie Hancock, Wayne Shorter, and Mark Turner. Holding a Masters of Music from UCLA's prestigious Thelonious Monk Institute of Jazz Performance, he also serves as a professor at the California Institute of the Arts. As the leader of his band, Boom Clap, Pinson's dynamic playing style spans jazz, R&B, and gospel genres. Here are Jonathan's choices...

Brian Blade & The Fellowship Band, *Perceptual* [2000],
"Perceptual"
**Drummer** - Brian Blade

Brian Blade Brian Blade Brian Blade. This man is truly an inspiration to me as a drummer and a person. When this album came out, it was a culture shock for music lovers. This track shows his artistry as a bandleader and, of course, as a drummer. He has a special place in my heart because he's always supported my journey in music. The same can be said about his playing style; it is just seen every decision he makes on the bandstand is super supportive and perfect.

## Jeff "Tain" Watts, *Citizen Tain* [1999], "The Impaler"
### Drummer - Jeff "Tain" Watts

Jeff "Tain" Watts helped spark the movement of the young jazz lions and the resurgence of jazz music in the 1980s. He is one of the greatest drummers alive and the first drummer I heard who fused the Elvin Jones and Tony Williams sound and made it his own. I chose this track from Jeff because it showcases how brilliant he was as a composer and a drummer. Jeff's approach was innovative, from the flams to the Swiss army triplets to the polyrhythms.

## The Billy Cobham George Duke Band, *Live on Tour in Europe* [1976], "Almustafa The Beloved"
### Drummer - Billy Cobham

Billy Cobham is a strong influence on how I play the drums and how I lead my band. When I think about Billy, I genuinely see him as a superhero—the way he plays, the head wrap, the 500 toms, the powerful singles, all of it. He plays with so much power and force and command. I first heard him on an album with McCoy Tyner, *Fly with the Wind*, which blew me away; I love how he structures and shapes the whole tune. He is a fantastic storyteller on the drums. Cobham is an excellent example of a masterful drummer consistently doing masterful things, and this song is so good it's laughable.

## John Mayer, *Continuum* [2006], "Gravity"
### Drummer - Steve Jordan

Steve Jordan is a master scientist of sound when it comes to the drums. Funny enough, the same time I started to focus on Billy Cobham was also the same time I was listening to Steve Jordan. His pocket in playing is unmatched, and you hear the drums' history within his musicianship. "Gravity" is a clear-cut example of Steve showing us how to play a simple deep groove by applying the right choices and colors in the song and, as a result, having us all in our emotions. It's storytelling at its finest, and even though it's a simple 2 & 4 groove, you immediately know Steve is on drums.

## Wynton Marsalis, *Live at The Village Vanguard* [1999], "Jig's Jig"
### **Drummer** - Herlin Riley

Herlin Riley is a New Orleans drumming legend (and a legend in general). He was the first drummer who sparked my creativity by combining a great feel alongside numerous percussive instruments to enhance his sonic ability with the band. This has been a practice in New Orleans drummers down to the great Baby Dodds. Still, this man has a unique creative imagination. My favorite drummers are great storytellers. And again, this is one of my favorite swing feels, period, in regards to jazz.

# Martina Barakoska

*"Listening to them is a journey; it always brings me to a different place."*

Martina Barakoska is an inventive drummer and musician based out of North Macedonia. From collaborations with acclaimed artists like Funk Shui and Duper to performances at prestigious festivals such as Alteisa Drumfest and the Yamaha Drum Days Festival, Martina has showcased her talent across Europe and the Balkans. Her debut solo album, *Weird Fishes*, and subsequent releases like *Sunrise* solidify her position as a rising star in the music industry. Here are Martina's choices…

Red Hot Chili Peppers, *Californication* [1999], "Californication," "Purple Stain," "Parallel Universe" **Drummer** - Chad Smith

Chad Smith is so important to me; every time I see him play, I understand why I started playing drums. He's just having so much fun and serves the whole song, specifically the melodies that Anthony is singing.

The unique thing about this album to me is that "Californication" was one of the first songs I tried to learn on the drums, and it was the perfect introduction to playing ghost notes. Also, the other subtleties of feeling his temperament and character translate into his playing are excellent, which you can feel through his hi-hat. He is constantly juggling between open and closed because he is tapping his foot all the time (as a result, the hi-hat opens at some very cool places in the groove) and playing ghost notes and filling in between because he's full of energy!

In "Purple Stain," especially the *Live at Slane Castle* version, I cannot get over how good that outro is and how good they sound and groove as a band!

In "Parallel Universe," I just like his songwriting and have learned so much from it.

Warpaint, *Warpaint* [2014], "Intro," "Keep Us Healthy," "Love Is to Die," "Hi," "Feeling Alright"
**Drummer** - Stella Mozgawa

I found out about Warpaint while I was still new to the drums. The most important thing about this band was how encouraging it was to see four amazing female musicians in the band, making beautiful music, touring, and loving each other so much. Seeing that, I knew I wanted to do this!

Listening to Stella Mozgawa's songwriting and how creative she was with her grooves inspired me to dig deeper into auxiliary sounds and dampening (e.g., "Biggy") dry cymbals; you can still hear how she influenced my playing. The songs wouldn't be the same without her playing.

"Intro" and "Keep It Healthy" have to be some of my all-time favorite songs because I love the production so much. There are some quite complex parts, but it's so delicate and detailed.

Of course, in "Love Is to Die," I love the groove but also how she's using the rims to add another dimension, layer, and melody to the song's breakdowns.

In "Hi," I enjoy how they start with a hybrid-sounding kit and then progress into a natural sound when the song opens up.

In "Feeling Alright," I feel like the drums are the centerpiece of this song, leading the piece melodically and rhythmically simultaneously!

---

## Radiohead, *In Rainbows* [2007], "Weird Fishes/ Arpeggi," "Reckoner," "15 Step"
### **Drummer** - Phil Selway

This album has a special place in my heart; I appreciate it for many reasons. Of course, the drumming is fantastic, but I love the sounds, guitars, lyrics, and singing—everything speaks to me, and I've been influenced by it so many times; you can hear it in my music.

It could be more refined but still very crunchy and natural; I love the production.

I enjoy the "Weird Fishes/ Arpeggi" drum beat and its natural sound. Another favorite is "Reckoner," a song driven by the drums and percussion, and the change in the middle of the song gets me every time (heart emoji). Listening to Radiohead is a journey; it always brings me to a different place. And I won't even get into "15 Step" because it's very evident why it's genius; the production and sounds are outstanding.

The album is incredible, but take time to listen to their *In Rainbows From The Basement* performance; they bring the songs to another level (which I didn't think was possible).

---

John Frusciante, *The Will To Death* [2004], "An Exercise"
John Frusciante, *The Empyrean* [2009], "Unreachable," "Central"
**Drummer** - Josh Klinghoffer

I've spent so much time listening to John's albums; I love his expression, honesty, and constant evolution as an artist. I could spend hours listening to *The Empyrean* and *The Will To Death* because they make you think and drift away with your thoughts; I also love the lyrics. Interestingly, the drummer for this album is Josh Klinghoffer, who is mainly known as a guitarist but also an excellent drummer. I always loved his "non-standard" drumming and sound; it's distinct. And a fun fact: he was the drummer for Warpaint as well.

A few of my faves are "Unreachable" and "Central" from *The Empyrean*; I enjoy how "big" the drums sound, and they are loose; the feel is fantastic.

"An Exercise" is a song I love from *The Will To Death* for the same reasons. I love his songs and the way he writes music.

---

Art Blakey & The Jazz Messengers, *Moanin'* [1959],
"Are You Real"
**Drummer** - Ark Blakey

Even though this is very different from the other albums, I spent a lot of time listening/playing along to Art Blakey while in music school. I love his buzz rolls when he introduces a change, the big sound of his drums, and the way he emphasizes the themes with dynamics. His swing pattern is quite distinct because it sounds very sharp.

My favorite from this album has to be "Are You Real." It has a fantastic theme, and Art's use of dynamics makes it very powerful; I can't even imagine how it would've felt to hear this live back in the day.

---

# Adam Chistgau

*"His ability to support the emotional drive of the music while sounding full and huge, even at pin-drop volumes, is always a goal every time I play."*

Adam Christgau is a Los-Angeles based drummer and percussionist. He's worked with Tegan & Sara, Troye Sivan, Sia, Weezer, John Scofield, Kacey Musgraves, Brandon Flowers, Ingrid Michaelson, Chaka Kahn, LP, Dan Romer, and multiple music scores, including Pixar's *Luca* and HBO's *Station 11*. In addition to musical endeavors, Adam owns and operates Christgau Design, a high-end custom furniture company based in Los Angeles, CA. Here are Adam's choices…

Chuck Loeb, *Chuck Loeb Live at 7th Ave South* [1982-1984], "Excerpt from Cookie"
**Drummer** - Steve Ferrone

I lived in northern NJ until I was nine years old. During that time, my dad studied guitar with a few people in NYC, namely John Scofield and Chuck Loeb. My dad would often bring a small Sony Walkman recorder to these shows and bootleg the performances. I specifically remember hearing Zach Danziger on one of these recordings when he was 16. I was blown away and decided from that time (at four years old) that I wanted to play drums for the rest of my life. This specific recording comes from a time when many of the musicians in NY were playing on studio recordings during the day and then playing small gigs at night in 50-person capacity clubs all over the city. I have listened to dozens of other recordings from this specific era, and it is always such an incredible demonstration of peoples' proficiency on their instrument and their ability to make the pocket huge simultaneously.

## Wayne Shorter, *JuJu* [1965], "JuJu"
**Drummer** - Elvin Jones

This recording is the first time I remember hearing Elvin's playing as a teenager. It's an undeniable freight train. This was the first time I recognized the difference between triplet and straight 8th feel, and I wanted to have the facility to capture it the way Elvin did. His playing would profoundly affect my playing, not only in the jazz world but in the pop and rock world. His ability to support the emotional drive of the music while sounding full and huge, even at pin-drop volumes, is always a goal every time I play.

## Busta Rhymes, *The Coming* [1996], "Still Shining"

Looking back on this, I'm curious if J Dilla produced this track, and he got credited under a different name since it was early in his career. I want to know if it was him or a separate producer.

I was deep in my jazz studies when I first heard this track. I wasn't actively listening to pop or hip-hop as much. I was so fascinated to hear how this track moved around the beat and how Busta Rhymes brought so much of the syncopation into the fold from his voice. It was the first time I heard drums following those syncopated landscapes in this music, and it sent me down a hip-hop and neo soul deep dive. I return to this record yearly to find new inspiration on the kit.

Chris Potter, *Chris Potter Bootleg Live at The Knitting Factory* [2001], "High Noon"
**Drummer** - Brian Blade

Once again, this is another bootleg that I have listened to hundreds of times on repeat. Brian Blade sounds ferocious on this recording at the Knitting Factory in NYC that my college roommate happened to capture during our first year at school.

While Brian sounds incredible on recording, there is something undeniable about his presence on the instrument in a live setting. His joy is infectious. It's rare to hear someone so clearly reacting to every musician on the bandstand in real time. Often, drummers with this kind of command tend to steer the ship in their own direction, and while it's powerful and moving, Brian constantly shows us that you can do that in a supportive way. In this recording, he has the audience in his palm and the band acting in concert.

I have transcribed this track to the best of my ability and taken everything I can from it to the bandstand whenever possible.

Jeff Buckley, *Grace* [1994], "Mojo Pin" (starting at 4:09)
**Drummer** - Matt Johnson

I'm sure many of you know this record well and know of Matt

Johnson's playing. There are countless times I listen back to something I have recorded and realize that I have repeatedly played fills directly from this record. There are feels I've tried to mimic time and time again from everything Matt plays here. Specifically, one of the biggest things I've taken away is his ability to play the widest time possible. I mean that he can give the maximum space between each note, no matter what the subdivision is. Each 16th note stretches the entire duration of that note, each quarter note, etc.

This is especially evident in the clip of this track here. You hear every note to its fullest extent, which is something that, no matter what style of music you're playing, is crucial to master. It's something I'm still working on every day.

# Ralph Alexander

*"This album taught me that being unique in your approach is always more important than being fast and loud."*

Ralph Alexander is a powerful American rock drummer currently touring the world with the artist Poppy. He is also recognized for his contributions to CRX (which features Nick Valensi of The Strokes) and the experimental duo The Dose. In The Dose, he showcases his multi-instrumental prowess by simultaneously playing bass and drums, incorporating a Moog Taurus III into his kit. Here are Ralph's choices…

Led Zeppelin, *How the West Was Won* [2003] (recorded 1972), "Immigrant Song"
**Drummer** - John Bonham

*How the West Was Won* was a live album my older brother Topher bought when I was 13. I had already started playing drums, but when I heard Bonham on that record, it made me take drums seriously for the first time. I wanted to figure out every fill and groove that I could. Playing along to every track was my practice time requirement, and I learned many of the early basics just by studying those parts.

## Slayer, *Seasons In The Abyss* [1990], "Seasons In The Abyss"
### Drummer - Dave Lombardo

In high school, I started getting into heavier bands with my friends. We had our band (Death Machine Weapons) and covered a lot of Metallica, Guns N Roses, Black Sabbath, etc. Once the door was opened to heavier stuff, it was only a matter of time until we discovered Slayer—and when we did, it blew our fucking minds. Dave Lombardo always seemed like the logical next step in the evolution of Bonham's playing—if it had gotten heavier and faster—so naturally, I loved it. Dave's style was chaotic yet rooted in confidently solid technique.

## Radiohead, *OK Computer* [1997], "Paranoid Android"
### Drummer - Phil Selway

I could write an entire book about how Radiohead—not just *OK Computer*—transformed my approach to drumming and musicianship. Like Led Zeppelin, my brother introduced me to Radiohead. This album taught me that being unique in your approach is always more important than being fast and loud. Being a well-rounded musician who pushes your boundaries was something I wanted to be, not just another "metal/rock" drummer. For the first time, I looked at songs as a whole- not just opportunities for me to try and show off.

## Mastodon, *Crack The Skye* [2009]
### Drummer - Brann Dailor

Mastodon is one of the most extraordinary bands because they

197

differ entirely from how they started. In one aspect, it's due to Brann taking on vocals for the first time on this record. I had already been a fan of their early work, but when this came out, it was the first time I had heard a drummer completely change a band seemingly out of nowhere. It gave me the confidence to constantly push myself and try to add to a band in ways I didn't think I could — beyond just drumming.

## Chris Stapleton, *From A Room: Volume 1* [2017], "I Was Wrong"
**Drummer** - Derek Mixon

Chris Stapleton alone is excellent, but his band deserves much credit for giving him his solid foundation. This record (and all of them so far) is a constant masterclass in dynamics, feel, and emphasizing space. So much of Derek's playing features an approach I envy as a metal drummer. What's funny as you get more experience is learning that playing fast is easy. Playing slow with good feel is the challenge.

## Metallica, *Live Shit: Binge & Purge* 1989]
**Drummer** - Lars Ulrich

I watched *Live Shit: Bing & Purge* to study how to put on a show as a performer. Metallica is in its absolute prime, and the energy is something I remember being blown away by. Not only do you have to play your parts, but you have to do it with attitude and energy. Anybody can stay home and listen to your songs — but when they come to SEE you, it has to be a show.

## Rush, *Moving Pictures* [1981]
**Drummer** - Neil Peart

Rush was an inspiration for multitasking. I loved Neil Peart, but Geddy always blew me away with how much he played on stage. His use of the Moog Taurus pedals inspired me to develop my approach to playing bass and drums simultaneously with the same pedals — a band of musician's musicians. It's hard not to find inspiration from all three.

# Dan Mayo

*"Suddenly, and for the first time, I felt utterly free; I could play however I wanted."*

Dan Mayo, an Israeli drummer and composer, is celebrated for his exploration of spiritual and avant-garde music. While leading the power trio TATRAN remains his primary focus, Mayo's impact stretches wide, with numerous solo projects and collaborations with notable artists such as Ester Rada and Mike Shinoda of Linkin Park. Here are Dan's choices…

---

### Karim Ziad, *Ifrikya* [2001], "The Joker"
### **Drummer** - Karim Ziad

Karim played a massive role in my musical journey. Through Karim, I learned these three valuable lessons:

1. I learned how to see the song and its energy in much more depth; I learned how to be its guide, to see where the final destination is, and to take the band there smartly and organically while still supporting the musicians. They can fly away, but my role as a drummer is to fly with them as far as they want while knowing where we are going and how to return to the track.

2. I discovered how to free myself from the "one" on the kick drum. I feel comfortable floating in the music while my internal "one"

is stronger than ever.

3. I learned the ability to play freely over odd time signatures. It should feel like 4/4, natural. There's no need to play the "one" every bar; feel the internal clave and sail away.

## Two Fingers, *Fight! Fight! Fight!* [2020], "Razzy Beat"

To this day, Amon Tobin is one of my favorite artists; his music is an excellent example of how electronic music can feel live; in my opinion, it sounds more live than other "real" live music.

His understanding of the instruments' transients, tone, and character is beyond this world; he captures the moment. His album *Fight! Fight! Fight!* is how I discovered him and his music; through that, I got to know all his other projects.

## Christopher Dell, Christian Lillinger, Jonas Westergaard, *Beats* [2021], "Configuration II"
**Drummer** – Christian Lillinger

Christian is my favorite now because he brings something to the drum set I've never seen before. Not only does he have a clear voice you can immediately recognize, but the way he thinks of sounds is beyond the drums, which is reflected in his phrases, too.

I know a lot of free jazz drummers, and most of them sound like they are playing the free jazz genre; Christian sounds like he's playing himself with 100% honesty and intent. When I hear him play, I immediately get sucked in.

## Miles Davis, *Nefertiti* [1968], "Pinocchio"
## **Drummer** - Tony Williams

What an album! When you listen to it, you hear a collective of musicians. Each has their voice in the most extreme way, but it creates one beautiful brush stroke.

**In our initial chat, you shared a story about how a performance at just 17 years old, as part of a gifted young musicians' camp, had a profound impact on you. Could you recount this story?**

At that time, I was pretty depressed; I felt like everything I played was never good enough. I tried to be what my teachers wanted me to be and not myself. Then, I went to the audition for this young gifted music camp. The teacher there was Eli Degibri (a brilliant sax player!), and he saw something in me; he especially loved what I played naturally, by mistake.

For example, we would talk about the songs with the band without even playing anything, and while we spoke, I used to play along with my fingers on the snare quietly. The teachers would yell at me at school for "interrupting the whole class," but Eli responded differently; he loved it. He would stop and say, "Wow, this amazing idea," and I could tell he meant it. I finally felt like my voice had a place.

At our final concert, I asked him during the soundcheck, "Am I playing too loud?" He said, "It's only loud when you want it to be loud." Then I realized that being loud is a musical choice; it's so beautiful. Suddenly, and for the first time, I felt utterly free; I could play however I wanted. It's my musical choice, and when I played quietly, it didn't feel like a punishment; it felt good. It was my choice, and I was 100% in the music.

# Zach Jones

*"If you want to learn how to play drums in a band behind a singer-songwriter, I'd recommend studying every note that he plays... "*

Z ach Jones is a musician, drummer, producer, singer, and songwriter rooted in Brooklyn, NY. His resume includes artists such as Sting, Ingrid Michaelson, A Great Big World, Secret Someones, and Elle King. Zach also spearheads his own musical project, Zach Jones & the Tricky Bits. Here are Zach's choices…

---

**The Beatles, *With The Beatles* [1963], "It Won't Be Long," "All I've Got to Do," "All My Loving," "I Wanna Be Your Man"**
**Drummer - Ringo Starr**

I started playing drums when I was nine years old. For my 10th birthday, my parents gave me a boombox and two CDs—the soundtrack to *Willy Wonka & The Chocolate Factory* and *With The Beatles.* I love both, but only one features Ringo Starr.

Ringo's playing on this album is phenomenal. Yes, The Beatles would go on to make more innovative, groundbreaking recordings, but Ringo's sound and feel were never more exciting and raw than they were on *With The Beatles.* His sense of the song and his ability to craft unique parts are evident here, and his one-in-a-million feel— that beautiful, slightly swung right hand is inimitable. If you question

Ringo's abilities, I invite you to play "I Wanna Be Your Man" from top to bottom while singing lead and get back to me. Peace and love.

---

### '60s Soul: When A Man Loves A Woman {1997}, "Soul Man," "Knock On Wood," "Chain Of Fools"
**Drummers** - Al Jackson Jr., Roger Hawkins

I hadn't thought about this gem of a compilation in years before appearing on the podcast, but as soon as I was asked to list five albums that impacted my playing, this CD immediately sprang to mind. This record introduced me to several key figures and branches of American R&B music (Aretha, Muscle Shoals, Stax, Curtis Mayfield…) as well as two of my very favorite drummers—Roger Hawkins and Al Jackson, Jr.

If I had to define "pocket," I might point to Roger's work on "Chain of Fools" and Al's on "Knock On Wood." My little boombox would practically break a sweat when these cuts came roaring through. Al's commitment to a groove is unmatched, and when he chooses to play a fill, it's catchy, musical, and MATTERS. I got an Al Jackson, Jr. baseball card at the Stax Museum, and I keep it on my bass drum as a reminder to get out of my head, get into the groove, and make the music feel great. Listening and playing along to this compilation was an invaluable education. It still blows me away and keeps my priorities straight.

---

### James Taylor, James Taylor Live [1993], "Your Smiling Face," "Mexico," "Country Road"
**Drummer** - Carlos Vega

I grew up in southern New Jersey, but my mom is originally from

204

southern Vermont, and once or twice a year, we'd make the 6-hour drive to visit our family in the Green Mountain State. That gave us PLENTY of time to listen to music, and this album was always in the rotation.

If you want to learn how to play drums in a band behind a singer-songwriter, I'd recommend studying every note that Carlos Vega plays on *James Taylor Live*. This record captures an iconic artist at the top of his game, backed by a band of absolute monster musicians. Carlos holds the whole thing together with elegance, humility, and taste while still managing to light the music on fire. He nods to JT's classic studio recordings featuring drummers like Russ Kunkel and Rick Marotta. Still, he makes the music feel fresh and vital and always lets us know who he is — Carlos's take on "Country Road" is the definitive version. You can hear the joy and excitement in James's vocal performances; he clearly feels free and comfortable enough to lift off. That's the feeling Carlos taught me to chase when I'm behind the kit — the high that comes from making your fellow musicians feel supported and inspired.

The Police, *Every Breath You Take: The Classics* [1995], "Can't Stand Losing You," "Every Little Thing She Does Is Magic"
**Drummer** - Stewart Copeland

I had already drummed for about 4 or 5 years when my dad recommended this compilation. I was primed for music that challenged my ears and my playing, and OH BOY, did this record deliver.

The whole sound of this band was and is a revelation — Sting's voice, his bass playing, his darkly funny lyrics, Andy Summers's tone and chord voicings, and of course, Stewart Copeland's drumming, which turned my brain upside down and inside out. The Police created accessible, radio-friendly music comprised of completely unorthodox ingredients, and Stewart's singular feel, sound, and approach to composition and instrumentation were essential to the mission. I have the great honor of playing drums in Sting's touring band, and it's a joy to approach these timeless songs from a fresh angle. But while these tunes have lived many lives since they were first recorded, I find the originals just as thrilling as the day I first heard them.

---

Steely Dan, *The Royal Scam* [1976], "Kid Charlemagne," "The Caves of Altamira," "Green Earrings"
**Drummers** - Bernard Purdie, Rick Marotta

*The Royal Scam* and *Aja* were my introductions to Steely Dan. While I nearly chose *Aja* for this list because it features a cavalcade of '70s session greats, the truth is that Bernard Purdie's playing on *The Royal Scam* will always make it my favorite.

I had the opportunity to take a few lessons with Purdie when I was 14 or 15, and there is nothing like experiencing his playing in close proximity. The man has more pocket in his little finger than many drummers do in their whole body, and I mean that literally—he can play whisper-quiet with only his fingers, and it's the funkiest thing you'll ever hear.

*The Royal Scam* captures the many facets of his greatness—his feel, his subtlety, how he kicks the band, and the absolute joy radiating from him when he plays. It's infectious. Just try to sit still when "Green Earrings" comes on. The only thing missing here is the Purdie Shuffle, so go ahead and put on *Aja*, too, and bask in the undeniable genius of The Hitmaker.

---

# Joe Bagele

*"... this music was so impactful that I ended up moving to the San Francisco/Bay Area in search of this funk."*

J oe Bagele is a San Francisco-based producer, artist, multi-instrumentalist, songwriter, and educator. His sound is fresh, but tangibly rooted in nostalgia. Originally from Rochester, NY, Joe has produced and released several albums under his name, followed by a project he calls Otis McDonald, writing audio library music for YouTube. In addition to producing/recording, he's shared the stage (and I might add not always on drums) with Stevie Wonder, Mickey Hart of Grateful Dead, Fred Wesley and PeeWee Ellis (members of James Brown's band) Dave Schools (of Widespread Panic), Mike Gordon (of Phish), Martin Luther (of The Roots), Gift2Gab, Lyrics Born and many more. At the end of the day, Joe just wants you to dance. Here are Joe's choices...

Herbie Hancock, *Thrust* [1974], "Palm Grease"
**Drummer** - Mike Clark

When I was in 5th grade, my two older brothers were digging through our father's record collection and stumbled upon a wild album cover. It depicts Herbie Hancock flying a spaceship through another world, and his flight controls are keyboards. I was ten years old, which would mean it was 1993 when I saw this, and at that point, this album was almost 20 years old. I was immediately transported to another time just by looking at this artwork. But when the needle dropped and the first track, "Palm Grease," started, my life was forever changed. The track begins with the drums playing a syncopated funk groove, then, gradually, each layer is introduced, finishing with the bass line before the song moves past the first section. My mind melted. I had never heard grooves like this or bass lines so melodic yet funky. Every element was so meaningful.

I needed to know how it was done, so I fired up my dad's Yamaha keyboard, which had tons of sounds and the ability to multitrack, record, or sequence. I had never recorded anything; this was my introduction to many things. I was transcribing, recording, layering, and learning new instruments. "Palm Grease" was one of the first bass lines I ever tried to play, and this music was so impactful that I ended up moving to the San Francisco/Bay Area in search of this funk. Sixteen years after moving to SF, I took over the same room where this album was recorded, Studio D at Hyde Street Studios (formerly Wally Heider Studios). It is now the room where I make all of my records. Full circle moment.

## Mahavishnu Orchestra, *Inner Mountain Flame* [1971], "Vital Transformation"
**Drummer** - Billy Cobham

Not long after hearing Herbie Hancock's *Thrust*, my oldest brother Adrian was on a holiday break from college, and he played *Inner Mountain Flame* by the Mahavishnu Orchestra. The first track he showed me was "Vital Transformation," which opens with a bombastic drum intro performed by Billy Cobham. This song is in 9/8, and it never dawned on me that this was in another time signature until I tried to play it myself. That started a whole new journey, where I fell in love with playing in odd meters. I love off meters because you can always find a way to feel 4/4 over it, which teaches you how important the one is when going back to play something more straightforward. I'm unsure what drew me in at such a young age. What I do know is that these five musicians conveyed some overwhelming energy while blasting off into outer space. There is still nothing quite like it to this date.

## John Scofield, *A Go Go* [1998]
## **Drummer** - Billy Martin

John Scofield's album *A Go Go* was a serious game-changer for me. I was a freshman in high school and studying jazz drum set. The drums were the instrument to express myself as a musician best. If I wanted to go to college for music, it made more sense for me to focus on jazz so I could play the drum set rather than studying classical music on concert percussion. I was not a jazz aficionado by any means, but I loved improvisational music, and one of my favorite improvisers growing up was John Schofield. As all the other jazz fusion records and artists introduced to me, Scofield was one of those guys that both of my older brothers adored, and of course, I heard it all the time, so I loved it. But this album, *A Go Go*, was different. As a listener, I always leaned more toward music which made me want to dance. I grew up in the '80s and '90s, and the first music I heard was Michael Jackson. As I became more interested in music, I always gravitated towards funk and R&B. So when John Scofield teamed up with Medeski, Martin, and

Wood, it immediately gave me nostalgia. It made me feel the same as when I discovered Herbie Hancock as a ten-year-old, Parliament Funkadelic as a 12-year-old, or James Brown as a 13-year-old.

Now I was 15, studying jazz music, and here was this jazz legend, giving his listeners a dose of rhythm and blues and funk music. It was my favorite record that year, setting me off on a journey I'm still on. I loved jamming, and I love jam bands, but this was cooler than any jamming I had heard at that time. It informed me and my musical preferences as a high schooler and led to me starting a new band with like-minded friends. We played improvisational, jazz-influenced, and funk-influenced grooves until we were blue in the face. Billy Martin's drumming was reminiscent of Clyde Stubblefield and Zigaboo Modeliste. It was this open drum sound, but it was funky and felt so fresh to me. I went on to see this band perform live over 20 times. To this day, I'm still chasing that high.

---

## Erykah Badu, *Mama's Gun* [2000], "Penitentiary Philosophy"
### Drummer - Questlove

After three years of studying jazz drum set and becoming a jazz snob, I dated a girl around the year 2000 who introduced me to Erykah Badu's music; I was a senior in high school. I remember when Erykah first came out, but I didn't pay much attention to her. R&B in the '90s could have been better. But the little bit that I had heard from her, I liked, and my high school crush's influence helped me discover her music and check it out more thoroughly. That year marked the second studio album by Erykah, which was *Mama's Gun*. It was at the end of my junior year and the beginning of my senior year of high school when I started to revisit a lot of hip-hop music that I used to listen to as a middle schooler—artists like A Tribe Called Quest, Dr. Dre, Snoop Dogg, and Digable Planets. Around that time, one of my best friends introduced me to the Roots. I had never heard of a live hip-hop group before with live drums. So that piqued my interest and got me wanting to check out Questlove. When I went to the record store to check out *Mama's Gun*, I looked up the credits and found that Questlove was drumming on it, so that piqued my interest even more. From the moment I pressed play on "Penitentiary Philosophy"(the first song), I was hooked. I didn't know people were still making records that sounded like this. It reminded me of both Funkadelic and Stevie Wonder, but it also reminded me of A Tribe Called Quest and some of the other classic hip-hop groups from the early and mid-'90s.

Man, I wore that tape out. I listened to it daily for most of my senior year of high school. The funny thing is, I was obsessing over getting my chops together and understanding the jazz vocabulary so I could audition for schools. When I eventually ended up going to the Eastman School of Music, my head was so deep in these neo soul records that I knew my time at college was limited. I knew that I would not learn how to make records that sounded like that, and that made me feel the way I felt when listening to it. Once I absorbed everything I could on *Mama's Gun*, I was introduced to *Voodoo* by D'Angelo, which also had Questlove in the drum chair. That was it for me. Two weeks before my sophomore year of college, I took a leave of absence and moved to San Francisco, started learning ProTools, and set off on my next journey learning how to produce records. *Mama's Gun* was life-changing for me. It's still one of my favorite albums of all time.

---

Stuff, *Live at Montreux 1976* [2008], "Signed, Sealed, Delivered"
**Drummer** - Steve Gadd

Steve Gadd! Enough said. Lol. I was born and raised in Rochester, New York, and I'm a drummer. If you grow up a drummer in Rochester, New York, it's hard for Steve Gadd not to be your favorite drummer. I was fortunate to work with Steve several times while attending the Eastman School of Music. He would come back and visit once a year and do a clinic with the drummers in that program. I loved everything he did. Still do! But it was when I was about 30 years old I discovered the band, Stuff. My introduction to Stuff was looking up Steve Gadd on YouTube, and I came across an entire concert, *Stuff: Live at Montreux*. Holy smokes, did I discover gold! That band starts with this laid-back groove but somehow excites you while bathing in their laid-back swag.

As that concert progresses, there are a couple of times when Steve takes a solo. It's his second solo on that concert, which comes out of them jamming on "Signed, Sealed, Delivered" by Stevie Wonder. The drum solo that Steve takes is a master class in groove, vocabulary, and time. Never once does he lose time. And everything Steve plays is so easy to listen to because he solos in phrases. It's almost as if he simultaneously writes and performs a brand-new piece of music before you. The pocket is so funky that when the camera pans over to their bass player, Gordon Edwards, his shoulders are moving back and forth, and it's so intoxicating that your shoulders start moving with him. It's not a lengthy drum solo, but it is perfect. Steve Gadd is a master at groove and technique. He's inventive, and he always plays the correct part. That is not an easy thing to do, and that is why he is one of the most recorded drummers in history — my number one influence as a drummer.

# Adam Deitch

*" ...when the aliens make contact, we should blast [This Album] to create a peaceful interaction."*

A dam Deitch, a Grammy-nominated record producer and drummer based in Denver, Colorado, is renowned for his work with Lettuce, John Scofield, Break Science, and The Adam Deitch Quartet. His versatile style encompasses hip-hop, funk, electro, pop, and jazz. Deitch has also collaborated with acclaimed artists like 50 Cent, Talib Kweli, Les Claypool, and Ledisi. Here are Adam's choices...

Earth, Wind & Fire, *Earth, Wind & Fire - In Concert: Live at the Oakland Coliseum 1981* [1981], "Jupiter"
**Drummer** - Fred White

From Earth, Wind & Fire to Donny Hathaway's *Live* record, Fred is the most simple-styled yet driving force in funk, R&B, and soul history. Earth, Wind & Fire was a gift to humanity, and when the aliens make contact, we should blast *That's The Way of the World* to create a peaceful interaction. Fred drove that giant band with a fervor—often imitated, never duplicated. My favorite jam is "Jupiter". Iykyk

## Don Blackman, *Don Blackman* [1962], "You Ain't Hip"
**Drummer** - Dennis Chambers

Dennis is the King of Drums. There are zero gigs he couldn't do. His recordings with Sugarhill Records kicked off this genre called hip-hop. His performance on THE *Don Blackman* album is some of the most deadly funk ever. "You Ain't Hip" is just next level groove for dayz. Then there's his Scofield, Brecker Bros, McLaughlin, Santana, and 1000 more situations and records — he's an undisputed Mike Tyson-level heavyweight champion.

---

**What makes David Garibaldi's contribution to drumming so groundbreaking?**
David Garibaldi combined the James Brown/Purdie beats seamlessly and freshly with some Afro-Cuban and salsa rhythms prevalent in the Bay Area. He turned the drum world, AND the downbeat, upside down. I took a lesson with him when I was 12 — a life changer.

---

**Why are Clyde (Stubblefield) and Jabo (John Starks) so essential to the foundation of funk drumming?**
There is no funk music without these two. Both Jabo and Clyde have iconic styles. Their time and feel are exquisite! The drum sound and lack of fills made the music even heavier — inventors on a da Vinci level.

---

**How would you describe Zigaboo Modeliste's unique contribution to drumming as a whole?**
Zigaboo is the sound of New Orleans funk. He created a hybrid of

214

2nd line parade beats on a drum set that the world had never heard. His kick and snare work is untouchable, while his hi-hat flavor is entirely original. I only really heard him play a tom tom once I saw him live, and he still kicks ass today!

# Darshan Doshi

*"I've watched all of his drum solos to date, and I love how he pushes/pulls the groove...his vocabulary is mind-blowing."*

D arshan Doshi, a fusion-leaning Indian drummer and composer, tours with Salim Sulaiman, Farhan Akhtar, Adnan Sami, Diljit Dosanjh, and Amit Trivedi. He's played drums for Bollywood hits like *Rock On!!, Black, Dhoom 2,* and others. Starting at age 2, he has held the record for the youngest Indian drummer in the *Limca Book of Records* since 1997. Based in Mumbai, Darshan is a notable figure in the music scene. Here are Darshan's choices...

Dave Weckl Band, *Rhythm of Soul* [1998], "Access Denied"
**Drummer** - Dave Weckl

In my first class, my teacher Ranjit Barot gave me five albums, one of which was this record. From then on, my approach to drumming completely changed.

Dave Weckl is the master of rhythm for me. His drumming style is characterized by his impressive command of complex rhythms, incredible technique, and ability to blend various genres into his playing. I love how he tunes his drums and how they sit on the mix of each album. The first song I heard Dave play was "Access Denied" from the album *Rhythm of Soul*; that intro fill is insane.

## Billy Cobham, *Spectrum* [1973], "Spectrum"
### **Drummer** - Billy Cobham

The teacher I mentioned earlier, Ranjit, was a big fan of Billy Cobham with The Mahavishnu Orchestra and showed me the album *Birds of Fire*; when I got to know more about the maestro Billy Cobham, I wanted to check out his solo album, *Spectrum*. I loved the groove in 7 in the title track. The band was a pioneering force in jazz fusion, combining elements of jazz, rock & world music. Cobham's drumming style is characterized by its power, precision & innovative use of odd-time rhythms & techniques.

## Benny Greb, *Grebfruit* [2006], "Grebfruit" (the solo)
### **Drummer** - Benny Greb

Benny Greb is one of my favorite drummers and educators in the scene; I love his versatility and unique style. *Grebfruit* is a phenomenal album showcasing his drumming skills, musicality, sense of humor, and overall positive attitude toward music. As a drummer, I enjoy his stack cymbals, signature snare drum & floor tom tuning. I have watched all of his drum solos to date, and I love how he pushes/pulls the groove, and overall, his vocabulary is mind-blowing.

## Niacin (Billy Sheehan, John Novello, Dennis Chambers), *Niacin - Live in Tokyo* [2005]
### **Drummer** - Dennis Chambers

I first saw Dennis Chambers in Mumbai in 1996 at the Zildjian Day event, and that performance utterly blew me away. I also loved every tune on the *Niacin* album. The trio sounds powerful, and I love how they blend jazz, rock, and funk elements, creating a uniquely dynamic sound. Dennis has incredible technique, and the speed/clarity around the kit is phenomenal. He is one of the goats who has played with some of the biggest names in the jazz world and is still touring the world at 64.

## The Dave Weckl Band, *Synergy* [1999], "Wet Skin"
**Drummer** - Dave Weckl

As I mentioned, I love every song on the Dave Weckl album *Synergy*. The drums' mix and tuning were top-notch on this album. I got to spend some time with Dave at the Drum Fantasy Camp in 2015 in Chicago and learn about the Minor 3rd tuning he follows for his toms. Even his signature snare drum is quite unusual, with two springboards and a damper fitted inside the drum, which creates the perfect balance for the snare drum tone. His hand and foot technique helps him to get the best style and sound from his Yamaha drums.

# Liberty DeVitto

*"I learned that whatever you choose to play, make sure it fits the*
*story and the mood the writer is trying to capture."*

L iberty DeVitto is an American rock drummer best known for his longstanding collaboration with Billy Joel. His drumming has played a fundamental role in crafting Joel's legendary sound. Beyond his work with Joel, DeVitto has contributed his talents as a session musician to various projects, with credits on records selling over 150 million units worldwide. Here are Liberty's choices…

### Elton John, *Caribou* [1974], "Don't Let The Sun Go Down On Me"
**Drummer** - Nigel Olsson

I can remember sitting with guitarist/vocalist/songwriter Richie Supa. He played the song and pointed out the triple fill (I think that's what it is) going into the last chorus (there was one in the chorus before, but it's less intense). This fill, and the rest of what Nigel plays, is a lesson in constructing the perfect drum part for a pop song. The drumming on this song is as great as anything a Weckl or a Colaiuta plays.

219

## James Taylor, *Sweet Baby James* [1970], "Fire and Rain"
### **Drummer** - Russ Kunkel

Again, Richie Supa showed me this. If you listen to the song, it's all acoustic instruments. Russ uses brushes but plays like he is using sticks. This gives the drums the perfect "acoustic" sound that doesn't overtake the music and fits perfectly with the other instruments. His fills are to the point, keeping the song (with no bridge) moving and building to its climax.

I once asked Russ how he came up with the idea of using the brushes. He said he was having difficulty hearing the others while they were rehearsing the song while playing with sticks. So he went to brushes so he could hear them better. Sometimes it's not being afraid to try something different that will make people think you're brilliant!

## The Rascals, *Collections* [1967], "Come On Up"
### **Drummer** - Dino Danelli

When I first started playing, Ringo Starr was the king of the drum throne. When I first heard the Young Rascals, Dino Danelli pushed him right off the seat. The Rascals were the first band I had ever seen play live. When Dino played, I saw for the first time that a drummer could be as much of a focal point as a lead singer. He played to the song. I once asked him how he came up with playing the conga drum on their number one hit "Groovin." He said the song's about sitting on the grass in a park with the sunshine, beautiful weather, and the one you love. He said he'd be playing a conga drum if he were there. He wouldn't bring a full set of drums to the park! I learned that whatever you choose to play, make sure it fits the story and the mood the writer is trying to capture.

**Can you talk about watching Carmine Appice live with Vanilla Fudge and how the sound of his drums impacted you?**

There was the shovel (Ringo), then there was the backhoe (Dino), and then came the bulldozer (Carmine). When I first saw Carmine, I saw the drums as a focal point like Dino but with more intensity. He had more giant drums, both visually and sounding. He hit harder. He was competing for volume in a very loud and forceful band. Carmine made every drummer on Long Island step up their game or drop out of the race.

**You mentioned that songs like "Parchman Farm" and "Hot For Teacher" made you never want to play double bass drum...**

There are two reasons I don't play double bass drum. One is a song on an album by Cactus called "Parchman Farm" with Carmine Appice on drums. The other is "Hot for Teacher" with Alex Van Halen on drums. After listening to both those songs, I thought, "What can I do that would be better than what they have already done?." So, I stuck to what I was good at and what fit into my playing style (can you imagine double bass drum on "Piano Man"?). No matter what you do with your double bass drum pedal, you will always be compared to "Hot for Teacher." Many young drummers today love the double pedal. The problem is they overuse it and become dependent on it. They're completely lost if they have to sit in on a set of drums with a single pedal.

# Jessica Burdeaux

*"It's rare to write drum parts that are so easily recognized by drummers and non drummers alike..."*

J essica Burdeaux is a Chicago-area-born-and-raised touring and session drummer known for her online social media presence and contributions to bands such as Covet and City Mouth. In addition to her drumming skills, she hosts several video series on reverb.com and collaborates with YouTuber Rob Scallon, demonstrating her versatility both on and off the stage. Here are Jessica's choices...

blink-182, *blink-182* [2003], "Violence"
**Drummer** - Travis Barker

When this record came out, I remember hearing the hits like "Feeling This" and "I Miss You" on TV, but when my brother bought the full record, I ended up loading it onto my Sony MiniDisc Walkman and listening to the album on repeat for years after. I really can't stress enough how much of an impact this record had on my approach to drumming. Travis had already established himself as someone who could write catchy and creative hooks on the drums before *blink-182* [the album]. Still, hearing the attention he put into crafting these parts to make each song come alive really stuck with me and helped me think outside the box when I began writing drum parts of my own. It's rare to write drum parts that are so easily recognized by drummers and non drummers alike, but this was a skill that seemed to come to Travis so naturally.

---

## toe, *The Future Is Now* [2012], "Run For Word"
## **Drummer** - Kashikura Takashi

The first track I ever heard by toe was their song "C." The opening groove grabbed my attention immediately with its big, boomy drum tones and intricate sticking. I've loved instrumental music for a long time, but this band had something extraordinary that made me want to hear more. I soon discovered their EP, *The Future Is Now*, and was blown away. Kashikura's musicality is next level. His grooves are so masterful and always fit the music perfectly. He manages to play such complex rhythms and make them sound so simple. This ability is on full display for the entirety of the EP, but the opening track, "Run For Word," has some of my favorite moments. Kashikura is so good at shaping his parts to fit seamlessly with the melodic layers happening in each song, and as the drummer for a primarily instrumental band, I draw much inspiration from Kashikura. I strive to play with the same precision and inventiveness.

---

## Paramore, *Brand New Eyes* [2009], "Careful"
## **Drummer** - Zac Farro

When I was a freshman in high school, a friend mentioned Paramore and played a few songs from *Riot!*. It is wild to me that I wasn't aware of Paramore yet because they are now one of the most monumentally influential bands in my life.

The sheer power of *Riot!* was incredible. Everything about it was huge: the riffs, the melodies, the lyrics, and Zac's monstrous drumming. He packed a punch that not many drummers I had heard before had. His ability to craft a drum part perfectly accompanying and accentuating what was happening in the track stood out to me the most. He played with authority and brought a level of energy and intensity to the kit that was unmatched.

I can't say I have a favorite Paramore album because they are all so special to me, but when focusing on the drums, I have to talk about *Brand New Eyes*. When I heard the album opener "Careful," I was in total awe, and it helped me identify elements of Zac's playing that make him such a remarkable musician. Zac follows what's happening in the song very closely with his kick and snare in a way that makes everything pop out and outlines things for the listener. Additionally, he has some of the strongest and tightest fills I have ever heard. I always strive to deliver the same power and energy in my performances as Zac did on this record.

---

## +44, *When Your Heart Stops Beating* [2006], "Lillian"
### Drummer - Travis Barker

It should be no surprise that Travis Barker has made my list again. When Travis formed +44 with Mark Hoppus after the blink-182 split, I was excited to hear what that project would sound like. They only released one album, but it was perfect. If I were to charge up my iPod Nano and see the play count on these tracks, I can assure you it would be A LOT, but one song in particular, "Lillian," might have the most. The album *When Your Heart Stops Beating* had many interesting electronic and synth elements, and I loved hearing how the drums paired with them. Hearing "Lillian" when I was just a teenager and being so obsessed with deciphering what was happening in every layer of the track profoundly impacted my musical phrasing. At this point in my career, I've studied many different drumming styles, but I have internalized this album so that it will always be a massive part of the foundation of my playing style today.

Bad Suns, *Language and Perspective* [2014], "Dancing on Quicksand"
**Drummer** - Miles Morris

I first heard of Bad Suns through a comment on my Instagram post in 2018 requesting a cover of their song "Dancing On Quicksand." I immediately fell in love with the track and knew I had to dive into their albums. Their dancy, groove-oriented style was fun and different from many bands I grew up listening to. Since being introduced to the group, Miles has become one of my favorite drummers. Their album *Language and Perspective* showcases his rock-solid timing and feel on every song, but "Dancing on Quicksand" is still one of my absolute favorites. Miles has such a knack for playing grooves that let the music breathe while being able to sprinkle in the most tasteful fills. He has a linear style to his playing that I was starting to explore around the time the band was introduced to me. Listening to him and learning his drum parts helped me grow and become comfortable with a new style that I often incorporate into my playing now.

# Mark Stepro

*"This stuff was an exotic delicacy for a kid who grew up on Tom Petty, and I lustily ate it all up."*

**M**ark Stepro stands as the archetype of a Los Angeles-based working drummer. His career includes recording and performing alongside esteemed artists such as The Wallflowers, Ben Kweller, Butch Walker, Courtney Love, Jackson Browne, Keith Urban, Dwight Yoakam, John Prine, and many others. Here are Mark's choices…

### John Scofield, *Groove Elation* [1995], "Kool"
### **Drummer** - Idris Muhammad

Scofield, to me, has always been a little bit like *Saturday Night Live*: everyone has a strong opinion about which is the best era, and almost invariably, wouldn't you know that the "best era" corresponds directly with one's own adolescence? So the formative Scofield of my youth includes those mid-'90s records, beginning with his 1994 collaboration with Pat Metheny, *I Can See Your House From Here*, then 1995's *Groove Elation*, followed by the Medeski, Martin and Wood-backed *A Go Go* in 1998. To me, that era of Scofield is like the '90s *SNL* era where Sandler was crushing it with *Billy Madison* and *Happy Gilmore*, and you had *Tommy Boy* going with Spade and Farley, and oh crap, I'm doing it.

226

I considered writing about some stuff from *A Go Go*, but then it dawned on me that even at a young age, I "got" Billy Martin's playing on that record. Don't get me wrong, I'm a HUGE fan, but fundamentally and mechanically, even at a young age, I could understand what was being played on that record. Idris Muhammad's playing on *Groove Elation*, though, particularly the track "Kool," was like the first time I ever went to a foreign country or ate Indian food or something. What IS this? It was a completely new discovery. It's like a new country just popped up on the map.

*Groove Elation* is an excellent gateway record for a youngster interested in improvised music because it's harmonically pretty straightforward and bluesy. It's not *Giant Steps*. Like those Frisell records with Viktor Krauss and Keltner, it's very rootsy and organic. True to its name, it's very groove-based. It feels great, the melodies are easy to sing, and then in the middle of it all, you have the ornery Idris Muhammad just DEALING some crazy New Orleanian nastiness.

The groove accompanying the tune's head is syncopated, unique, twisty, and slinky. I spent a lot of time just trying to get the coordination down. Up to that point in my playing, learning a groove meant memorizing some variation of the basic 4/4 rock beat, which I could do with no problem. This pattern, however, was light years beyond what my 14-year-old rock drummer brain had ever encountered. Then there are the SOUNDS: that snare is popping like crazy, and the kick drum is WIDE open (can anyone say Keith Carlock?).

Check out the little drum and guitar duet between Idris and Scofield that happens at just 0:45. Deceptively, the notes on the hi-hat are mostly either on the quarter note pulses or the &'s, so it's not like there's any crazy "horizontal" chopsy stuff going on, meaning he's not in 32nd note triplet territory or anything like that. It's incredibly complex, yet not "shreddy." The hands' interplay with the bass drum in that particular, overlapping way that only New Orleans guys can do gives this drum break its magic. Whereas the gospel and pop stuff that we love and obsess over can be "horizontal" in the form of blistering hand/foot linear combinations, this stuff is VERTICAL, if that makes any sense: lots of double stops between the kick and snare in all sorts of unexpected (read: syncopated) parts of the beat. This stuff was an exotic delicacy for a kid who grew up on Tom Petty, and I lustily ate it all up.

---

Jonatha Brooke & The Story, *Plumb* [1995], "Inconsolable"
**Drummer** - Abe Laboriel Jr.

When I was a teenager growing up in rural Ohio, I had an extremely influential teacher named Jim Ed Cobbs. My mom would drive me to his house in Columbus, "the big city," an hour and back every week. I looked forward to those lessons more than just about anything.

Because I was a relatively "advanced" 14-year-old rock drummer growing up in a place with very little diversity or access, I was convinced that learning Rush songs and Neil Peart stuff, in general, was the apex of drumming. If I could tackle THAT, I'd be "good." I mustn't come off like I'm dogging on Neil Peart. He was one of my first drum heroes and with good reason. But there's something very maximalist about Neil's playing that makes a novice drummer think that Neil is the greatest in the same way that Donald Trump's gold toilet makes a specific type of person believe that he's a wealthy and successful man (I'm not trying to get political here, nor am I trying to compare Neil Peart to Donald Trump). Rush songs are in odd time signatures, and they have busy fills cascading over many drums, so obviously, that stuff is "good" and "hard."

228

So there I was, ready for my lesson, asking Jim Ed to help me learn more Rush stuff when he politely called a timeout. "Hey man, (I'm paraphrasing because this was a long time ago), I know you like Rush, and I know that you think of that stuff as being advanced, but I think it might be good to learn that there are different types of 'advanced.' It doesn't always mean 'fast' or 'in odd time signatures.' Why don't you listen to this "Inconsolable" track, and let's play along."

The tune "Inconsolable" is a lush 6/8 ballad on Jonatha Brooke and The Story's stellar 1995 album *Plumb* that begins with the drums laying out entirely, then blooming into a simple cross-stick pattern, then to a more muscular backbeat, culminating with a full-on blowing vamp at the end. The record is an absolute master class of '90s studio drumming. Abe Laboriel Jr., Jay Bellerose, and Shawn Pelton are all over this thing. There are no odd time signatures. There are no fills with subdivisions (subdivisions!...jokes) faster than 16th notes.

I was so unprepared and out of my depth. This was like the living, breathing manifestation of the Dunning Kreuger Effect. I knew so little about what I was doing; I didn't even know what I didn't know. It was borderline IMPOSSIBLE to play along to this track because I'd never been asked (nor had I considered) to execute something with so much space. There was a mile between these beats, yet there was Abe, nailing every impossibly slow subdivision. This was an excellent setting for an invaluable lesson: if you're going to play slow, THINK fast. If you're going to play fast, think slow. It took a while for my ears to develop to where I could even RECOGNIZE that I wasn't locked up with the track; I was early here, late there, out of control, and spinning out all over the road. I stuck with it over the next several months and finally started honing my time and eventually began to come up with something resembling consistency.

But this wasn't JUST a slow-burning, great-feeling groove. At the end of the track, the band opens up for an outro vamp that catches fire while paradoxically STILL crawling along at an agonizingly slow tempo. But within that tempo, Abe is demonstrating some serious vocabulary, interplaying expertly with the piano, which is increasingly becoming more harmonically dense and jazzy.

I STILL practice playing along to this thing. I'm not saying I'm some groove master by any stretch. Still, I'm eternally grateful to my teacher for turning me onto this track and to Abe for playing so beautifully. As a result, I learned this invaluable lesson on timing and feel at age 14 and not 24 or 34. Nail this track, and you will always get hired.

---

### Soul Coughing, *Ruby Vroom* [1994], "Mr. Bitterness"
### **Drummer** - Yuval Gabay

Soul Coughing made me want to move to New York. The '90s Williamsburg/Zebulon/Jojo Mayer/Zach Danziger/NuBlu thing may as well have been Mars compared to where I grew up, surrounded by cornfields and Creedence. I saw Soul Coughing perform in Cleveland as they opened up for the Dave Matthews Band, and I couldn't believe what I was hearing: was this dance music? Club music? Trip hop? Beat Poetry? Live drum'n'bass? The decadent and hedonistic Godless out-of-touch sounds of Blue State Coastal Elites (sorry, the guy in front of me on this flight has Fox News on his screen)? Now that I think about it, I probably wouldn't have been asking myself those questions in those terms because, at that point in my life, I'd probably never even heard of those styles of music or those arty scenes. I just knew that this was way cooler than the fuckin' Eagles (I'm sorry for cursing).

Yuval Gabay belongs on the '90s New York Mt. Rushmore

alongside guys like Jojo and Zach, who pioneered the art of "A human guy recreating a drum machine that was itself recreating breakbeats performed by human drummers, in many cases sped up to the point of oblivion by DJs who had zero concern for whether or not it was within the limits of human drumming capabilities."

"Mr. Bitterness" is a dance-y house beat like you'd hear in a club, but filtered through the lens of a Bernard Purdie or Jeff Porcaro because it's played live on an acoustic kit by a human. The left hand plays all those 16th-note off-beat ghost notes, and the right hand plays the hi-hat but then crosses over to play the backbeats. The whole thing is orchestrated in a beautiful, loping two-bar phrase. Again, this is the kind of thing that SEEMS simple until you try to do it, like "The Funky Drummer" or "I Keep Forgetting" by Michael McDonald.

I got to New York well after Yuval disappeared (I assume he's around somewhere, but I went looking for him and never could find him), and Williamsburg became a playground for the rich. While I would never even attempt to place myself in the same league as those players in that scene, studying this music leveled up my playing beyond boom-bap-boom-boom-bap.

---

## Son Volt, *Trace* [1995]
### Drummers - Mike Heidorn, Craig Krampf

I've probably listened to this record more times than any other record in my life. Son Volt came out of Belleville, Illinois, in the mid-'90s, following the dissolution of singer Jay Farrar's previous project Uncle Tupelo, which he co-led with future Wilco leader Jeff Tweedy. This music was originally in a bit of an odd ghetto; it was referred to as "alt-country," "insurgent country," or sometimes "no depression" (primarily by journalists; *No Depression* was the name of a magazine that covered left-of-center roots-based artists which would now be referred to as "Americana.").

If Soul Coughing made me want to move away from the rural midwest, Son Volt made me feel less alone there. The music and the themes in the songwriting reflected my physical and cultural environment in an honest way: highway travel, industrial decay, rural poverty, loneliness, and despair, all delivered with very traditional American instrumentation: fiddle, banjo, pedal steel, acoustic guitar, and vintage, warm, Neil Young-style electric guitar tone. I used to drive from my tiny hometown an hour and a half west on Route 30 to visit my girlfriend in college in another small town. I would listen to the record while driving, and as I looked out the window, what I saw and heard seemed to disappear into one another. Listen to the tune "Live Free" while driving past cornfields, squinting through the muddy windshield of a 1988 Ford F-150, and you'll see what I'm talking about.

No disrespect to Mike Heidorn whatsoever, but this isn't a "drum record" for me, but I wanted to mention it because, in a way, it's more important than that. The record is a significant influence on me as a MUSICIAN way more than as a drummer. One thing that my old teacher, Jim Ed, and a future teacher, Glenn Kotche (more on him in a bit), really imparted to me was that the ultimate goal is to be a great MUSICIAN who HAPPENS to play drums, NOT to be a "super sick slammin' drummer" (although I still try, with much futility, to be sick and slammin'.)

My exposure to this music and similar artists (Jayhawks, Lucinda Williams, Big Back Forty, Old 97s) would come in very handy down the road because the song-based, simple playing on this record and in this style of music in general shares a lot in common with my current gig with the Wallflowers, so it's good that I unknowingly became so prepared by spending a couple of thousand hours listening to this stuff when I was a kid. For whatever reason, this style of music, rebranded as "Americana," seems to be very popular now with artists like Jason Isbell, Sturgill Simpson, and Nathaniel Rateliff doing large numbers, and I'm fortunate to have been listening to and playing and living this music since 1996 or so. Comes in real handy sometimes.

---

### Wilco, *Yankee Hotel Foxtrot* [2002], "I'm The Man Who Loves You"
### **Drummer** - Glenn Kotche

Around the time Jay Farrar formed Son Volt in the wake of Uncle Tupelo's dissolution, co-frontman and Uncle Tupelo bassist (!) Jeff Tweedy went on to form Wilco. Originally a no-nonsense, workmanlike rock outfit out of Chicago, Wilco gradually evolved into a truly unique and unparalleled institution of musical experimentation. As a result, Wilco, to me, has always been like that older brother or sister who I grew up with but who then went off to college in a cool, faraway place and came back at Thanksgiving with all kinds of radical political opinions and a nose ring, engendering sneers from conservative uncles at the family dinner table. What was once a band firmly grounded in the Stones, the Byrds, and the Bottlerockets was now deploying the influences of modern classical composers like Karl Stockhausen and the krautrock of CAN and Neu! I loved all of it.

In 2003, I watched Wilco perform "I'm The Man Who Loves You" on *Late Night With Conan O'Brien*. Their former drummer, Ken Coomer (who I loved), had seemingly been replaced by some kind of hipster mad scientist whose setup included crotales, prepared snare drum heads with springs and noisemakers attached, and contact mics attached to metal fruit bowls to be struck with rubber mallets. It was Glenn Kotche, and I was all in. I read an article about Glenn in *Modern Drummer* shortly after that, and he mentioned in the piece that before joining Wilco, he was a teacher and had a robust roster of students. I immediately emailed Wilco's manager to see if I could contact Glenn to ask for a lesson. I assumed the manager's assistant's intern would get back to me in three months with a non-negotiable "No," instead, he forwarded my email to Glenn, who instantly got back to me and said, "Sure, let's do it." I had a couple of lessons with him in Columbus, Ohio, where I lived when Wilco came through town. I treasure those memories and Glenn's influence, guidance, and instruction. I'm a kid who was raised on a steady diet of Classic Rock Radio (not ashamed of that at all), and here's this guy showing me John Cage phase pieces and Balinese gamelan melodies adapted for the drum set.

Wilco, particularly Glenn, has been a North Star for me. I understand their origins because I come from the same place but always strive to know where they're going. Their journey and evolution inspire me, particularly their 2001 record, *Yankee Hotel Foxtrot*. My friend Aaron Lee Tasjan and I used to sit around and watch Sam Jones's 2002 documentary about the band and the making of *YHF*, "I Am Trying To Break Your Heart," over and over and over, and we can quote the whole film line by line. As was a prominent theme of the documentary, if you strip these songs down to their simplest elements, they're essentially still folksy, Americana-ish, Bob Dylan-adjacent tunes. But with *YHF*, Jeff's lyrics contained a dreamy, abstract opacity that propelled the lyrical content away from weary highway travel and whiskey and shot it deep into the subconscious.

Additionally, the real genius of the band as a collective (led in no small part by the late great Jay Bennett, in my opinion) is how they took those simple songs, deconstructed them, and sonically re-animated them in the image of the future. Wilco is like Walter White's evolution from mild-mannered school teacher to take-no-prisoners drug kingpin. They started as one thing and ultimately became another bigger thing. I'm not saying it's cool to be a drug kingpin. I'm just saying I like Wilco a lot, and *Yankee Hotel Foxtrot* rounds out the list of records or tracks that have profoundly influenced me.

---

# Noa Kahn

*"I always think about telling a story through the drums and sometimes try to imagine myself playing a different melodic instrument while soloing. That is all thanks to him."*

N oa Kahn, a Grammy-nominated drummer with a tendency towards jazz, fusion, funk, and R&B, swiftly made her mark on the music scene upon moving from Israel to the US in 2019. As of the writing of this book, Kahn's recent tours include stints with Adam Lambert, Jax, and Big Wild. Here are Noa's choices...

Tower of Power, *Tower of Power* [1973], "Soul Vaccination"
**Drummer** - David Garibaldi

This record was first introduced to me by Billy Buss, my professor at the Tower of Power ensemble at Berklee College of Music. David Garibaldi, the drummer in this record, influenced my drumming in many fields. His style opened my mind to linear drumming and improved my creativity and feel on the drums.

I also love that in recorded live shows of Tower of Power, Garibaldi slightly yet constantly changed his grooves each time he performed, proving his endless creativity and musicality.

## Dave Weckl, *Master Plan* [1990], "Festival De Ritmo"
### Drummer - Dave Weckl

My former ensemble teacher at my high school, Yuval Tabachnik, introduced this tune to me. At that time, I wasn't good enough at the drums or mature enough to have the courage to start digging into Weckl's drumming. I thought it would be impossible for me to transcribe his drumming, so I left it aside. Only a few years later, in Berklee, I had a deeper understanding of drumming and the courage to look back into this tune, so I transcribed and learned this piece and other tunes from Weckl's catalog.

Weckl's drumming has a fantastic flow; it's expressive, full of dynamics, and sounds effortless to the listener. His drumming has improved my own flow, vocabulary, and technique.

## Kim Burrell, *Live In Concert* [2001], "I'll Keep Holding On"
### Drummer - Robert "Sput" Searight

This song certainly contributed to my approach to gospel drumming. The drummer, Sput (also a fantastic keyboard player and an arranger), plays a tasteful groove here and sneaks in incredible polyrhythmic and mind-blowing fills now and then. He is extraordinarily creative and musical, and you can tell by his drumming that he plays a harmonic instrument as well, thanks to his innovative ideas, which are composed of much more than great technique alone.

## Joshua Redman, *Elastic* [2002], "Jazz Crimes"
### Drummer - Brian Blade

In high school, I only played and listened to bop music (mostly swing-based), but thanks to my brother, Dor Kahn, I was introduced to Joshua Redman and the modern jazz world.

This tune is full of groovy kicks and complex yet beautiful harmony while keeping a steady groove. Blade's drumming is highly melodic, and you can hear that from the way he tunes his drums, his melodic phrases during his solos, and the way he accompanies the soloists while playing a groove.

He sounds like a saxophonist or trumpet player, not a drummer since I can always sing the phrases in his solos. His solos are full of dynamics and feel, and he sounds like he is telling a story through them.

His drumming influenced me, and it still affects me whenever I play a solo. I always think about telling a story through the drums and sometimes try to imagine myself playing a different melodic instrument while soloing. That is all thanks to Blade.

## Oz Noy, *Fuzzy* [2007], "Fuzzy"
### **Drummer** - Keith Carlock

My brother, Dor Kahn, also introduced me to this record during my high school years, but when I met my former teacher (and mentor) Shlomi Cohen a few years later, I started exploring Keith Carlock's drumming.

Carlock plays the drums effortlessly with an insane speed and creative ideas while maintaining the song's groove. It sounds to me that he always keeps the foundation of the feel in his head and lets his creativity lead, but I can still feel the presence of the groove while he solos.

His playing is also incredibly accurate yet loose. It never feels tense. He has this incredible flow in his drumming that makes every note sound amazing. His drumming influenced me as I often try to keep the groove foundation while soloing, especially when playing funk/fusion music.

# Dave Scalia

*"...it was a prime example of what music is about. They had already played together for 25 years and developed a language."*

D ave Scalia is a Nashville area-based drummer, producer, and songwriter. Currently in his eighth year with Elle King, he has also collaborated with artists such as White Rabbits, Maude Latour, Dawn Richard, Veritè, and many others. Known for his nuanced and elastic playing style, Dave is highly sought after in the music industry. Here are Dave's choices...

### The Beatles, *Help* [1965], "Ticket To Ride"
### **Drummer** - Ringo Starr

I first heard this song from The Beatles' *Red Album* compilation CD *1962-1966* — I "stole" it from my brother on a road trip to DC with my family when I was 9 and 10. It then led me to the actual '65 release, *Help*. The song "Ticket To Ride" was unique and radical for its time. It's through-composed and ends with a different, sped-up refrain section. The drums and guitars are heavy — some even say it was a precursor to heavy metal. Of course, a lot of why this song is fantastic can be attributed to Ringo's drumming. The beat in the verse with that flam on the rack tom is a unique counterpart to the guitar part, and placing the flam in the right place with the right feel is where a ton of the song's entire feel lies. The fills are interesting (many of them just straight-up rolls), just like in the drum entrance on the rack and in the middle of the tune where he splits the roll with the snare; it's so hip.

It's undeniably a unique, distinctive Ringo groove that wasn't heard in pop music before. Ringo is not only cultivating a singular, groovy drum part; he's composing and likely composing in real-time. And I have to mention the drum tones! When I heard this, it wasn't only a great song with good drumming; it gave me this sense of excitement in playing drums and a drum part. It made me realize that having a personality on the kit and a distinctive approach can elevate the music.

## James Brown, "Funky Drummer" single [1970]
### Drummer - Clyde Stubblefield

I grew up in Madison, Wisconsin, where Clyde Stubblefield lived for more than 40 years, although he was born in Chattanooga, TN. I no doubt would have been exposed to his playing if we hadn't overlapped, but since we did, I feel a special connection to him. He lived in Madison long enough to become a pivotal part of the music scene. I feel so lucky to have seen him play regularly in town; however, I'm still kicking myself for failing to get a proper lesson!

We could talk about many other James Brown tunes he contributed to or other artists he played with, but the "Funky Drummer" break changed music history. Clyde played with James Brown for six years and had no formal training, and he likely improvised this beat at a session with Brown in 1969. The groove is timeless, nuanced, novel, and the most sampled drum groove ever. The syncopation and nuance of the snare drum ghost notes make this special to me. There's an entire universe in this beat—in all four limbs. I can hear New Orleans' second line swinging in the snare drum, and the 16th hi-hats have a straighter feel. There is a fusion of styles with Clyde's approach; it is a lightning-in-a-bottle groove and moment.

It's a fantastic accomplishment for Clyde to improvise a 20-second groove with such a vibe and have it essentially birth hip-hop and revolutionize funk/soul. Knowing it is the most-sampled groove of all time, it's an incredible shame that Clyde struggled with medical bills toward the end of his life.

When I first heard this groove in high school, it changed me, and hearing Clyde play the first time did the same. After all of that, I got into funk music and still, to this day, practice the "Funky Drummer" beat. It's one of those grooves you can never really get to sound like Clyde plays it. It's deceptively complex and is a measuring stick for any drummer to play and make feel good/natural. If you can make it feel great and play it for minutes at a time unwavering, you got some shit together.

My first gig after moving to Brooklyn was with former James Brown bassist Fred Thomas. It came full circle for me when I went to his apartment in Bed Stuy to rehearse before the gig. After playing some funk tunes on the setlist, he smiled, so I knew I had done just a little of my homework. Or maybe he was just being nice!

Miles Davis, *Four And More* [1966], "Seven Steps to Heaven"
**Drummer** - Tony Williams

I was in my first year of college at Indiana University in the music school dorms when someone put this record on. I'll never forget that moment; it was like time stopped. I was familiar with Tony's playing then, but only for his records with Miles, such as *Nefertiti, Miles Smiles,* etc. I hadn't heard this live record with the quintet, but it is one of the best live jazz recordings ever. First of all, the drums sound so, so good. I don't know how it's mic'ed, but few were likely used. I'm sure he's playing a Round Badge Gretsch—18", 12", 14"—and probably some old K's. Anyway, for me, the drum tones alone became the archetype for what jazz drums should sound like. It blows me away that Tony was 19 years old at the time of that recording (Herbie was 24). The entire band was on absolute fire that night. That lineup had been around for about a year before that recording, and the communication, interplay, space, pure energy, and creativity are all top-notch. Tony was undoubtedly the fire behind that quintet.

"Seven Steps To Heaven" stands out because it is so lyrical. Of course, it's got all those drum breaks and the open solo right towards the top of the tune—that's a drummer's vibe. It's a beautiful, lyrical, musical drum solo; you can hear Tony forming his unique voice at 19.

## Frank Glover & Claude Sifferlin, *Siamese Twins* [1999], "Confirmation"

So, I always include this record when discussing what has influenced me. I'm not trying to be clever or coy by picking a tune without drums for this discussion about drumming; this record shaped me significantly because I got the enormous pleasure of playing in a band with these guys in college. They are jazz musicians in Indianapolis, and, starting in my Sophomore year, I began subbing in and eventually became their regular drummer at the Jazz Kitchen in Indianapolis. I got to play with Frank and Claude for about four years before Claude passed. They would play duo all over town, mainly at a jazz club called Chatterbox. Before playing with them, I'd watch these guys play as a duo; to me, it was a prime example of what music is about. They had already played together for 25 years and developed a language.

Frank is playing clarinet on this record, but he plays tenor and soprano. Each has a unique voice, but they can come together as one. That may be where the *Siamese Twins'* name came from. I may be wrong about that. Watching these guys play duo and later having an opportunity to somehow play with them for years was incredible; it gave me so much. They have this elastic time, too. As you listen to the form, you might ask, "Oh, my god, wait, are they not together?" But their phrase points are perfect, as are their harmonic language and lyrical interplay. And also, their time is elastic. So, one of the "challenges" (it was very advanced) for me was figuring it out while on the gig. I never really talked to these guys about it, either. My "ear" got better. Even though their time was elastic, they always knew where everything was.

With the song "Confirmation," I had to listen repeatedly and figure out what the drums could be doing. It got my ears and listening skills fine-tuned. The drums were not-so-metronomic in this case, so I learned to be creative and confident in my time and solid within the group. It was freeing to realize that their time concept was not a literal thing on the grid (music is very much in that realm now.) Listening to them converse in their language and being comfortable with their sense of time greatly impacted me. This would influence anybody on any instrument, particularly for drums. The absence of drums on this record made me think about ideas and time differently. The lessons I learned playing drums in their quartet shaped my playing. It taught me about the depth of music relationships. Knowing those relationships existed gave me something to strive for in my playing. Listening to them play was spiritual for me. So, even though there are no drums in this piece, it taught me a lot about playing and interacting with other musicians.

---

## J Dilla, *Donuts* [2006], "Lightworks"

This is not a drummer; it's just samples.

I also heard this one when I was in college. It was another one of these epiphany or light bulb moments. I hadn't listened to this type of production or this rhythmic concept before. It's Dilla time; it's its own unique thing; There's a book that friends have shared with me in which the author and other people have analyzed what is happening here, i.e., what Dilla did and what he accomplished. What makes it so cool? It's innovative hip-hop production, but it also has a different rhythmic and time feel, cool harmonic stuff, excellent production, incredible textures, all kinds of things. I remember hearing it when drummers like Chris Dave were physically putting this into action. It's a genre in and of itself, and it's hard to articulate because there are multiple time feels at once. There's a beautiful diagram in the book, *Dilla Time* by Dan Charnez; The graphic image in the book illustrates different rhythmic time: there's 1980's straight time (a straight grid— like playing along to a drum machine), then you have swing time (like Count Basie), and then there's Dilla Time in which you have all these times at once, but it still grooves so hard that it does something to you. Hearing how Dilla approached his production really influenced my drumming.

I don't consider myself a drummer specializing in this kind of drumming, but I identify with it, so it influenced my playing. Because, above all else, every drummer has a beating heart and has swing to it. And every musician has it. And that's what is so special about playing music, especially a highly rhythmic instrument like drums. In the song "Lightworks," the paradigm shifted because of the kind of production that Dilla created; it made me think about drums differently. "You mean that the snare drum and bass drum don't have to come at the same time?" It's brilliant. You're thinking of groove drumming, with the bass and snare, and you think, "You mean everything is floating in space, and you are going to place it in a certain way that can make it feel this way?" I WAS AMAZED when I read more about how this record was finished. It was Dilla's last record; he did it while he was in the hospital as he was dying.

Around 2006-2007, I was listening to all kinds of music while in school, lots of jazz and hip-hop, all kinds of music but only a little electronic music. But hearing Dilla's production, I discovered a whole new world. It's like finding a new solar system out there. Although there's not a drummer on it, rhythmically it's fantastic. They're breaking boundaries and making music electronically and with sampled music in a new, organic way. "Lightworks" has always been my favorite. In this record, all the tracks are short, like short stories with a new rhythmic feel and the beat has that Dilla thing. Brilliant.

## Nobukazu Takemura, *Scope* [1999], "Kepler"
### Drummer - Nobukazu Takemura

This is an excellent follow-up to *Donuts*. There are no traditional drums on this record. Takemura is an electronic musician from Japan, and he generates all the sounds by himself or from manipulated samples. I first heard this around the same time that Dilla was introduced to me. After being introduced to electronic music in college, I got into minimalism and composers like John Cage, Steve Reich, Phillip Glass, etc. I was impressed by the composition, but also the rhythmic content that came out of minimalistic music. This Takemura track has many cool rhythmic layers, and the composition is thoughtful, patient, and minimal. The one sound in this song that is particularly exciting is the "CD skipping" sound—I don't know how he does it or what it is, but it's rhythmically exciting. As a drummer, listening to this music without traditional drums gave me so many ideas. For instance: What would I play along to this? Also, we spend a lot of time as drummers thinking about how the snare drum sounds, the tuning, the tone of the bass drum, etc., but when you hear music like Takemura's, you realize anything can be rhythmic. Takemura is using different sounds than I was used to for the kick drum, the snare, the hi-hat—and they're all electronically generated. Most of all, this music asks whether we are drum set players or musicians playing rhythmic instruments. This record helped me think outside the box as both a drummer and a composer/musician whose primary instrument is the drums. As far as I understand, Takemura made all of this music out of his apartment in Japan, and at that time, being a fellow "bedroom" producer, it spoke to me in that sense.

---

## Al Green, *Let's Stay Together* [1972], "So You're Leaving"
## Drummer - Al Jackson Jr.

I couldn't do this without including Al Jackson because he's Mr. Taste. He played on pivotal hits with Sam & Dave, Aretha Franklin, and Booker T; he was a Stax house drummer. Al Jackson epitomized a drummer who knew restraint, played to the song, and had a deep pocket and backbeat. My dad, a huge Stax fan, an R&B and soul fan, and a drummer, undoubtedly exposed me to his playing at a young age. His groove shaped me from the beginning. This record is famous and one of the best soul and R&B records ever made. As a later contribution from Al Jackson, it's great to hear him on a record where the technology has advanced a bit from his earlier recordings; there is more clarity. You can hear that Jackson came from a jazz background; his dad led a big band, and he sat in. I love the jazz and soul/R&B connection in his playing and many of the Stax and Motown players. In my journey, that connection of jazz and blues to R&B/soul is what I was exposed to early on, so I love it and try to honor it in my playing.

# David Raouf

*"This shifted how I thought about my drumming...I started to write drum parts instead of just drum beats."*

Davi Raouf, the mastermind behind the YouTube channel *rdavidr*, seamlessly and humorously blends his passion for percussion with his craftsmanship abilities. Through his channel, he showcases his talent for building, creating, and repurposing second-hand percussion instruments. In addition to his YouTube endeavors, David dedicates his spare time to crafting hip-hop beats, producing play-along tracks, and curating sample libraries featuring the drums he's created or modified. Here are David's choices…

Iron Maiden, *Powerslave* [1984], "Powerslave"
**Drummer** - Nicko McBrain

In the early 2000s, I saw a commercial on VH1 where a 2D cat cutout sang "Run To The Hills". I had no idea who Iron Maiden was, but I would leave the TV on VH1 to catch that commercial and hear the infamous 16th-note descending tom fill from "Run To The Hills" again. When I learned it was Iron Maiden, I went straight to the record store to find more of their music. Many people may call Iron Maiden's aesthetic cheesy, but little 13-year-old Dave was mesmerized by it. I bought a used copy of *Powerslave* just because of the album art. That

249

CD reeked of cigarette smoke and stunk up my room after I brought it home. I didn't care; once I put it on my boombox and heard the intro fill in "Powerslave," I knew I needed a giant drum set with 12 toms to play fills like Nicko McBrain.

This ultimately led to my interest in heavier music because these drummers had big kits. Bands like Iron Maiden, Metallica, Megadeath, and Pantera were all I listened to. I would go deeper into the metal genre, but the further I went, the more I hated it. Something about the drumming in these surface-level metal bands had me hooked. It was simple, but every note they played fit the song perfectly. Their beats were simple, and their fills were catchy. Catchy yet straightforward, which to this day, are the two things I aim for whenever I sit behind a kit. The only difference is that I despise power toms and am behind a four-piece. Sorry Nicko.

## Steve Reich, *Drumming* [1970]

Steve Reich's *Drumming* may seem like an oddball for those who only know me through my YouTube channel, but this piece, or album if you want to call it that, played a massive role in what I do with drums today. My first drum teacher, Scott Clark, played a few minutes of "Drumming: Pt.1" for me in a lesson one day. I had no idea what to think or why he played it for me. It just sounded like a bunch of dudes beating on some bongos. Scott is the kind of guy who would drop so much knowledge and wisdom in a 30-minute drum lesson without you even noticing, and then a day later, it would hit you like a ton of bricks. In this case, those bricks came hurtling toward me about two years later during my junior year of high school.

Sitting in music theory class, flipping through the textbook, I came across a chapter about minimalist music. "Steve Reich? That name sounds familiar." I thought. After making the connection that this was the guy Scott told me about, I went down the most bottomless minimalist music rabbit hole. What does plucking a cactus's spikes with contact mics hooked up sound like? John Cage has got you covered. What about a drum solo with crickets chirping in the background? Ask Glenn Kotche. Or how about mics hanging from the ceiling swinging across speakers to create weird feedback patterns? Reich is your man. Those are extreme examples and may sound like the beginnings of a noise band. Still, that rabbit hole indirectly made me realize the vast sound possibilities with only a drum set. It's the wacky gear, crazy mods, and left-field sounds that keep me glued to drums and why picking up another instrument never once crossed my mind.

---

### Nas, *Illmatic* [1994], "NY State of Mind"
**Drummer** - Produced by DJ Premier (who sampled George Brown of Kool and the Gang)

In 2011, I finished my first year of college. Long story short, I didn't really like school and ended up dropping out to move back home and attend community college. A buddy and I were driving to class one day when he took the aux and started playing "New York State of Mind" off Nas' *Illmatic*. The grittiness of the beat combined with Nas' storytelling was something I had never heard in rap before. Remember that I grew up in the era of crunk and trap, so '90s rap was new to me. I had assumed all older rap sounded like Sugar Hill Gang, but I was wrong. This was all around the time I was getting bored of playing drums. I wasn't playing in any ensembles in school and all the friends I played music with weren't around because they were busy getting degrees. I had no reason to play or practice drums outside of my own will. But after hearing *Illmatic* and going down a '90s hip-hop rabbit hole and learning about sampling, I knew that beat-making was the perfect thing to fill the void of drumming.

I became obsessed with sampling. Every other day I would go to a record store, buy a stack of the most random albums you could think of, go back home, and listen to them all in hopes something was interesting enough to sample. As you can imagine, I amassed a rather large vinyl collection. I loved the beat-making process, but listening to these random albums was probably the best thing I could have done to re-spark my interest in drums. I heard music and drum beats I didn't even know were possible to play. My favorites were the foreign records since most weren't in 4/4. Watching a YouTube lesson about playing in odd times is one thing, but hearing it done in a musical context puts it all in perspective. You may have heard the saying "drum machines have no soul," but that statement couldn't be any more false, at least when sampling real humans playing real instruments. '90s hip-hop beats are pretty simple, but they don't lack feel. This phase of my life was more eye-opening for my drumming than I ever could have imagined. I thought my timing/feel was solid, but when trying to drum along to these simple boom-bap beats, I quickly learned that I was the one who had no soul.

## Passport, *Cross Collateral* [1975], "Homunculus"
### **Drummer** - Curt Cress

One of the albums I found during record digging was *Cross Collateral* by Passport. I was always drawn to albums with the craziest cover art, and *Cross Collateral* had precisely that; a skeletonized airplane flying in the clouds with a big pair of glasses and eyes coming out of it. Of course, I had to buy it even though I had no clue what the music sounded like. Sidenote, this is the BEST way to find new music, haha. Passport is a German jazz fusion group with hints of krautrock sprinkled in. When I dropped the needle on the song "Homunculus" and heard the drums come in, I stopped thinking about whether I could sample anything and just sat and listened. Jazz fusion was nothing new to me, but something about the sounds of the drums was so foreign. The way they were tuned, recorded, and physically played sounded different. The toms were tuned high but sounded low and thuddy, the cymbals were crisp but trashy at the same time, and the drums felt on top of the mix but in a way that blended the band. Everything about these drums felt so wrong yet so correct simultaneously.

My beat-making phase was around the same time I started taking my YouTube channel more seriously, leading me to ditch the idea of becoming a producer. I play a lot of different drums on my channel. New kits, old kits, weird kits, kits made from random objects, you name it, I've played it. Typically when going into a recording session, you want to match the equipment to the sound you're after, but I'm forced to do things backward. I find the kit and have to find a track that matches. For example, Ben [Hilzinger] found me a weird old Impact drum set from the '80s where the toms look like the big helmet from *Spaceballs*. I could have played to some basic drumless funk play-along track, but that doesn't do the kit justice. The kit screams the 80s, so an upbeat retro-synthy track is what the kit deserves. "Homunculus" is a song I still think about when I do any drum recording. If the kit doesn't match the style, the magic is lost.

Saves The Day, *Through Being Cool* [1999], "Last Lie I Told"

## **Drummer** - Bryan Newman

The timeline is a little screwed at this point, but the friend who played me Nas was the same one who got me into my first real band back in high school. I say "real" because this was the first time I played in a band where we played shows, rehearsed regularly, and recorded/released music. I got the gig because my friend was the drummer but got kicked out by his parents for having bad grades. No wonder we ended up in community college. He asked if I could fill in while he was busy trying to get smarter, so I accepted. The only issue was they played pop-punk music which was NOT my thing. The rest of the band didn't seem to have a worry in the world and assured me that once I listened to *Through Being Cool* by Saves the Day, I would be fine. Sure enough, they were right. "The Last Lie I Told" stands out the most because the beats were so catchy and seemingly technical but were beyond simple at the same time. Again, I gravitated towards catchy and straightforward. These beats had a different charm and were a more evolved version of the simple beats by Pantera, Iron Maiden, etc.

I had always considered pop punk to be lame. I was never a huge fan of Blink 182, Green Day, New Found Glory, etc. Sure, they have some hits, but I never was able to sit down and listen to one of their albums the whole way through. With Saves The Day, though, I was hooked (and later helped me appreciate the more mainstream bands I mentioned). The drumming in Saves The Day felt like a part of the song, not just a beat with some fills to transition into different sections. I don't consider the drumming to be more musical, but it served more of a purpose to the songs. I was so impressed with the drumming in *Through Being Cool* that some of the first videos I posted on YouTube were drum covers from that album. This shifted how I thought about my drumming, especially in this band. I started to write drum parts instead of just drum beats. Even today, I write parts that will leave the same impression on anyone listening. The type of drum part where people can't help but air drum since it's such a vital part of the music.

# Scott McPherson

*"There aren't many things I remember as clearly as the different encounters I've had with this record... "*

S cott McPherson is a legendary drummer who has worked alongside Elliott Smith, Sense Field, M. Ward, Bright Eyes, Neil Finn, She & Him, and others. He is also the founder of Tackle Instrument Supply Co., a Minneapolis-based boutique renowned for its durable and stylish gig bags and accessories. Here are Scott's choices...

Emmylou Harris, *Wrecking Ball* [1995], "Where Will I Be"
**Drummers** - Brian Blade, Larry Mullen Jr.

I remember getting this record when it was first released. I heard it on the radio while living in LA. KCRW's *Morning Becomes Eclectic* with Chris Douridas shaped most of my musical preferences through his show and his picks. I've loved Daniel Lanois' production aesthetic since his work in the '80s with U2. It was a time when liner notes were the gospel. So I got the record, and the opening track blew my mind. Since then, I have incorporated the nuance, subtlety, feel, and sound of the drums into my approach to playing whenever possible. I saw Emmylou perform two times during the time this record cycle. Once, I saw her at a bookstore called Borders Books in Santa Monica. Another time, I saw her with the full band consisting of Brian Blade, Daniel Lanois, Buddy Miller, and

Darryl Johnson. This band left nothing more to be desired. There aren't many things I remember as clearly as the different encounters I've had with this record and seeing it performed masterfully live. Brian Blade is at the heart of it and has left an indelible impression that survives to this day as my favorite musician.

---

Elliot Smith, *From A Basement On A Hill* [2004],
"Pretty (Ugly Before)"
**Drummers** - Scott McPherson, Steven Drozd,
Aaron Sperske, Fritz Michaud

This song was recorded during the 2000 *Figure 8* tour cycle in which I was the live drummer. We first learned this song during the pre-tour rehearsals, and it was one of a few new songs that Elliott had written but hadn't recorded or fully fleshed out. It came organically to us; each corresponding part wrote itself to this song. We came up with parts that Elliott liked and locked them in. We performed this song live almost every night for the whole year of this tour, and, eventually we had a day off in Boston. Elliott asked if we wanted to go in and track this song at Fort Apache. This was an exciting prospect for me as I loved quite a few records that came out of that place, such as Pixies, Juliana Hatfield, Throwing Muses, Belly, and Tanya Donelly, to name just a few.

---

# Joe Seiders

*" ...you can put this song on at any party, and the vibe goes straight to ten."*

J oe Seiders is a multi-instrumentalist best known as the drummer for acclaimed indie rock band, The New Pornographers. He has also performed with Neko Case, Emmitt Rhodes, John Oats, Tracy Bonham, and many more. With his precision and versatility behind the kit, Joe's collaborative style is a songwriter's dream. Here are Joe's choices…

Wilco, *Sky Blue Sky* [2007], "Walken"
**Drummer** - Glenn Kotche

What can I say about Glenn Kotche that has yet to be said? He's a true master of his craft. I was always a Wilco fan, but when I heard the *Yankee Hotel Foxtrot* record for the first time, it was an absolute revelation. I loved how he approached the kit from such a beautiful, orchestral angle.

One particular fill on the song "Walken" off the *Sky Blue Sky* album slays me. The entire song swings, and after the third chorus or so, this sort of solo guitar riff happens. When Glenn brings the song back in, he plays this long, 8th-note straight-against-swing snare fill that slowly falls back to swing as he finishes the fill on the toms. I think it's so simple yet brilliant and natural.

We played a show with Wilco in Denver a few years back, and when I looked to side stage left, Glenn was there watching me during our set. To say I was nervous would most certainly be underselling it.

---

### Wings, *Wings At The Speed of Sound* [1976], "Let 'Em In"
### **Drummer** - Joe English

"Let 'Em In" is one of the greatest, most simple grooves ever. With the hi-hat accents and the basic kick-snare pattern, Joe English knocked it out of the park on this one (with a little help from Denny Laine on the military drum bits). I've had multiple sessions with different bands and artists where they've asked for the "Let 'Em In" beat. It's timeless.

As a bonus, you can put this song on at any party, and the vibe goes straight to ten. I swear it's because of the feeling you get from the tempo of this one. "Let 'Em In" has the PERFECT tempo. Put that on my gravestone.

Also, I love the story that Joe English answered the call for what he assumed was an ordinary audition for a rock band in some basement and ended up face-to-face with Paul McCartney. It's safe to say he got the gig.

---

### Deerhoof, *Friend Opportunity* [2007], "The Perfect Me"
### **Drummer** - Greg Saunier

Greg Saunier of Deerhoof is the best drummer I've ever seen live. I can't think of anyone else with such a unique and incredible playing style. His fills are unmatched. The way he pushes the rhythm without rushing gives you this intensity that's wildly addicting to listen to.

Put on the record *Friend Opportunity*, press play (specifically "The Perfect Me"), and boom, you hear drumming like you've never heard before. Then look up videos of him smashing kick and snare with giant hi-hats. Greg is such a student of music and composition. The pure madness he can bring to a song without trampling the vocals is incredibly inspiring.

## Radiohead, *The Bends* [1995], "Nice Dream"
**Drummer** - Phil Selway

It's a very controversial take, but *The Bends* is my favorite Radiohead record. I'll never forget the first time I listened to the album, specifically the second chorus of "Nice Dream" when the entire chord progression happens, and I thought, "This is my new favorite band."

Philip Selway's drumming was criminally underrated at the time, in the mid-'90s, when loud, busy drums were in fashion. I always look to Phil as a drummer when I think about ways to "serve the song." He never gets in the way, yet his ideas are always innovative and chosen with the greatest taste.

## Nirvana, *MTV Unplugged in NY* [1994], "About A Girl," "Come As You Are"
**Drummer** - Dave Grohl

It seems cliche to put Dave Grohl on any influential drummer list but come on, it's fucking Nirvana. I was a teenager looking to bash the hell out of some drums, playing along to the first few records (thank you, Dale Crover as well), when I discovered the *MTV Unplugged in NY* show. I had never heard drums sound like this; he was playing similar parts from the records but with this cool, acoustic, chilled drum sound!

This is how a fourteen-year-old Joe Seiders discovers dowel sticks and jazz brushes. I had no idea they existed until I saw Dave Grohl use them on MTV. Hearing songs reworked in such a way blew my mind.

# Neal Daniels

*"...I stopped playing for the drummers in the audience and started playing for the song."*

N eal Daniels, a Chicago native now based in Los Angeles, has built an impressive career as a drummer, touring with artists like LP, Liz Phair, Matchbox 20, Post Malone, Booker T. Jones, Rachel Platten, DAYA, Bea Miller, and more. When he's not on the road, Neal runs Whitefish Studios in LA, where he records remote drum tracks for clients around the world. Here are Neal's choices...

## Pearl Jam, *TEN* [1991], "Alive"
**Drummer** - Dave Krusen

My dad passed away when I was 17 years old, and I was in a strange place around that time, musically speaking. I was playing in metal bands and listening to some questionable music. I regret not being more open to some music my dad was trying to show me at a young age. I have great memories of him showing me this record when we would drive around together. He loved Pearl Jam, and I specifically remember him singing and air drumming to the song "Alive." I remember us tapping along at stoplights and him laughing when I nailed the occasional drum fill. So, more than just loving this song and recording for the obvious musical reasons, it brings me back to a great time in my life.

## Metallica, *Master Of Puppets* [1986], "Battery"
**Drummer** - Lars Ulrich

"Lars Ulrich is overrated." "Lars Ulrich sucks." "Lars Ulrich can't play double bass," Etc etc. Listen here and relax, pal. Lars was and will forever be the man and driving force of Metallica. Sure, his double bass drumming in the song ONE in 2023 sounds like a wet PB&J hitting a cement floor, but who cares? In the '80s and early '90s, Lars was unstoppable. *Live Shit: Binge & Purge*? Come on. He was a massive inspiration to me and thousands of other drummers worldwide. I saw Metallica in 2004 at Allstate Arena in Chicago, and that concert changed my life. It was the first time I said, "Yeah, I wanna do that!" I picked "Battery" because they opened with it at Allstate Arena, and I remember being so blown away while, at the same time, being crushed by 300 lb animals in the pit. Black eye aside, it was a true game-changing moment for me. This record and song bring me back to my early high school days, and it was around this time when I started to play and focus on drums full-time.

## Umphrey's McGee, *Anchor Drops* [2004], "Ja Junk Part 1"
**Drummer** - Kris Myers

Umphrey's! If I say that three times in the mirror, I'll start tripping on acid again. Kris Myers was one of my biggest drum influences growing up and was a true drum hero of mine. (This is also true for most of my friends who played music in Chicago in the mid-2000s).

I was musically attracted to Umphrey's because they rocked a little harder than the other popular jam bands around that time. Kris had amazing double bass chops and played some really interesting parts in a music scene that didn't have any of that happening. Coming from a metal background, this opened me up to a new scene because I didn't realize that this kind of drumming could cross into the jam band world. I was immediately hooked and saw them over 50 times throughout high school. Umphrey's also significantly influenced my high school band called "Chicago Green." We used to cover many of their songs and would drive to the Aragon Ballroom in Chicago to see them together. It was an enjoyable musical time and certainly my most creative, drumming-wise. I have great memories of driving to school at 7 a.m. with my friends blasting the song "Ja Junk" before stumbling into math class.

## Frank Zappa, *Over-Nite Sensation* [1973], "I'm The Slime"
### Drummer - Ralph Humphrey

I had a significant Frank Zappa phase. The entire reason why I moved to Los Angeles at 19 years old was to study with Ralph Humphrey at the LA Music Academy. (Now called The Los Angeles College Of Music). After my so-called "jam band phase," I graduated to the next level...ZAPPA. My high school band used to cover "Montana" and "I'm The Slime," featuring Ralph Humphrey on drums. Listening to and playing this music at a young age was exhilarating. I explored odd times very early on, and although I probably should have been more focused on playing a simple beat well, I had a pretty deep understanding of how to break down odd times. Besides being a great song, "I'm The Slime" brings me back to a time when I made the biggest and best move of my life, from Chicago to Los Angeles in 2009. Studying with Ralph for those next few years was an unbelievable experience I'll cherish forever. Ralph had a few books on odd times, my favorite being *Even In the Odds*. It's about breaking down odd times in groups of 2s and 3s. He hammered those groupings into my head while at school… 2s and 3s, 2s and 3s, 2s and 3s. After some ongoing health issues, Ralph passed away this past April. As the universe's tribute to Ralph, he died on 4/23/23.

---

## Parliament, *Clones Of Dr. Funkenstein* [1976], "Everything Is On The One"
### **Drummer** - Jerome "Bigfoot" Brailey

After attending music school, I started focusing more on playing the parts needed to "get the gig." I felt lost musically and needed to learn the steps to make a living playing drums. I was overplaying and not focusing on what matters most—GROOVE. FEEL. POCKET. TIME KEEPING—not chops and technique, like I once focused on so heavily. I heard this song and record for the first time when I needed it the most, and boy, was it enlightening. I stopped playing for the drummers in the audience and started playing for the song. I started getting more impressed by drummers having fantastic timekeeping and feel, rather than a fast chop they played in the bridge. That mental shift truly started from hearing some of these songs, and I'll never look back. "Everything is on the one today, y'all, and don't forget it."

---

# Donnie Marple

*"I wore this particular tune out and practiced it until I learned every note. And I still keep a lot of the licks in my back pocket!"*

Donnie Marple rose to prominence in 2007 as the Guitar Center Drum Off Champion. For over a decade, he has been a cornerstone of Lee Brice's band, showcasing his impressive soloing and solid rhythm. He has contributed to numerous #1 hits and is known for his gentlemanly demeanor both on and off the stage. Here are Donnie's choices…

Ron Kenoly, *Lift Him Up* [1992], "Ancient Of Days"
**Drummer** - Chester Thompson

I'll always remember when my Mom came home from the Ron Kenoly/Don Moen concert in the early '90s. I was probably five years old, and that's all she listened to for a couple of years. She even brought home a VHS tape, the audio from which later became the record *Lift Him Up*. This record shaped my development as a young drummer, inspiring me to play different genres at a young age. It was one-of-a-kind music with some of the most excellent musicians in the world on the same stage. Each musician brought their flavor to the table, making it such a worldly sound that anyone from anywhere could relate to it musically. These world-renowned musicians had one goal: to "Lift Him Up."

The rhythm section included Chester Thompson, Abraham Laboriel, and Alex Acuña. It's just a powerhouse sound of groove and rhythm. The music moved the listener in such a way they had no choice but to dance and move. I would call it anointed because I felt listening/watching that this was something bigger than I could comprehend. This record had a one-of-a-kind sound that inspired me to be myself and create my voice in the drum world.

---

## DC Talk, *Welcome to the Freak Show* [2003], "So Help Me God" Drummer - Will Denton

This live record was one of the first CDs I ever owned. I felt so cool owning a CD like this because there were guitar solos, heavy-hitting drums, rap, harmonies, and full-blown energetic melodies. Because I was limited in what I could listen to as a kid, this record created a loophole into the world of Rock and Roll. The power chords, heavy rock beats, and a positive message gave me hope as a preacher's grandchild to listen to music that moved me without the guilt of secular lyrics.

Looking back, I don't regret being a little deprived of the classic rock/pop records that most of my peers grew up listening to. The reason for this is because it helped me create my sound. The funk/rock elements of DC Talk's *Welcome to the Freak Show* were such a different thing to me. I wore the record out, head banging and air drumming in the car's back seat wherever my parents drove me. This was a live record, so recognizing the rawness of a live rock show vs. a clean, perfectly mixed studio record significantly impacted the performance and energy in my playing. Even as a middle schooler, I realized that beauty is sometimes in the imperfections. Drummer Will Denton brought so much energy that you could almost see him playing while listening to this album.

---

## Dave Weckl Band, *Live (And Very Plugged In)* [1984], "The Chicken"
### **Drummer** - Dave Weckl

I went to see Dave Weckl at the age of 14. I'll never forget seeing the flyer in our high school band room. I honestly didn't know then that there was such a thing as a "professional drummer." I assumed drummers were a dime a dozen—playing their part to fit the gig appropriately. But then I saw Dave Weckl and had my former mindset blown to smithereens. Thinking this was a glorified jazz concert, my expectations were low. From the first to the last note of every song, I was invested—studying every ghost note and dynamic of the show. It was the first time I heard a drum set make its own music and even create melodies. It reminded me of the movie *Transformers*, but the drums came to life instead of a car coming to life.

From that day forward, I changed my mindset regarding my goals, and all I wanted to do was to make other people feel the way I felt at Dave's concert. I also remember crying in disbelief that he could pull off some of these "superhuman" grooves, fills, and overall sounds on that Yamaha kit. Every cymbal, bongo, tom, and snare had a voice like a choir of heavenly percussion. Some songs sounded as if five drummers were playing at one time. I couldn't wait to get home and add some of these elements to my playing. It's been some process, and to this day, even playing for a county artist, I can see how Dave Weckl inspired me to be a drummer and a full-rounded musician.

---

## Dave Matthews Band, *The Central Park Concert* [2003], "Grey Street"
### **Drummer** - Carter Beauford

After moving to Nashville, I joined a band called Elmwood. After the first three months of being a band, we got signed to Paradigm—a booking agency based out of Nashville. They had several bands that I looked up to on their roster, including Dave Mathews Band. I was skeptical of DMB starting out because I mostly listened to their hits that came on the radio occasionally. Luckily, I got invited to see a DMB show by Elmwood's lead singer, Ruston Kelly. To say their performance floored me would be a colossal understatement. Carter played with his thunderous double pedal, fast toms fills, hitting china cymbals, chewing gum, blowing bubbles, smiling, fist pumping, encouraging his band to bring all they had, etc. It was such an inspiring sight because they were so in sync. They played this show as if it was their last. Dave's fans are also one of a kind and feed off of their energy from the beginning to the end of the show.

After seeing them live, I went on a DMB binge—listening to all their records. My personal favorite is the *The Central Park Concert* record. For a band to pack out this kind of park in the middle of New York City was just mind-blowing to me. This record captured their live show so well that it made you feel like you were in the front row, cheering them on and soaking in every note from every band member.

---

## John Mayer, *Room For Squares* [2001], "Neon"
### **Drummer** - Nir Z

This record practically went viral in my high school, but I was the only one who didn't know any of the words; I can blame Nir Z for this.

The feel and sound of the drums on this record were so infectious, to the point that there were times when Nir was the only musician I could hear. I learned so much from this record because I realized that less can be more. The musical maturity throughout this record also helped me mature when supporting an artist. Before this record, I wanted to be the next Buddy Rich. After digging into this record, I tried to find a gig where I could support and make the singer and band sound as good as possible. If John Mayer was the golf ball, Nir was the tee. He set every verse, chorus, bridge, and guitar solo up so perfectly that you couldn't help but appreciate the final product of this album.

Nir has also recently influenced me because he has played on several Lee Brice records. It's so fun to learn the parts that he comes up with, mainly because there is nothing predictable about Nir. I also enjoyed playing alongside Nir on the number 1 single, "Rumor," by Lee Brice. To share a track that was a smash on the radio with my favorite session drummer of all time is such a surreal feeling. If I were to model myself after a studio drummer, it would be Nir. He's not afraid to go for things and create grooves and fills that make the song what it is.

# Tucker Rule

*"...he's got so much swagger. It's infectious, and you can't help but feel cool when you listen to him play."*

Tucker Rule is a founding member of the legendary emo/post-hardcore group Thursday and recently started a supergroup with fellow emo-scene members called L.S. Dunes. Over the years, Tucker has collaborated with Ageist, Franko Iero & The Future Violents, and Murphy's Law. He has also toured with Yellowcard, My Chemical Romance, and The Wanted. Here are Tucker's choices...

### Usher, 2006 *Modern Drummer* Festival DVD, "Caught Up"
**Drummer** - Aaron Spears

Aaron Spears's performance of "Caught Up" was legendary; I've probably watched that video a zillion times. His timing is impeccable, the fills are creative and blazing, the kit sounds beautiful, and the dude is smiling ear to ear. Drums are fun, and there's no ceiling when you work hard, practice, and have a great attitude. Aaron Spears demonstrates all this, and it's inspiring.

### Quicksand, *Slip* [1993], "Fazer"
**Drummer** - Alan Cage

I grew up as a skater listening to fast punk and hardcore, and Quicksand is my favorite band of all time, hands down. My entire world changed when I turned on MTV's *120 Minutes* and saw the video for "Fazer" — heavy yet melodic guitars, beautiful vocals, and monstrous drums from my man Alan Cage. We've been lucky to tour with Quicksand over the years, and their live show absolutely rips. These dudes are heroes and wonderful human beings we can call friends.

## Deftones, *White Pony* [2000]
## **Drummer** - Abe Cunningham

Deftones' *White Pony* is one of my favorite records from front to back. Abe's got so much swagger. It's infectious, and you can't help but feel cool when you listen to him play. Thursday has been lucky enough to do a bunch of touring with Deftones, and I would always sit behind the riser and watch him annihilate the drums and watch the crowd bob their heads in appreciation for Cool Breeze's greasy grooves.

# Tim Very

*"You cannot talk shit on them; please don't try to, or you'll look like a fool."*

Tim Very is the highly creative drummer for rock band Manchester Orchestra, known for his powerful and playful drumming style. Apart from his work with the band, he has collaborated with artists like B.o.B, Bad Books, Chris Staples, and Brother Bird, showcasing his versatility and talent as both a musician and songwriter. Here are Tim's choices...

Foo Fighters, *The Colour and the Shape* [1997], "Hey, Johnny Park!"
**Drummers** - Dave Grohl, William Goldsmith

Of course, I had to pop in the Granddaddy of rock & roll drumming himself, Dave Grohl. I know he gets a lot of attention in the drummer world, but just like Lebron, you'd be a fool not to put him in the greatest of all-time category. Sure, tons of drummers can play insane blast beats or incredible chops, but no one wants to listen to that shit. What's wanted and needed is perfect drumming and fills for excellent songwriting, and Grohl nailed it TWICE. He was so good that he replaced his drummer because it had to be done correctly. I just saw Will play with Sunny Real Estate, and he's a BEAST, so it's no disrespect; it's just that Dave writes the best parts EVER. He's got drum parts that allow you to take away the rest of the music and still know what song it is; that's a particular skill. Who cares about your paradiddles? This dude controls the feel of some of the greatest songs ever written. So he's in at #1. No apologies.

## AC/DC, *Highway to Hell* [1979], "Highway to Hell"
## **Drummer** - Phil Rudd

Phil is my 2nd choice and on the other side of the spectrum from the all-out assault drummers that plague our ilk. This dude must be some gentleman with the selfless way he lays back and lets the guitars take you on a ride. The music is timeless, and the drumming is a huge part. The perfect drink is made with just the right ingredients, and that's Phil's drumming in AC/DC. He makes it sound so simple, but it's excellent taste. Drummers need to learn to get out of the way of the song. Just do it for everyone's sake, and your band will love you.

## Wilco, *A Ghost is Born* [2004], "At Least That's What You Said"
## **Drummer** - Glenn Kotche

Now, Glen is another story. He's like style, chops, and finesse wrapped into one perfect drummer for a pretty perfect band. You cannot talk shit on Wilco; please don't try to, or you'll look like a fool. Glen jumped into that band and took the drumming to an overcharged level. I saw them on the *A Ghost is Born* tour, and it almost blew my little 22-year-old drummer brain out the back of my head. If you've seen them, you know what I mean. Wilco's drummer was already dope, and they got Glen because he was THAT good. I get it. As a drummer, he's what I aspire to.

---

### Refused, *The Shape of Punk To Come* [1998], "The Deadly Rhythm"
### **Drummer** - David Sandström

Now, here's my slight curveball. I am surprised sometimes by how many people have yet to hear Refused, but if you were a fan like I was (and still am), then you understand that this band is lighting in a bottle, and the drumming is the catalyst. This dude has such a tremendous style, and it's completely BADASS. The fills rip your face off, as does the music, and it was music to my teenage angsty soul. They do a lot of unconventional stuff you find in heavy music, and each song is a fresh new journey. Gotta scream.

---

### Colour Revolt, *Plunder, Beg, and Curse* [2008], "Ageless Everytime"
### **Drummer** - Len Clark

Having my good buddy Len Clark on this list seems strange, but he deserves this spot. Another hybrid of sorts, he could hit the drums like an absolute animal and write the most sensitive and simple parts perfect for the song. He's written some of my favorite drum stuff to this day and is the absolute homie. Color Revolt was a force to be reckoned with. I hated playing shows with them back in the day because they steamrolled everyone who got on a stage with them! Let's talk them back into a reunion one day. Until then, if you haven't heard this band, enjoy some of the finest rock songs you'll ever hear!

---

# Guy Licata

*"...it sounded like a PLACE; it felt like my city, but sort of a hazy nostalgia of a city and a culture. It was dark. It was sexy. And it had this sheen over it."*

G uy Licata wears multiple hats as a working drummer and the Manager of Core Business Innovation at Zildjian Company. With a rich history in touring and session work, he has collaborated with notable artists such as Bill Laswell and Museum of Love. Additionally, Guy is the founder and creator of the Reflexx Practice Pad. Here are Guy's choices...

The Headhunters, *Survival of the Fittest* [1975], "God Made Me Funky"
**Drummer** - Mike Clark

When you're very young, you're entirely influenced by things culturally because you don't have any real agency. You're born into a family/community and inherit or grow up around and experience many things. Your influences are as big as these experiences. From the ages of 5-10, there were only a few CDs around our house. It was primarily tapes, and they stayed in the car for the most part.

Outside that, I used to go through my mom's record collection. Most of the records didn't speak to me, but a few did.

This record hit hard, confused me in a good way intellectually, and just tickled me; I felt it in my body. While it was a pure cultural influence then, today, this is something that ticks all the boxes along with emotional and intellectual.

---

Primus, *Sailing the Seas of Cheese* [1991], "Jerry Was A Race Car Driver"
**Drummer** - Tim "Herb" Alexander

---

From the ages of 10-15, I mostly listened to rock, and the first tape I bought with my own money was Guns and Roses' *Appetite For Destruction*. From there, grunge happened—Nirvana, Soundgarden, Pearl Jam, and all of Seattle exploded.

MTV was the way I discovered most new music, and when the "Jerry" video popped up on *120 Minutes* with Matt Pinfield, it broke my brain. I couldn't figure out what was happening, but I loved it. It was heavy but funky, with some complexity, and wholly absurd. It was its own thing.

I found many bands through Tim and his influences. That's how I got into Rush and The Police, and that process can continue infinitely through those bands and drummers.

---

Maceo Parker, *Life on Planet Groove* [1992], "Pass The Peas"
**Drummer** - Kenwood Dennard

---

For me, ages 15-20 were very formative, and the first time I heard this tune, I was cutting class; it was my sophomore year.

I was at a buddy's house with a handful of friends, and this song came on. When it dropped, my body started moving uncontrollably; it hit me like a truck and had a weight I'd only felt from heavier music. I immediately started mining everything remotely funky, e.g., James Brown and the JB's, The Meters, P-Funk, Herbie Hancock, Tower of Power, Gap Band, Zapp and Roger, etc.

At this point, we're also in a golden age of hip-hop careening into the shiny suit era, but this was also when you saw hip-hop's cultural influence going wildly mainstream. We stopped calling it rap, as that was a massive distinction at this point.

From funk, I inevitably found the wildly exciting world of fusion. Fusion brought in more of an intellectual component missing from pure funk, and I found myself down another massive rabbit hole. My teacher, the late Kim Plainfield, had a name for this kind of drumming; he called it Sophistafunk. Dave Garibaldi was also one of my biggest influences during this time and everything from the East Bay.

## Renegade aka Ray Keith, *Vintage Dread 2000* [2009], "Terrorist"

In 1998, I was living in New York, having just returned from college in Oregon. I knew I wanted to pursue music more seriously, but needed to figure out how. I was living in my parents' house and experiencing crushing existential dread.

All my friends in the area were gone, so I got a job at Sam Ash in the drum dept. I met many people through that job and those in my network who were still around. I also went to raves and parties in the area, which was like nothing I had ever experienced; it felt dangerous and new. The music wasn't anything I had heard in a real way, but the culture was exciting.

Everyone was there to dance and have a good time. It was removed from the standard music culture I was used to, and as a musician, it was a brave new world. There weren't any bands. There were DJs and producers, and you couldn't find most of this music outside of 12" vinyl, so this was the only delivery system.

At most parties at the time, you had Main Room, which was mostly four on-the-floor genres like house or techno; then you had the smaller side rooms where you'd hear jungle, drum bass, breakbeat, etc. (dubstep didn't even exist yet). I remember walking into a jungle room for the first time and it being total chaos. The bass was massive and hit you in the chest; the beats were frenetic and seemed like a giant through-composed part. People were losing their minds and DANCING TO IT.

It was aggressive but smart and funk in a way I'd never heard before. After that, I was hooked. And being that you couldn't just go down to Tower Records and find this stuff, I was out at parties and making friends with DJs and producers within the scene. I remember the first time I heard Terrorist. It had all of these active ingredients of jungle that I loved but was put together in an interesting way. It had complexity but a simple song form, and everything sat perfectly.

## Burial, *Burial* [2006], "Southern Comfort"

The ages of 25-30 were interesting. Grime and dubstep were slowly coming to the US and living in a space that usually played jungle (in the side room). It was not the dubstep we know today; the term EDM didn't even exist.

And then Burial happened.

Some people describe it as Hauntology: retro-futurism. It had elements of all these things I loved, but it was put together in a new way.

In it, I heard bits of Tony Allen, elements of jungle, more cinematic things, foley, etc. I was confused yet again. Burial sounded like a PLACE; it felt like my city, but sort of a hazy nostalgia of a city and a culture. It was dark. It was sexy. And it had this sheen over it.

# Nate Morton

*"The details...are hazy, but suffice it to say, in 1978, a seven-year-old Black kid rocking out to KISS wasn't exactly the norm."*

N ate Morton, known as the drummer for NBC's *The Voice*, boasts a lengthy career performing with notable artists including Paul Stanley, Madonna, Chaka Khan, Natalie Cole, Vanessa Carlton, Miley Cyrus, Poe, and others. Renowned for his infectious energy, Nate holds an unmatched ability to play for the song while maintaining a distinct personal voice, pun intended. Here are Nate's choices...

KISS, *Dynasty* [1979], "I Was Made For Lovin' You"
**Drummer** - Anton Fig, Peter Criss

In 1978, I lived with my mom on her parents' family farm in Gordonsville, TN. At the time, I had a bicycle, a Tonka dump truck, a shoebox full of Legos, and a drum set. On a typical summer day, I'd play with my Tonka truck and/or ride my bike outside until it became unbearably hot, which would've been around 10 am in the South. When I succumbed to the heat, I'd go inside and build something with my Legos, and then Grandma Edwena would make me my favorite, Beanie Weenies, for lunch. After licking the bowl, I'd stay in my room and play drums for the rest of the day.

I had access to my mom's green, fold-out suitcase record player and all of her old 45s, which included The O'Jays, The Temptations, Booker T. & the M.G.'s, and more, but the first album I ever owned was KISS' *Dynasty*. The details of when and how I acquired it are hazy, but suffice it to say, in 1978, a seven-year-old black kid rocking out to KISS wasn't exactly the norm.

*Dynasty* came into my possession right around the time my interest in drums had led to me attempting to hear what guys were playing on all the music I was listening to. The beauty of *Dynasty* for me was that the drumming was relatively straightforward. Straightforward enough that my ear could listen and draw connections between what I was hearing and my limited vocabulary...or so I thought. *Dynasty* quickly became my go-to play-along record, and I would jam out to it all day; THAT is why KISS' *Dynasty* is on my list!

## Grandmaster Flash and the Furious Five, *The Message* [1982], "The Message"

I am old enough to remember the dawn of rap music. There was a point during my lifetime when rap music WASN'T... followed by a time when suddenly, rap music WAS! Released in 1979, historians might give the nod to "Rapper's Delight" for the first rap song, but for me, the first rap song to peg the needle was "The Message" in 1982. As previously mentioned, my parents separated when I was six years old. There was no custody battle or legal proceeding; my mom basically "went back home" and took me with her. My home was Gordonsville, TN, where I lived with my mom and my grandparents, Cecil and Edwena Carter, on their family farm. Eventually, my parents reconciled and ultimately chose to cohabitate once again—so it was back to Kent, OH. We lived in an apartment complex called Silver

Meadows, more commonly known as Silver Ghettos. I was a chubby, nerdy, ten-year-old black kid with a pronounced Southern accent and a penchant for the band KISS... so obviously, I fit right in.

I did my best to actively lose my accent, which is surprisingly easy when you put your mind to it. I connected with my peers less through KISS and more through hip-hop; we would even bring out the cardboard and make terrible attempts at break dancing. In the way a clothing fiber gets caught, and twists into your beard, the song that wove itself into the tapestry of my new "urban" existence was "The Message" by Grand Master Flash. It wasn't just the song on the boom box; it represented my transition from farm kid who picked strawberries, shucked corn, and blew up wasps nests with firecrackers to wannabe "urban" kid who learned to roller skate, listened to hip-hop, and sucked at breakdancing.

The significance of "The Message" goes even deeper; I learned it word for word. On bus rides home from the 4th grade, I would stand up on my bus bench and start from the top, "Broken glass, everywhere / people pissin' on the stairs you know they just don't care / can't take the smell, can't take the noise / got no money to move out, I guess I got no choice..." — and I swear, I'd perform the entire song down, word for word. That is the importance of that song in my life, and THAT is why "The Message" is on my list!

## Yellowjackets, *Four Corners* [1987], "Postcards"
### **Drummer** - Will Kennedy

*Four Corners* by The Yellowjackets represents the first time I heard the combination of jazz fusion intellect with pop music sensibilities wrapped in a sheen of impeccable musicality. The Yellowjackets didn't reinvent the wheel, but some might argue they reinvented Weather Report. If memory serves, I saw The Yellowjackets live before being familiar with their music. My father took me to a Yellowjackets concert, and I was immediately blown away by their drummer, Will Kennedy. Will possessed so much technical facility, but at the same time, he displayed such dynamic and creative phrasing.

*Four Corners* isn't just drumming ear candy; there are harmonic complexities that tickle your ear in addition to soaring improvised melodies that you walk away singing. *Four Corners* was a reminder that music doesn't have to be chops OR musicality. This record juxtaposes the strength level of The Rock with the beauty level of Mother Nature, and THAT is why *Four Corners* is on my list!

John Scofield, *Blue Matter* [1986], "The Nag"
**Drummer** - Dennis Chambers

During high school, while living in Columbia, Maryland, a suburb of Baltimore, I had the privilege of taking private lessons with an all-time great instructor, Grant Menefee. Grant threw EVERYTHING at me — time stuff, technique stuff, groove stuff, fill vocabulary stuff, and MUSIC stuff! Within a moment of MUSIC stuff, Grant said, "I want you to listen to this." What he shared was a tune by John Scofield called "The Nag." "The Nag" is a track from the *Blue Matter* record featuring Dennis Chambers on drums. I sat. I listened. I absorbed. And when the track was over, I asked, "So, who's the percussionist on that song?" Grant said, "Percussionist?" I replied, "Yeah... the percussionist... obviously that's not one guy... who's playing all the other stuff?" Grant said, "That's ONE guy... the drummer, Dennis Chambers." We had a fight which I lost. I couldn't believe ONE person was generating all that information from the drums department.

*Blue Matter* was my first exposure to the bone-crushing chops of the one and only Dennis Chambers. I had never heard anything like that, and at that moment, my head exploded. Around that same time, I was told, "Don't only listen to your heroes, also listen to your heroes' heroes." By way of that philosophy, I discovered Billy Cobham and Zigaboo Modeliste; I have Dennis Chambers to thank for that. *Blue Matter* was my introduction to Dennis Chambers and some of his influences, which in turn influenced me, and THAT is why *Blue Matter* is on my list!

---

## Fishbone, *In Your Face* [1986], "Knock It"
**Drummer** - Philip 'Fish' Fisher

In 1988, I was a sophomore at Oakland Mills High School in Columbia, Maryland. As a freshman, I had worked very hard to make the marching band snare line, and now, as a sophomore, I was hoping to try out for jazz band. After school, I was alone in the band room, practicing on the drum set, when a head popped into the band room door. The head belonged to a student named Dave, and he said, in short, "We should jam together sometime." Cut to: I loaded the kick, snare, and hats of my Pearl BLX drum set into my mom's 1978 Firebird and she delivered me to Dave's house, where I set up my drums in the living room. Dave had his guitar plugged into an amp there, and he started playing who knows what... and along with him, I started playing who knows what, and just like that, I was playing music with not a record but another actual person. At that moment, Dave Sitek became the first ever musician I played with.

That day, we played and played... jammed, rocked out, whatever idea either of us threw out, the other threw one back. It went like this until the neighbors called the police, who eventually showed up and asked us to keep it down. And we did...until we didn't, and the police were called by the neighbors again. This jam day led from one connection to the next, ultimately forming a kick-ass high school rock band called Akamilli.

Akamilli played talent shows, clubs, backyards, community centers, and pretty much anywhere there was a stage. It was quite a fantastic ride through my high school years, and much like rapping "The Message" years earlier on my fourth-grade bus, being in Akamilli garnered attention and, on some level, helped keep me from getting beat up...

One day, my bandmate Dave says...

**DAVE:** You have to check out this band?!
**NATE:** What band?
**DAVE:** Fishbone
**NATE:** Fishbone? That sounds so dumb
**DAVE:** Trust me
**NATE:** Okay, dude

Dave played me "Knock It" from the Fishbone record *In Your Face*, and within eight bars, I was convinced this was the best band I'd ever heard! Eight more bars went by, and then another and another, and when the song finished, I had an all-time favorite band, which remains as such to this day!

Fishbone is meaningful on multiple levels. ONE is that all the members are incredible musicians. TWO is that they have historically been committed to creating that which they are moved towards rather than that which is most financially advantageous. THREE, Philip

Fisher on the drums is a monster! I have been a fan for ages, and I've stolen much of what I play from Philip. Frequently, when I listen to Fishbone records, I remember where I stole things from.

Fishbone is my all-time favorite band. They were introduced to me in high school, resulting in a lifelong influence, and that is why FISHBONE, *In Your Face*, is on my list.

# Ian Maciak

*"As time passed and I got deeper into electronic styles, I was pleasantly surprised at how well the rhythms and style I learned from him transferred over."*

I an Maciak is an independent drummer and producer celebrated for his precise, machine-like playing infused with a touch of humanity. Specializing in electronic music genres such as D&B, breakbeat, footwork, UK garage, and IDM, he crafts drum sample packs for platforms like That Sound, Test Press, Bandlab, and Splice. Ian also collaborates with numerous sensational artists including Machinedrum, Shigeto, Tony Grey, and Roman Bulakhov, showcasing his versatility and expertise in the electronic music realm. Here are Ian's choices…

**First of all, can you talk about your immediate family and how they contributed to your development?**

I started with my immediate family because I grew up in a house where everyone played music, which seemed like a no-brainer. My mom, dad, and older brother are all multi-instrumentalists, so from an early age, I had seen them all play band or solo music. My parents exposed us to a wide range of music and never forced their taste on us so that I could consume a wide range of styles. While I was young, my parents would often take us to see the Pittsburgh Philharmonic Orchestra, and that's when I caught the bug of wanting to play percussion, so I enrolled in our school system band program. I started out playing mallet percussion *cue a line of 3rd graders smashing "Hot Cross Buns" on glockenspiels* then eventually moved to battery percussion and much later graduated to the drum kit.

## Mr. Oizo, *Analog Worms Attack* [1999], "Flat Beat"

French music producer/DJ Mr. Oizo was my second pick. My older brother always had 411 skateboarding videos growing up, and I'd always want to watch the one with this particular song, which I obsessed over. It had a driving distorted bass line, laser-focused electronic drum parts, and bright syncopated synths; I fell in love with it. I learned it was "Flat Beat" by Mr. Oizo. I later found the album *Analog Worms Attack* and would listen to that album constantly. It was my first introduction to electronic music, which I don't think I was aware of then because of how organic the album feels and sounds. Fast forward twenty years, and it's still one of my all-time favorites.

## Battles, *EP C/B EP* [2006]
### Drummer - John Stanier

Third was the powerhouse drummer for the band Battles, John Stanier. I first heard him with that group during my first year of college, and he's still hands-down one of my favorite players. The frenetic pace and power that he played with absolutely enthralled me. He's the only player that I decided to emulate. I first heard him on the Battles EP, and when their debut album, *Mirrored,* came out, I immediately bought it to start learning all of his parts. As time passed and I got deeper into electronic styles, I was pleasantly surprised at how well the rhythms and style I learned from him transferred over.

---

**Can you talk about the "perfection" of electronic music?**

The fourth pick was more of an idea about electronic music and its precision; I was highly motivated to recreate the "perfection" of those drum parts, leading me to better understand my relationship with time and manipulate it. I had a relatively healthy obsession with "being the drum machine" for a long time. As I learned more about electronic music and how the styles I liked were made, I realized they weren't as perfect as I thought. So, my focus shifted to manipulating my time against and between the click/grid rather than the click controlling what I played.

---

**Can you discuss your experience seeing Die Like a Dog Trio (Hamid Drake, William Parker, Peter Brötzmann) and free/avant-garde music?**

For my last pick, I chose a performance by the Die Like a Dog Trio, which I attended and had a chance to talk to the drummer Hamid Drake. After the show, we were smoking cigarettes, and he planted a simple idea in my head that is still rattling around. I told him that I was also a drummer and that his performance made me so excited to return to my studio and practice. He stopped me dead in my tracks, took the cigarette out of his mouth, and said, "Don't go back and practice. Go back and play." I'm not religious, but that was a "come to Jesus" moment for me. The entire two-hour car ride home, I kept thinking about "go and play," repeating it to myself. To be clear, he was not telling me NEVER to practice but to focus more on being in the moment and practicing performing. It completely changed how

I thought about using my time in the studio and preparing for live shows. Out of all of my picks, I think this one has affected me the most. So with that, go and play.

# Joe Plummer

*"I noticed he took a deep breath when he sat down, so I did the same. And from then on, I watched him build the most beautiful pieces of improvisational music I had ever seen."*

J oe Plummer, a drummer from the Pacific Northwest, has made significant contributions to indie rock. He's collaborated with renowned bands such as Cold War Kids, Modest Mouse, The Shins, Man Man, Mister Heavenly, and a newer project called The Coromandelles, alongside Matt Maust from Cold War Kids and Daniel Michicoff from Tijuana Panthers. Here are Joe's choices…

Wilco, *Yankee Hotel Foxtrot* [2002], "I Am Trying to Break Your Heart"
**Drummer** - Glenn Kotche

I was sitting on an orange couch in my living room in Portland when I first heard this. There are a few different drum grooves in this song. It starts with a distant, more atmospheric groove that's simple but not hard-hitting. It's almost like you're grooving unconsciously — a simple, open ride/kick/snare pattern; I will always love that. Then the AMAZING phrase in the verses is off-kilter yet sticks with the bass guitar. It sounds sporadic, but it's not; it's a groove!!!! This is one of Glenn's most genius moments in writing, and if I am forced to pick one of the millions of genius moments Glenn has brought to us, this is it. Mid-song, he settles into a straight beat that includes most of the phrase from the first verse and the opening groove. He's illustrating three sections in one beat. It lifts and carries the tune.... then....it all falls apart in beautiful percussion freedom. It was completely eye-opening. I may have heard something like this before, but it did not stick like this. There is no way I will ever be able to get this out of my drumming brain. Did I say genius enough yet? Probably not. GENIUS.

---

**Would you like to discuss seeing Mark Guiliana at the Revival Drums' Anniversary show?**

I had moved to Seattle, and José (owner) invited me to the Revival Drum Shop (in Portland, OR) for their 10th anniversary. The shop has always meant a lot to me, and I was psyched that I wasn't on tour so I could go. I found Mark Guiliana on the internetosphere and was psyched about his playing. His freedom and openness inspire me, and I often think about his style and sonic delivery when practicing alone. On my way down, I talked with a fellow drummer who had heard about the party but could not make it, and he told me Mark was playing. I must have overlooked the lineup or not looked at all. Either way, I was beyond excited. I intentionally stopped myself from imagining what or how he would play to keep it as much of a surprise as possible.

For whatever reason, I was in a weird mood when I got to Portland, and until Mark played, I was mainly hanging by myself despite all my Portland drumming homies being at the show. I planted myself close to the stage left when he started playing to get a good view of his hands. I noticed he took a deep breath when he sat down, so I did the same. And from then on, I watched Mark build the most beautiful pieces of improvisational music I had ever seen. His patience and skill worked in tandem. His knowledge of sonic projection was on point, and his looseness responded to his technical rigor and vice versa. His playing kept me "in" by implying and reminding me of what I'd just heard and what might come next. It touched me like no other piece of live music. I may have teared up. I probably did — I definitely took another deep breath.

Minutemen, *Double Nickels on the Dime* [1984], "Anxious Mo-Fo," "Jesus and Tequila," "#1 Hit Song," "Martin's Story" **Drummer** - George Hurley

*Double Nickels On The Dime* is significant because George Hurley redefined punk and punk drumming for me. Along with Watt and Boon, this record showed me that punk was not all just style and aggression but actual energy. You didn't need to play 40 million miles an hour to deliver "fuck you" anymore. You could do it with a funk beat, a no-wave groove, or even classic rock vibes, ala CCR or Blue Öyster Cult. Punk and music were officially bonded for me once I heard the Minutemen.

**Anxious Mo-Fo:** It starts with heavy, open toms before switching to a thin, funky verse. It all sounds so fierce to me, and the attack on the drum screams as loud as D. Boon. **Side nerd note**. Consider that Alex Van Halen and George were both using Black Dots around this time; compare the two, and you'll know what I'm talking about when I say George had punk energy.

**Jesus and Tequila** and **#1 Hit Song:** Probably the first time I recognized groove. The ride work in both songs taught me a lot.

**Martin's Story**: Again, punk-funk. At this point, I had yet to hear no wave or James Chance. I couldn't believe that this type of aggression and energy could live in a beat like this.

---

**Can you talk Tony Allen's influence on your playing?**

Naturally, Tony Allen came to me with my interest in Nigerian and other "nontraditional" African artists. When I first started listening to Fela Kuti, of which Allen was the musical director and drummer, I listened to the band's overall sound rather than just "the drummer." I was looking for cohesiveness and a "sound"; I quickly found it with Fela and other '60s- and '70s-era African artists. It wasn't until I started picking apart this sound that I discovered, obsessed over, and ultimately fell in love with Tony Allen. NO ONE can make a drum set sound like one instrument like Tony. Imagine a truck is a drum set. In the back of the truck is the band. Imagine that truck starting up and driving the band into an infinite sunset with a limitless amount of fuel. Each bump, hill, and corner maneuvered in the smoothest, most humble, most confident way imaginable, leaving you with a distinct rhythmic memento, bar after bar, bar over bar. And then, of course, all his work with Damien Albarn is incredible.

---

Public Image Ltd., *The Flowers of Romance* [1981],
"Four Enclosed Walls"
**Drummer** - Martin Atkins

This beat is simple and spacious with the power of Bonham, and a "tribal" groove that became a must-do for all the gigantic '80s new wave bands. I credit Atkins with being the first (or one the first) to show us the light and power of this kind of drumming in synthetic and angular Western pop music. These drums and this whole record, in general, got me thinking about and experimenting with reverb and

295

room sound. On the flip side, playing the "Four Enclosed Walls" beat a little faster with a tighter sound becomes an excellent hip-hop beat. As a youngster, it didn't hurt that someone told me that Dale Crover soundchecked with this beat.

# Tim Baltes

*"...I come back to this album, again and again, to help recenter my session playing as more music-focused than self-serving."*

T im Baltes is a multifaceted talent, excelling as a drummer, writer, social strategist, and self-proclaimed drum history enthusiast. His online persona is characterized by humor and authenticity, drawing in a dedicated fan base. With a blend of skill and personality, Tim has carved out a niche for himself within the drumming community, ensuring his lasting presence and influence for years to come. Here are Tim's choices...

The Weakerthans, *Hopelessly Devoted To You, Vol. 4* [2002]
"Aside"
**Drummer** - Jason Tait

I was 12 or 13 years old when I went to a shop at the local mall and bought *Hopelessly Devoted To You, Vol. 4*, a five-dollar music compilation CD from Hopeless Records. It introduced me to many great bands, including Atom And His Package, Samiam, Fifteen, and The Weakerthans. Hearing John K. Samson's songwriting with Jason Tait's drumming immediately formed a strong bond between me and the music of that last band. The Weakerthans' song "Aside" is a punk rock anthem that brought an emotional maturity to that genre that I'd never heard before, and the feeling I got from listening to that music kept me combing through the band's discography for the next decade. The Weakerthans quickly became a favorite of mine, and Jason Tait became a drumming hero to me, but I'd never imagined how my own drumming would connect me with Jason in my late twenties.

When early 2018 rolled around, I was surprised to see that Jason followed me on Instagram. I immediately sent him a message and told him how his work on the Hopeless Records compilation mentioned here changed my drumming and my life forever. He sincerely thanked me and offered to meet me when he was touring through the states later that year. I picked him up from a venue in Milwaukee, Wisconsin, and we spent time driving around the city. He wound up buying a vintage Ludwig Pioneer snare from the music store I used to work at, and he played it that night with the band. We went thrifting together at Antiques on Pierce. And on the way back to the venue, we grabbed tacos from a great little food truck. I even hit the drums later that night—the same ones he used on so many Weakerthans records.

Throughout the entire experience, it felt like two normal dudes just hanging out, catching up, and enjoying time together. I'll always pinch myself about that day because I continue to remember it as one of the most wonderful times I've ever had, and it all started with one amazing song on a CD I bought as a kid.

---

## ...And You Will Know Us by the Trail of Dead, *Worlds Apart* [2005], "Will You Smile Again For Me"
**Drummer** - Jason Reece

In college, I worked at a music shop where the crew would sell gear and listen to their favorite tunes all day long—and this is where

I first heard the ...Trail of Dead record *Worlds Apart*. Unlike other music I'd enjoyed at this point in my life, this wasn't just a set of songs. This album played out like one single connected, cinematic-like composition. As a drummer, I appreciated the album's punk rock spirit and the two percussionists rhythmically rooting every track.

Many of my favorite records exhibit how to use drums in the most musical way; this is no exception. From the drum set to the tympanis and the auxiliary percussion, I took from all of these elements to better inform how I approach drumming. For this reason, I come back to this album, again and again, to help recenter my session playing as more music-focused than self-serving.

---

**Can you discuss the impact of Eric Moore's solo at the 2003 Guitar Center Drum-Off?**

YouTube was a game-changer for drummers in the early 2000s. It shattered so many barriers for anyone looking to learn the craft. Eric Moore's 2003 Guitar Center Drum-Off Final video introduced me to learning drums via YouTube. Moore's work in the video perfectly represents gospel chops, supreme showmanship, and musicality. Seeing this in my teens helped me get ahead of the curve on gospel chops, and I incorporated this into disparate music styles like hardcore, metalcore, and death metal. Those skills developed further and further as my music career went on, and I can thank this video from Eric as the catalyst for my flashy drum fill voicings.

Eric Moore makes gospel chops look effortless in his videos, and visually grasping this concept gave me the foresight to ensure that any stickings I use in my fills should feel the same. I appreciated the chops of drummers like Eric Moore, Teddy Campbell, Calvin Rodgers, and the like. From each drummer, I'd try to take little pieces that I loved from their drumming and incorporate them into my work. Pieces of

299

the inverted paradiddle, hertas, swiss army triplets, and blushdas became canon in my musical voice, spurred from the incredible solo Eric Moore posted on YouTube decades ago.

---

**Can you describe your experience at winter NAMM 2019 and how it impacted your drumming?**

In January 2019, I quit my full-time corporate gig of more than five years to turn my part-time music work into a full-time career. I walked out on my last day of work to immediately drive over two thousand miles to NAMM in Anaheim, California. NAMM ultimately showed me that all the work I'd been doing on Instagram in my mom's basement actually had an impact in the real world.

So many moments at NAMM gave me an understanding that my work mattered, and that realization continues to fuel my drumming today. During my first day at NAMM, education superstar Mike Johnston stopped me to say how much he loved what I do. Scott McPherson, Elliott Smith's drummer, believed in me so much that he introduced me to every big wig he knew at the show. People from around the world wanted a picture with me. Interactions like these were the first time I'd truly felt like the little videos I published on social media made a big difference in giving my work visibility. I have to reminisce on that time today because it's a great reminder that drives my content creation across many online outlets.

---

**Can you tell the story of your performance at Revival Drum Shop's 10th Anniversary Party in 2019?**

Just a month after Winter NAMM 2019 concluded, I performed to a sold-out crowd at Mississippi Studios in Portland, Oregon, surrounded by hundreds of drummers, including heavy hitters like

Matt Chamberlain and Mark Guiliana. That experience made me feel like I was on the level to continue performing professionally from that day on. After I gave a little speech about what Revival Drum Shop and the drumming community meant to me that concluded in a drum solo, Mark Guiliana came up to me and told me what I did was beautiful. As I approached the green room, Matt Chamberlain (a personal hero to me for his work on The Wallflowers' *Bringing Down The Horse*) said to me, "Hey, man. You can really play drums!" And while practicing in the back of Revival Drum Shop for the weeks preceding that day, José Medeles, a guy who played drums for The Breeders, Joey Ramone, Ben Harper, and Modest Mouse, would laugh hearing my gospel chops and repeatedly called me a shredder.

Receiving compliments on my approach to drumming from artists with such heavy histories in this industry felt like an acceptance of my drumming. Those experiences felt like permission to keep doing what I was doing the way I was doing it. I fostered a drumming voice that had value to these folks, and I can't describe that feeling as anything other than blissful. As such, I'm so thankful to José (Revival Drum Shop's owner) for giving me the opportunity, Jake (the shop manager) for giving me moral support and a bed to sleep in, and Keary (the shop's restoration expert) for his friendship and support during that time. I'll never forget those moments or those people for as long as I keep kicking.

---

### *HONORABLE MENTIONS:*

The records, videos, and moments above represent my story until the *Big Fat Five* released the podcast in 2021. In the years since, my work in drums has continued to shift. I work a day job again, allowing me to do drumming in a way that serves my spirit solely. My content creation has shifted from mostly silly to mostly serious, from short-form to long-form videos, and from entertainment to education. Today, I'm trying to use my decades of drumming to help the next generation find inspiration in the same way others before me inspired my work. And I hope that you take from this little section in a book that selflessness can drive your work forward more than anything else. And the side effect of positively pushing others forward in their careers is pretty cool too! On that note, I'd like to thank Ben, Kris, and BFSD for the opportunity to jump on their podcast to create videos in late 2021 and early 2022 for their social media accounts and for the inclusion of my words here. It's well-known that drummers are a wide-reaching, tight-knit community of folks who seek to bolster one another, and the BFSD team is a great example of that unfettered kindness and support.

# Quinton "Q" Robinson

*"...it inspired me to aim for a similar dynamic and captivating approach when I play the drums, making the listener want to pay close attention to every beat."*

Quinton "Q" Robinson is a studio and touring drummer, programmer, music director, clinician, and consultant. He currently serves as the touring drummer for Broadway's *Hamilton*, having previously toured with *Ain't Too Proud*, a musical centered around The Temptations. In addition to his Broadway work, Q has collaborated with artists such as Avery Sunshine, Bobby Brown, Anthony David, and many more. Here are Q's choices…

## Walter Hawkins, *Love Alive II* [1978], "Until I Found the Lord" **Drummer** - Joel Smith

When I began playing drums, I'd set up my drum kit next to my dad's record player. The first song I tried to play along with was "Until I Found the Lord" by Walter Hawkins. Back then, I had no idea who the drummer was, but the drums drew me in whenever that song played. Only later did I discover the exceptional Joel Smith as the mastermind behind that captivating groove.

Right from the first downbeat, his passion was palpable. Every note he played was infused with intentionality; it significantly influenced my approach to playing with purpose and conviction.

---

## Toto, *Toto IV* [1982], "Africa"
### **Drummer** - Jeff Porcaro

Growing up, we were limited to listening to gospel music. However, one summer, just before my family's annual vacation, my dad bought a new car for my mom, which came with a complimentary cassette tape containing the best songs of that time. During the ride from the dealership, I was permitted to listen to secular music for the first time. The very first song that played was "Africa" by Toto. The moment I heard the intro, I couldn't wait to return to my drum kit and try to recreate that mesmerizing groove. I was around nine and was unaware of Jeff Porcaro's status as a legendary drummer, but the song deeply touched me. Even now, whenever I play the drums, I aim to evoke the same impact that "Africa" had on me during that memorable moment.

---

## Yellowjackets, *Four Corners* [1987], "Sightseeing"
### **Drummer** - Will Kennedy

During my first year in college, my music knowledge beyond gospel was limited. It was Jonathan Joseph, my applied drum kit instructor, who introduced me to the incredible drumming of Will Kennedy and the music of The Yellowjackets. The first song I encountered was "Sightseeing" from their *Four Corners* album, and it left me completely astounded. I couldn't help but wonder, "What is this music?" This pivotal moment marked the beginning of my love affair with jazz.

From then on, I delved deep into jazz music and the drummers who played it. At 17, I couldn't quite articulate it, but something about Will's playing resonated deeply with me. Perhaps it was his remarkable musicality or ability to navigate through various time signatures effortlessly. Whatever it was, I knew I wanted to incorporate this style into my sound.

Over the years, I've been fortunate enough to have meaningful conversations with Will about life and music, and he has had a profound impact on my personal and professional journey. Now, coming full circle, I've been fortunate to release my debut single, titled "The QR Code." Anyone who listens to it will undoubtedly recognize the profound influence that Will Kennedy and Yellowjackets have had on shaping my musical expression.

---

## Mint Condition, *Definition of a Band* [1996], "Definition of a Band"
**Drummer** - Stokley and Chris "Daddy" Dave

Around this time, despite having played the drums for a few years, I was still quite impressionable. Mint Condition's *Definition of a Band* album was an absolute masterpiece, blending gospel, R&B, jazz, pop, and rock in the most tasteful way possible. I found myself listening to it every day, almost exclusively, and even when I had to listen to other music for school or church performances, as soon as I finished, I'd go back to that album.

It had such a powerful hold on me!

Every song on the album resonated deeply with me, making it

difficult to pick just one favorite. However, the first song, featuring a double drum solo with Stokley and Chris "Daddy" Dave, left a lasting impression. I had never witnessed two drummers play together in such a synchronized, dynamic, and musical way before. It inspired me to aim for a similar dynamic and captivating approach when I play the drums, making the listener want to pay close attention to every beat.

## Snarky Puppy, *We Like It Here* [2014], "Lingus"
**Drummer** - Larnell Lewis

At this point in my career, I became fully immersed in the music world with a keen awareness of both Larnell Lewis' incredible dynamic style and the powerhouse that is Snarky Puppy. What captivates me the most about "Lingus" is its musical ambition and flawless execution. The rhythmic virtuosity that Larnell demonstrates here is something I aspire to achieve. This performance is exceptional, from the perfectly tuned drums to the precise frequency of his cymbals. My ultimate goal is for my playing to resonate as deeply with others as Larnell's playing resonates with me.

## Kirk Franklin, *The Rebirth of Kirk Franklin* (Live) [2002]
**Drummer** – Terry Baker

Terry Baker is one of our most prolific gospel drummers, with a remarkable track record spanning over 25 years. Throughout his illustrious career, Terry has been consistently in demand, making him one of the music industry's most recorded and sought-after drummers. For the past 15 years, he has been the recording and touring drummer for the gospel music icon Kirk Franklin while collaborating with other industry elites.

Terry is widely recognized for his precision and purposeful playing. I've had the privilege of knowing Terry for more than 20 years. As time passes, our friendship continues to grow, and he has remained a steadfast mentor, a true friend, and an enduring presence in this dynamic industry.

Terry's charismatic drumming style has impacted all present-day gospel drummers. As the younger generation of drummers, our elevated position is thanks to the foundation laid by remarkable individuals like Terry Baker.

# Rod Elkins

*"Your mood will inherently poke through your playing...find the mood that puts the band and the people listening to it in an excited state. Somewhere where they want to be."*

R od Elkins, a native of Huntington, West Virginia, is the drummer for Tyler Childers and The Food Stamps and El Dorado. He is celebrated for his distinctive style that merges the influences of legendary drummers like Al Jackson Jr. and Levon Helm while maintaining his unique contemporary flair. Here are Rod's choices...

### The Band, *The Band* [1969], "Jemima Surrender"
### Drummer - Richard Manuel

I used to think this was Levon Helm on the drums, but this track features Richard Manuel, the piano player, behind the kit. Levon often stepped out front and played mandolin on different songs, and Richard was a fantastic drummer. In this case, Levon played the electric guitar.

His playing on this track still interests me, for it's naivety that is now present in my mind. Richard wasn't a gigging drummer who knew what certain things were on the drums; this was spirit and soul. The simplicity of the quarter notes on the hi-hat through the verses to only be matched by sudden 8th notes in the bridge uplifts the song without adding more than what was needed. His intention was song first. As a phenomenal piano player and an even better singer, Richard Manuel brought to the drums what we, as practicing players, search for every time we sit down behind the kit, and that's a certain carelessness in playing that you forget about being a drummer that may often worry about timing, technique, or perfect note placement. Richard makes you want to be a musician first on the drums.

## The Band, *Rock of Ages: The Band in Concert* [1972], "Don't Do It"
### **Drummer** - Levon Helm

Okay, but seriously, this IS Levon Helm. You can't deny it here. From the beginning, he and Rick Danko set the stage for the grooviest five minutes of your entire life. The horns enter with a slinkiness and draw that puts you directly south of the Mason-Dixon line.

Levon was fascinating in his orchestration in arranging this song, where he would often switch the hi-hat and ride cymbal patterns from what we usually see in terms of hi-hat in the verses and ride cymbal in solos and possibly over choruses. Levon was genius in putting the ride cymbal over the verses here and only giving you a glimpse of that in the choruses. As a Holland-Dozier-Holland cover done previously by Marvin Gaye, The Band elevated this tune to unbelievable heights of what groove and feel should be at all times. Levon Helm, probably one the greatest singers of all time, plays his drums as he sings, with a flair and punch that harmonizes with himself.

This song was the first time I ever heard by The Band outside of "The Weight", which to me was just the *Easy Rider* song. My first experience seeing and hearing Levon was the grainy YouTube video from this concert in the university music library in 2009, and it changed my life forever. I've chased his soul in performance ever since.

## Herbie Hancock, *Thrust* [1974], "Palm Grease"
**Drummer** - Mike Clark

In college, I studied jazz, and we had to take a Jazz History course, naturally. The tests included a list of songs from a particular era or decade, and you had to know the song, who played on it, where it was recorded, and its release date. In this instance, the test song was "Spank-A-Lee" at the end of this *Thrust* record, but the first track, "Palm Grease," stuck with me.

Mike Clark puts you on the path to greatness with a two-handed, 16th-note groove that displaces some off-beat stabs before looping back around to do it again. It's clean. It's funky. And it's perfect. There are no lyrics here, except for the beautifully woven interplay between Mike Clark's drumming and the auxiliary percussion throughout the song. It might be the first song where, after I got over the shock of hearing how deep a pocket could get, my ears immediately went to the different shakers, agogo bells, wood blocks, and what seems like multitudes of other toys layered on top. The call-and-response nature of the back-and-forth almost takes the place of vocals that could be there but are not. It's a great example of how to support instrumental music on the skins melodically.

## Steely Dan, *The Royal Scam* [1976], "Kid Charlemagne"
**Drummer** - Bernard Purdie

"Pretty" Purdie laid it down on this one. When I heard this, I had an apartment that I had to fix up to make livable, and I arrived at my new home with nothing more than a turntable and three records: a random Nat King Cole, Blackfoot's *Strikes*, and *The Royal Scam*. I must have repeatedly flipped this record for an entire summer.

Purdie's playing is effortless, and how he fills over the bar line with a quiet crash during one of the many hooks of the song demonstrates that it can be done and done tastefully. He incorporates an accented "and" hi-hat pattern with a solid backbeat to lay in with plenty of snare chatter to keep you interested. It's flawless and tough to try and do well. Interestingly, in country music, I utilize the "Waylon" beat with a similar "and" accented hi-hat pattern with plenty of space to groove. It works so well in many ways and can be disguised to look and feel however needed. I have to mention that besides Levon's kit, Bernard's tones are immaculate, and I hope to figure out what he used on this recording someday.

---

Billy Joe Shaver, *Unshaven: Live at Smith's Olde Bar* [1995]
"Hottest Thing In Town"
**Drummer** - Craig Wright

This entire record is a clinic on what a burning hot bar band should sound like—from the timeless songwriting of Billy Joe Shaver to the absolute must-hear, imitate country-rock performance of Eddie Shaver on guitar, to Keith Christopher and Craig Wright melding as one unit for them to flex their prowess.

I don't think Wright's playing reinvented the wheel, but how he locks in with the rest of the band and delivers the true meaning of these songs is pure joy. I still can't rhythmically comprehend the opening fill. I never hear the entrance at the particular moment it happens, but it sends you into outer space as if it were a beer-laden honky-tonk. It feels so mean and raw, with perfect nuance, grit, and intention. I gathered mostly from this recording how to harness your mood when you play. Your mood will inherently poke through your playing. As an

311

anxious individual, you can hear it in my playing if I'm not having a particularly good day. It's essential to find the mood that puts the band and the people listening to it in an excited state. Somewhere where they want to be. Somewhere that lets people think they can do anything.

This record is super special to me; I took two different copies of this record on two different formats from my dad and wore them both out beyond playability. I still have the CD, but it does not work anymore. It's transparent now; I tried to fill the scratches with toothpaste as a young man. All in all, this is a record best enjoyed in its entirety.

## Waylon Jennings, *Lonesome O'nry and Mean* [1973], "Lonesome O'nry and Mean"

"Lonesome, O'nry and Mean" is probably one of the most remarkable representations of the "Waylon" backbeat. I couldn't confirm who played drums on the song, but the entire record lists a who's who in the history of drumming in country music. Buddy Harmon was the famed Nashville A-Team session drummer who essentially invented country drumming; Ritchie Albright was the long-time live drummer for Waylon; Willie Ackerman has played on everything that most folks are familiar with, such as Marty Robbins' "El Paso" and rounded out with a tenure on HeeHaw. Then there's Larry London, who plays the title track (I believe). Larry came from Motown to Nashville and is credited for bringing the backbeat to country music; I can't think of anyone else it could have been because, as he was a former session drummer for Motown, this groove lives deep inside you. Rock beat #1 has never sounded better.

312

Creedence Clearwater Revival, *Willie and the Poor Boys*
[1969], "Down On The Corner"
**Drummer** - Doug Clifford

*Willie and the Poor Boys* by CCR is super special because it's the first music I remember hearing as a kid. I had a PlaySkool record player that played plastic records, and I put a greatest hits CCR record on it from my dad's collection, and it played! I remember being scared of how different and haunting it sounded...but in a good way. Fast forward some months, and I was at my grandparent's house, where my granddad had a 1951 Wurlitzer jukebox (that I now own), and I discovered that this scary music was on it, too. I hit play, but I needed to hear it louder. I stuck my head between the pillars in the front and got my head next to the speakers while "Down On The Corner" beat me to submission until I was freed. Luckily, it was a 45 single, so it didn't wholly become my first hearing loss experience, but I still love CCR. It's funny, but I can smell what CCR sounds like.

# Kellii Scott

*"...he sent me up to the bungalow on the property with my drums and a copy of [This Album]."*

K ellii Scott is Los Angeles-based drummer for American alternative rock band, Failure. Over the years, he's lent his powerful drumming to Blinker the Star, Campfire Girls, August Everywhere, Still in Rome, Linda Perry, Veruca Salt, James Blunt, and Christina Aguilera among others. Here are Kelli's choices...

## AC/DC, *Highway to Hell* [1979], "Walk All Over You"
### Drummer - Phil Rudd

This was the first record I ever played drums along to; it was shortly after my parents bought my first drum set when I was 12. It would show me the basics of the drum set and playing rock music. My older brother gave me this record, and I don't think he knew how important this album would be in teaching me the fundamentals of playing drums.

So, a funny story about this record — at the beginning of my career, I was doing a record with Michael Beinhorn, and there were two drummers in the band (myself and John Molo, who was also Bruce Hornsby's drummer). I was young, inexperienced, and in jeopardy of losing my part of the record if I didn't get it together quickly. So

Michael Beinhorn gave me one last shot at getting it together; he sent me up to the bungalow on the property (where we recorded for the weekend) with my drums and a copy of *Highway to Hell*. He explained to me that, as a drummer, your primary function is to make people dance, and if you could imagine that there's a race and a finish line, the first thing that should cross that finish line is your kick drum. *Highway to Hell* had all the information I needed to come back on Monday and successfully record my parts for the record. I begrudgingly obliged. I thought AC/DC was simple, and I knew every note inside and out on that record. But armed with Michael's words, I realized that, while I could play the notes, I wasn't playing the intention; I was forcing the energy and drive that Phil Rudd naturally brought to the music. Frankly, that's why all of those AC/DC records are so fantastic. I'd like to say that I came down from the bungalow transformed and won back all my songs from the clutches of defeat (that wasn't the case), but I learned an important lesson. It would take some experience to make this lesson part of my ethos. Thank You Micheal Beinhorn and also to John Molo. I would not be where I am today without those two gentlemen.

## Rush, *All The World's A Stage* [1976], "2112 Overture"
**Drummer** - Neil Peart

First, where would rock music be if Neil Peart didn't exist? No other drummer in modern history held the dreams and imagination of every teenage boy with a drum set in the way that Neil Peart did. He embodies what I love most about all my favorite drummers: they sound and feel unique. That, above anything, is the most important takeaway. If you are going to be IT, you have to be able to channel your insides and do that one thing that only you can do: BE YOU. Neil Peart was the opposite side of the coin for me. Where Phil Rudd showed me the basics, Neil Peart showed me how to be musical and technical and how to accompany music in its entirety instead of just being the backbone. *All The World's A Stage* was another album my older brother gave me, and I became obsessed and spent hours studying every note. I would take the bottoms off old snare drums and tune them up like high toms to play those huge fills. When I learned how to play a Neil Peart song, there was no greater accomplishment because it was so technical and otherworldly.

## KISS, *Destroyer* [1976], "Flaming Youth"
### **Drummer** - Peter Criss

My love of all things KISS goes back to before I played the drums, maybe around seven years old. I would run home every day from school to imagine myself as a rock star jamming for hours to KISS records, especially *Destroyer*. At first, I imagined myself a guitar player/singer, either Gene or Paul, but I would eventually play pots and pans to KISS records by default. So, an emerging theme is becoming clear here about my older brother's impact on my choices and direction early on. I would rock out with tennis rackets and smash them at the end of the "show" just like the band would, so when I ran out of tennis rackets, I picked hockey sticks, first demolishing my own, then moving toward doing the same to my older brother's. Just as my "show" was climaxing, in walked my brother, not happy with what I was about to do to his hockey stick; he proceeded to crack me over the head real good. Thus, I switched to pots and pans, eventually becoming a drummer. My early experience with Peter Criss was beyond my understanding as a drummer, but as a kid who had to become a Rock Star, there was no more considerable influence on me; I knew what I would do before I even played a single note on a drum set. That being said, Peter was a fantastic drummer; the hooks he wrote and the unique choice of notes he played on all of those songs were incredible.

## Iron Maiden, *Number of the Beast* [1982], "Prisoner"
### **Drummer** - Clive Burr

I saw this older kid wearing this crazy shirt with a long-haired skeleton man holding the devil on strings like a puppet. I was in awe and slightly freaked out, but I had to find out whatever this was. A musician buddy told me it was "EDDY," Iron Maidon's mascot, and he loaned me his copy of *Killers*. I instantly fell in love and set out to own and learn all things Iron Maiden. When I got *Number of the Beast*, it changed everything; I loved Clive Burr's playing, most notably his speed and intensity; it was so technical but also very punk rock and raw. I also found him very musical but reserved; he didn't overplay but certainly didn't underplay. The song "Prisoner" immediately captured my attention; that drum intro was fantastic. I chose this because I love Clive's playing and thought his use of space and melody perfectly connected to the music he was playing. He was reacting to the music, the purest way to write your parts. This is the Clive Burr influence I've carried with me ever since.

## Led Zeppelin, *In Through The Out Door* [1979], "Fool In The Rain"
### **Drummer** - John Henry Bonham

I grew up hearing a lot of Led Zeppelin coming out of my older siblings' rooms, but I would only make them my own years later. Although there was a moment or two when my older brother would make me learn a section of a Zeppelin song, and once I knew it, he would parade me in front of his friends to show them how cool I was and what a great drummer I was becoming. "The Rover" intro and "Rock and Roll" intro come to mind — I was definitely not playing either one correctly then. So, around 19 or so, I learned that John Bonham was considered the greatest rock drummer, and you had to know everything about Led Zeppelin, so I proceeded to learn everything I could, just like every aspiring drummer. I cleared my schedule and devoted my life to doing nothing that wasn't Led Zeppelin and John Henry Bonham; his contribution to the trajectory of rock drumming is unrivaled. In my mind, *In Through The Out Door* was the pinnacle of his skill; every note on that record is perfect. Are there better records? Maybe. But from my perspective, that one has the perfect amount of notes. His contribution to me is just that, trying to leave the perfect amount of space unfilled with drums while being as musical as you can be without ruining that relationship.

# Carson Gant

*"...you talk about falling down the stairs! It blows my mind and makes me feel like I still don't hear triplets correctly."*

C arson Gant, a Canadian drummer, excels in replicating the essence of early programmed hip-hop beats. His seemingly effortless performances conceal unmatched precision and groove. Moreover, he introduced an innovative twist to the traditional loop library system through his website, oneuploops.com. Here are Carson's choices…

### Salvador Dream, *UR* [1994], "Connection"
**Drummer** - Ray Garraway

I had the great fortune of studying with Ray Garraway before he passed in 2013. He's my favourite drummer, bar none. This groove has so much weight and gravity that it feels like repeatedly getting kicked in the gut. I don't know what else to say about Ray. He changed everything for me. This track is just the tip of the iceberg of the musical beauty that flowed out of Ray—check him out!

### Herbie Hancock, *Mr. Hands* [1980], "4 A.M."
**Drummer** - Harvey Mason

The drumming on this track is bouncy, light, articulate, and free as a bird. The interplay between Jaco, Herbie, and Harvey is straight-up telepathic. *Mr. Hands* was one of the four records my drum teacher, Andy Ericson, sent home with me after our first lesson. The others were *Voodoo* by D'Angelo, *Peace Beyond Passion* by Meshell Ndegeocello, and a live concert by Screaming Headless Torsos. Similarly to Jack DeJonette, Harvey has an incredible ability to zoom out and see the whole track, and then thread a beautiful line from start to finish.

John McLaughlin, *After The Rain* [1995], "Sing Me Softly Of The Blues"
**Drummer** - Elvin Jones

Elvin's first fill a few seconds into "Sing Me Softly Of The Blues"… it's like…you talk about falling down the stairs! It blows my mind and makes me feel like I still don't hear triplets correctly. It's just a great example of what makes Elvin Elvin. Thankfully, I was turned onto him at a young age with *A Love Supreme.* I just lucked out that I liked it when I heard it, and I've listened to it hundreds of times since. But, this record by John McLaughlin showcases an older Elvin and is recorded so beautifully. It's as heavy as you can get for me. Elvin riffs on the time so much, especially in this song. I still don't understand how he did it. It's pure voodoo.

Weather Report, *Weather Report* [1982], "Dara Factor One"
**Drummer** - Peter Erskine

320

Peter Erskine's sound is incredible. He plays with so much intention and vibe. His improvised breakbeat drumming at the beginning of "Dara Factor One" masterfully sets up the rest of the song. The whole arrangement floats; it's the best way to describe it. Peter is a master player, but I don't know if he gets enough credit. He is undoubtedly one of the greats, and this whole record showcases that perfectly.

Sly & Robbie, *Sly & Robbie Present Anniversary* [2009],
"Crazy Baldhead"
**Drummer** - Sly Dunbar

This song impacted me in the same way as Ray Garraway's drumming in the song "Connection" from earlier; it's all about gravity, weight, and separating the limbs into different universes. I'm pretty sure this beat is partially programmed (and I was going to choose the original "Crazy Baldhead" by Bob Marley), but this one is laid out more on a grid. It's gratifying to play along with, as it's very consistent. There are no true fills; it just has dropouts and whatnot, so you can sit there and focus on making your hi-hat float up top while your kick and snare slam deep into the abyss — or die trying anyway :)

# Ira Elliot

*"...I discovered that my right hand could easily do a bunch of random stuff wholly disconnected from the two other limbs that kept a simple, repeating pattern."*

I ra Elliot gained prominence as the drummer of Nada Surf, joining the band in 1995. In addition to his time with Nada Surf, Ira has performed with artists like Bambi Kino, Vulcan Death Grip, Drive-Ins, The Fuzztones, Headless Horsemen, The Deans of Discipline, Champale, Maplewood, and Harvey Danger. Here are Ira's choices...

Stevie Wonder, *Talking Book* [1972], "Superstition"
**Drummer** - Stevie Wonder

I have a very clear memory — I was about 12 or 13 years old, around 1975, and just beginning as a drummer. I was struck by the opening four measures which, unbeknownst to me, was Stevie playing drums, so I headed down to the basement with my sister's copy of *Talking Book*, put on my big, over-the-ear headphones with the curly cable, and spent about fifteen or twenty minutes figuring it out which some years later I realized was my first step towards independent coordination.

The kick and snare are simple and straight, but the hi-hat plays a little "melody" over the top with a lot of shuffle-y dotted 8th notes — sort of like the intro to "Poison" by Bell Biv Devoe.

This was the first time I experienced the feeling of my kick and snare doing one thing while simultaneously having my right hand play something against it that wasn't just 8th notes the whole time. I discovered that my right hand could easily do a bunch of random stuff wholly disconnected from the two other limbs that kept a simple, repeating pattern. For a self-taught player, it was a significant revelation. Even then, I remember feeling that I was suddenly a slightly better drummer; I had crossed into a new realm of possibilities.

Funny, I played it in a cover band recently, now almost 50 years later, and realized I've been playing the main beat wrong all this time. I always assumed the bass drum was just on one and three, which is how a typical rock drummer might play it, but it's four on the floor, and when you play it correctly, you get its full, funky pulse.

I'm still learning things from "Superstition."

PS—In 2015, at a New York charity event for AMFAR, I had an opportunity to meet and play with Stevie Wonder (a video does exist). Knowing I only had a few seconds to say something, just before we went onstage, I shook his huge hand and told him he was absolutely one of my favorite drummers of all time. Oh, that was a perfect day.

---

### Led Zeppelin, *Led Zeppelin IV* [1971], "Misty Mountain Hop" (the long fill at 3:56)
### **Drummer** - John Bonham

Over the years, I regularly return to Zeppelin recordings for drumming inspiration, like almost every rock drummer. Bonham's unique style and sound are fun to emulate, and among the vast arsenal of skills he possessed was a confidence that allowed him to pull off unorthodox, heart-stopping fills occasionally.

If I had to pick only one that exemplified his unique musical abilities, it would be the remarkable fill that leads to the outro of "Misty Mountain Hop" at 3:56. The song begins with four bars of the main riff with a fat fill at the end to kick things off. That riff happens for two bars between each verse, and Bonham plays a short, punchy fill to lead the band back in each time. On the fourth and final one, which is four bars like the intro, John begins his wind-up with a bar-long, smooth, and fast single-stroke roll, then transitions into a crushing snare and tom fill that's so brilliantly and boldly executed. It never ceases to amaze me. That's Bonzo in full flight. We should all aspire to this level of musical freedom and invention.

---

## The Knack, *Get The Knack* [1979]. "Your Number Or Your Name"
### **Drummer** - Bruce Gary

I was the perfect demographic for this band in 1979. Sixteen years old and along with being into punk and new wave, my Beatles fixation raged on unabated.

The nerve of these guys not only to have their first album cover resemble the cover of *Meet the Beatles,* but then the back cover was shot so not only could you see the band (posed) onstage in white shirts, black skinny ties, and pointy shoes but you could also see their guitar and mic cables on the ground and TV cameras pointed at them like a scene from *Hard Day's Night.* I loved it.

"Sharona" (with that propulsive beat lifted from Smokey Robinson's "Going to a Go-Go") sold the record, but to me, the stand-out drum track on an album loaded with incredible drum performances is "Your Number Or Your Name." Bruce Gary's playing is full of detail and personality—combining fiery energy and fierce precision recorded beautifully to capture the unmistakable quality of a one-time live band performance. Small ruffs on the snare in the verses, lightning-fast 16th-note fills across a four-tom kit, breathtaking stops, and subtle dynamics make it a thrill ride where the drums are concerned.

There's a video of the band playing this song in 1979 live at Carnegie Hall (another Beatles move), which I highly recommend watching. You rarely see a drummer firing on all cylinders like this.

---

## Elvis Costello & The Attractions, *Imperial Bedroom* [1982]
## "Beyond Belief"
## **Drummer** - Peter Michael Thomas

To many, the Geoff Emerick-produced *Imperial Bedroom* is considered Elvis' magnum opus (his *Pet Sounds*), which may or may not be the case. But there's no arguing that few bands can claim a run of albums the likes of *This Year's Model, Armed Forces, Get Happy!!, Trust, Almost Blue,* and *Imperial Bedroom*. Damn. And who sits at the center of the mighty Attractions?; The great Pete Thomas—another drummer who combines electric, spontaneous energy (which is not always easy to capture in a recording situation) with a musicality that allows him to shift between classic styles while remaining modern and inventive effortlessly.

The opening track, "Beyond Belief," sets the pace. Pete builds the track dynamically, starting minimally with just a hi-hat and kick drum falling on the "two" for three quick verses, then (building) playing the kick on two and four for one verse, then (building) playing four on the floor for one verse before finally exploding to a Latin rhythm on the bell of the ride and adding that fat, dead *Abbey Road* snare.

From there on, through the fading end choruses, he unleashes an array of rumbling tom fills and Copeland-esque, off-beat cymbal accents. I was truly inspired. Now that I'm thinking about it, I recall that when I joined Nada Surf in 1995, my first thought was that this band could use a fast and furious, Pete Thomas-style drummer, and, well, I tried for a while, but in the long run they just ended up with an Ira Elliot-style drummer. :)

## Cream, *Disraeli Gears* [1967], "Sunshine of Your Love"
## **Drummer** - Ginger Baker

Ok. I'll be completely honest. I don't consider Ginger Baker a major or minor influence on my playing. I never spent any time listening closely or playing along with Cream or Blind Faith albums. I wasn't drawn to Ginger's decidedly unique style for whatever reason...which is fine. I flourished despite my ignorance.

But, I can say that the sound of Ginger's drums on this particular song is a perfect example (along with the overwhelming majority of rock albums made between 1965 and 1975) of the "Ludwig sound." It's not an easy thing to describe, but "woody" is a term that comes to mind; "warm" and "attack-y" are two more. It mainly concerns the thin shell design and the round-over bearing edges, which allow more head-to-shell contact. To use a technical term, more thwack.

My first serious kits were Ludwig, and while I played several different brands through the '80s and '90s—Tama, Pearl, Premier, Slingerland, C&C—I eventually went back to Ludwig, and that's where I will stay.

# Jeremy Taggart

*"Listen to him in conversation; you are transfixed because you know you will learn something important. He performed the same way."*

J eremy Taggart is a prominent Canadian drummer, radio host, and author. He gained widespread recognition for his tenure as the drummer for Our Lady Peace from 1993 to 2014. Alongside his work with OLP, Taggart has collaborated with several esteemed Canadian musicians, such as Tom Cochrane, Geddy Lee, and the Arkells. He remains a respected figure in the Canadian music scene. Here are Jeremy's choices...

John Coltrane, *A Love Supreme* [1965], "Resolution"
**Drummer** - Elvin Jones

My father was a jazz drummer, so I grew up listening to John Coltrane. I was almost afraid of what sounded so chaotic and aggressive hearing it as a youngster. Once I started drumming, I realized how controlled and technically sound it was. Elvin was so far ahead of his time in how he played, adding so much motion with his polyrhythmic approach. He was transported from the future, leaving jaws on the floor for generations. I'm happy to have met him and know his genius up close; it was truly the highlight of my career.

## The Band, *The Band* [1969], "Up On Cripple Creek"
### Drummer - Levon Helm

In my first band, we played several Band songs, which quickly made me a better drummer. With the way Levon chopped up faster tempos into halftime grooves, and how the drums led the music, I don't think any drummer in history had his conviction. Listen to him in conversation; you are transfixed because you know you will learn something important. He performed the same way. He was and always will be the coolest of the cool!

## The Who, *Quadrophenia* [1973], "The Real Me"
### Drummer - Keith Moon

When I first heard The Who, the reckless abandon of the drums immediately drew me in; Keith jumped to the forefront of the music. I'm not sure if it was because Keith was the best musician in the band or if the songs were designed to let him shine via the simplicity of Pete's writing. Whatever the case, I thought Keith was the first proper rockstar. He was head and shoulders above the rest of his band and got attention by being insane. That connected with me.

## Frank Zappa, *Joe's Garage* [1979], "Token of My Extreme"
### Drummer - Vinnie Colaiuta

I studied with Rick Gratton, who studied with Gary Chaffee, Vinnie [Colaiuta's] teacher. Rick taught me so much about odd-note groupings, where you chop up bars with weird combinations between your hands and feet. You can get lost fast in that world, and listening to how Vinnie used just enough of it changed the game for me. I realized you can be fancy occasionally, as long as it has taste and groove. "Token of my Extreme" is an excellent example of that.

---

## Soundgarden, *Badmotorfinger* [1991], "Searching With My Good Eye Closed"
**Drummer** - Matt Cameron

Matt was the first drummer I got into when I first started in OLP. I love how he carves out accents within fills and plows through complex sections, always stomping his hats in perfect measure. His time is super strong—crushing simply through odd tempos in such a stylish manner. He's a sweetheart, a true punk, and the nicest guy you would never want to fuck around with. I would say that he's the most individualistic modern rock drummer ever.

---

# Randy Cooke

*"...I still hear the downbeat and the phrase opposite to where it is. I've talked to other drummers about this to see if I'm the only one with this glitch."*

R andy Cooke, a Canadian-American session/touring drummer, has collaborated with artists like Dave Stewart of Eurythmics, Ringo Starr, Billy Joel, Five For Fighting, Smash Mouth, Colbie Caillat, Kelly Clarkson, and numerous others. As the quintessential sideman, Randy's guiding principle is succinct: "It's not about playing more things; it's about playing the right thing." Here are Randy's choices...

## Rickie Lee Jones, *Rickie Lee Jones* [1979], "Chuck E's In Love"
### Drummer - Steve Gadd

I was first introduced to this track/album by my parents. They both loved singer-songwriter-style music, so I grew up listening to a lot of that, one of those artists being Rickie Lee Jones.

Gadd was known for iconic grooves like "50 Ways to Leave Your Lover," which is a drum lesson nestled inside a two-bar phrased groove.

This song was Rickie Lee Jones' bona fide hit, and the drum performance throughout serves the music perfectly, but it's the fill out of the breakdown into the last chorus that had me lifting the needle off and on the record a few hundred times.

As always, Steve plays the track musically, but when the kit is featured, his signature style and approach to some of his killer linear groupings come out in that fill.

The way he uses his hi-hat foot as a 16th note just before a hi-hat strike with a stick, creating those different tonal textures, shows up in this one moment, in this one drum fill. (The hi-hat foot before a hi-hat stick hit can also be found in his "50 Ways" groove.)

I was able to take away more than one lesson from that drum fill, which was not just lifting and learning the mechanics and the feel of it, etc., but playing a song throughout and only choosing one moment to feature yourself on the kit—creating a moment where your ears perk up. You notice the drummer has slipped a little diamond into the song, and in just that one spot, and that's what I felt was so special about this particular song. It's a lesson in musicality, restraint, and control.

## The Police, *Reggatta De Blanc* [1979], "Walking On The Moon"
### Drummer - Stewart Copeland

Growing up in Toronto (primarily a rock n roll city), I found myself in my first band, playing exclusively funk and reggae, which made me stand out a little bit as a player.

When I was first exposed to The Police, I immediately latched on because Copeland incorporated reggae fills into punk and pop songs, which was incredible to me as I hadn't heard anything like that before. I instantly loved the band and Stewart's approach in general. One of the things the band did frequently was use delays on the kit, which created all of these new counter rhythms in the song.

Other than loving this song, there is a section where Stewart plays off the delays, creating new rhythmic motifs, etc. This choice prompted me to try and emulate those effects without the delays and create new sticking challenges, rhythmic challenges, and phrasing challenges, which I still incorporate in my playing.

---

### Prince, The New Power Generation, *Diamonds and Pearls* [1991], "Diamonds and Pearls"
**Drummer** - Michael Bland

OK, do I need to say it? The triplet fill going into the last chorus of this song is one of those fills that every drummer who loves Prince mentions. The groupings of four over the triplet fill were genius while incorporating flams at the beginning of each phrase; it was like an '80s arena rock drum fill stuck in the middle of an R&B ballad, which just elevated the energy tremendously. Bland's drumming performance on this track exemplifies playing the right thing in every section of the song.

This song, in particular, did that thing to me where, to this day, I still hear the downbeat and the phrase opposite to where it is. I've talked to other drummers about this to see if I'm the only one with this glitch. You know that thing where a guitar player or a keyboardist starts an intro with a rhythmic phrase, and you hear it in one spot, yet it's actually in another? And now it's imprinted in your brain, and you can't hear it any other way? This is what happens to me throughout this song for some reason.

---

### Prince, The New Power Generation, *[Love Symbol]* [1992], "Sexy M.F."
**Drummer** - Michael Bland

This is another favorite track of mine with the aforementioned mighty Bland on the kit. It is another example of an out-of-the-ordinary groove that entered the mainstream.

The fact that the snare is on the downbeat alone tells you you're in for an exciting journey from bar to bar. It swings, has internal dynamics as far as accents and ghost notes, and, just like Gadd's "50 Ways," is an iconic drum groove that every drummer should strive to lift. This is another one of those "drum lessons inside a groove" that became a signature song drum feel.

## The Time, *What Time Is It?* [1982], "777-9311"

The "777-9311" groove is an anomaly in that it was never a real drummer playing it, but it's become almost a right of passage, a challenge for drummers to lift it. It comprises two Linn drum samples joined together based on linear Garibaldi-esque feels. The displaced kick & snares falling on the second 16th note of each beat also proved challenging. As expected, a few incarnations are floating around out there, but they're all super hard, both sticking and technique-wise—a must-have groove in your arsenal.

# Willy Rodriguez

*"This is the purpose of music. A spiritual ritual. It is what we feel that we cannot describe. It is being able to talk to our creator."*

Willy Rodriguez is a Latin Grammy-winning drummer, percussionist, and bandleader. He's performed with jazz and Latin jazz greats like Jason Palmer, Papo Vasquez, Dezron Douglas, and Dave Liebman. Willy also collaborated with diverse artists such as Omar Rodriguez-Lopez, Mon Laferte, and Domino Saints. In 2019, he won a Latin GRAMMY for his work on Mon Laferte's album *Norma*. Notably, Willy recorded The Mars Volta's self-titled seventh album released in 2022. Here are Willy's choices…

Rage Against the Machine, *Evil Empire* [1996],
"People Of The Sun"
**Drummer** - Brad Wilk

As a drummer, a period of growth is crucial for every professional. Those first albums that won your heart are the musical foundation for your technical and artistic development. During my childhood in Puerto Rico, I was surrounded by many musical genres with Afro-Caribbean influences from Cuba, Jamaica, Panama, the Dominican Republic, and Mexico. In turn, US television became prevalent on a larger scale during the 1990s. Musically, MTV and VH1 greatly impacted Puerto

Rican youth, creating a musical change for the local market. The salsa genre was declining, and the younger generation was captivated by these new musical genres. *Evil Empire* mainly caught my attention because of the mix of hip-hop with a hard rock accompaniment. It was the perfect record to study simple rhythms with a certain degree of difficulty. The requirement to maintain a solid and energetic pulse that this record provides makes it a tremendous exercise that personally helped me develop rhythmic muscle memory and stamina.

The album's political message resonated with me as well. Puerto Rico is an imperial colony, and the political limbo in which the nation finds itself continues to impact the daily lives of all Puerto Ricans in a total economic recession. The courage to fight for the truth through music is admirable and noble.

## John Coltrane, *A Love Supreme* [1965], "Pursuance"
**Drummer** - Elvin Jones

Music is magic. It is a mesmerizing and intoxicating power. But more importantly, music is spiritual. As a student, I immersed myself in all the musical genres that this instrument requires. Jazz is the genre that brought the drum set to the musical universe, which was totally enchanting. It was related to my folklore and that of the other Caribbean countries. I felt at home. John Coltrane's *A Love Supreme* was my spiritual awakening. The record made me declare this is what I want to do. With his energy and empathetic accompaniment, Elvin Jones provides Coltrane with the perfect canvas to communicate with the afterlife. This musical connection separates itself from anything visual, physical, or earthly. This is the purpose of music—a spiritual ritual. It is what we feel that we cannot describe. It is being able to talk to our creator.

Chick Corea, *The Chick Corea Elektric Band* [1986],
"Silver Temple"
**Drummer** - Dave Weckl

Dave Weckl should have a bust in the White House. His musical ability and technical input to the instrument cannot be overstated. The success of this group was quite influential in sacred and popular music. It was instrumental, complicated, and sometimes danceable. This album was a headache to transcribe. A single theme could take me months to decipher. But the musical and technical enrichment was evident and real. Its linear combinations and Afro-Caribbean nuances surprised me in the transcription process. Everything is possible to use if you know its history. As soon as other musical genres start to plant themselves in your muscle memory, the musical reactions begin to navigate in different places making your performance richer and more entertaining. As drummers, we can fall into the prisons of musical genres. As musicians, this is precisely what we should not do. We should be able to accompany anyone.

Michel Camilo, *Triangulo* [2002], "Descarga For Tito"
**Drummer** - Horacio "El Negro" Hernandez

It is impossible to ignore Cuba's significant influence on my island of Puerto Rico. I grew up listening to son montuno, guarachas, cha-cha-cha, guaguancó, abakua, and local rhythms like the plena and the bomba. At the same time, I rarely saw these rhythms played on a drum set. Percussionists always surrounded me, but when I met Horacio "El

Negro" Hernandez and his charming execution and interpretation of all these rhythms, my life changed forever. His independence and respect for the Caribbean vocabulary taught me to appreciate much more what the Latin color is and its possibilities. The ability to cover the work of several percussionists with just two sticks and their ostinatos is an example of his genius. This album represents that for me. The Caribbean drummer is a musician who should be able to cover any musical style with a wide-ranging vocabulary. It is essential to mention that to master this musical style, knowledge of percussion is crucial to understanding and executing these genres.

Squarepusher, *Hard Normal Daddy* [1997], "Beep Street"
**Drummer** - [Boss] DR-660 drum machine, Yamaha QY700 sequencer.

When electric musical instruments began to emerge around the 1940-1950s, it caused a tremendous musical revolution that significantly impacted the drums. The size of the drums started to vary, and the construction of cymbals was adjusted to create more volume and definition. In turn, new genres formed; the rest is history. When the drum sequencers began to appear, everything changed. Its clarity and consistency create a perfect pulse for the dancer. What Tom Jenkinson, aka Squarepusher, achieved with a QY700 for this album was innovative. Producers usually use these instruments in a very conservative way, and for some genres, they are chosen with a solid and precise pulse to support their composition. In the case of Squarepusher, it is the opposite. His use of the sequencer interacts with his musical motifs and even brings a degree of improvisation to the drum sound. The clarity the sequencer brings to this interaction presents a great challenge for conventional drummers. By imitating drum machines, many new styles have been brought forward. This will continue to influence future generations of drummers globally.

# Mike Dawson

*"In effect, he was my first drum teacher, and I'm forever grateful for those lessons in simplicity, power, and control."*

Mike Dawson is the Chief Creative Officer at Drum Factory Direct and former Managing Editor of *Modern Drummer* magazine. Dawson's multifaceted career in both journalism and music solidifies his status as a respected figure in the drumming world, influencing and inspiring drummers of all levels worldwide. Be sure to check out his gear-focused podcast, *Drum Candy*. Here are Mike's choices…

Tone-Loc, *Loc-ed After Dark* [1989], "Wild Thing"
**Drummer** - Alex Van Halen

"Wild Thing" was a huge radio hit shortly after I got my first drum set. I remember playing along to the beat and fills on the back of the headrest of my parent's Chevy Cavalier. It was the first time I figured out how to play a drum part note-for-note, which got me super-stoked to learn more songs. It didn't hurt that the main fill in "Wild Thing" was sampled from the song "Jamie's Cryin'" by Van Halen, who I had already been obsessed with due to their constant airplay on MTV. This is the song that started it all.

## The Ramones, *Road To Ruin* [1978], "I Just Want to Have Something to Do"
### **Drummer** - Marky Ramone

I got my first set of drums, a cheap three-piece kid's kit from the Sears catalog, the Christmas of 1988. My brother also got an electric guitar and already knew how to play a few songs from the Ramones' classic album *Road to Ruin*. So the first thing we did was jam to the riffs of the opening cut, "I Just Want to Have Something to Do." After a few minutes, my brother said, "You have to play the bass drum too." (I was only playing the song with my hands on the tiny 10" splash and snare.) After a few minutes of struggling with the independence, I finally figured out how to play the beat with the bass drum added. It was a major breakthrough, and I spent the next few weeks learning all the beats and fills on this album. In effect, Marky Ramone was my first drum teacher, and I'm forever grateful for those lessons in simplicity, power, and control.

## U2, *War* [1983], "Sunday Bloody Sunday"
### **Drummer** - Larry Mullen Jr.

I'm left-handed, but I forced myself to play a right-handed setup. For the first couple years of drumming, I played two-handed hi-hat grooves and all my fills, starting with the left. But when I tried to play the classic intro beat to "Sunday Bloody Sunday," I kept getting tripped up by the sticking. One day, I tried to play it starting with the right hand, and it was exponentially easier. From that moment, I committed to relearning how to play everything with a right-hand lead. The cool side-effect is that now I can start patterns and fills with whichever hand creates the most logical flow. Thank you, Larry Mullen Jr!

---

## KISS, *Dressed to Kill* [1975], "Love Her All I Can"
## **Drummer** - Peter Criss

My first band was with my uncle Ryan. He grew up playing '70s and '80s hard rock, so we learned a lot of classic songs by Led Zeppelin, AC/DC, and KISS. The track "Love Her All I Can" from KISS' *Dressed to Kill* has a funky cowbell groove and a handful of short drum breaks towards the end. I learned the beat and breaks note-for-note, which instilled confidence in me. I was twelve years old. I've since transcribed hundreds of beats and solos across many different genres. KISS was the first.

---

## Dennis Chambers, John Scofield, Gary Grainger, Jim Beard,
## *Serious Moves* (Instructional Video) [1992]
## **Drummer** - Dennis Chambers

I ordered *Serious Moves* after seeing an ad for it in *Modern Drummer*. I didn't know who Dennis Chambers was, but the cover of the VHS reeled me in. Dennis looked cool, and he was playing a badass Pearl kit. I had just gotten a Pearl Export set and was a massive fan of Will Calhoun (who played Pearl at the time), so it was a done deal. Once I got the video, I watched it from start to finish daily for five years straight. Dennis became my all-time favorite drummer, and his playing in this video set the bar for how technical, funky, and musical one could be on the drum set to the stratosphere. Unrivaled, still to this day.

# Jesse Kongos

*"His playing seemed to embody a particular type of emotional cocktail, including aggression, humor, cool, nonchalance, and utter commitment."*

J esse Kongos is the drummer, as well as one of the primary songwriters and singers, for the band KONGOS, which comprises Jesse and his three brothers. While Jesse handles multiple instruments in the studio, his live performances primarily feature him on drums, where he also takes on lead vocals for several songs. A self-taught drummer with a diverse heritage spanning from England to South Africa to Phoenix, Jesse brings a unique approach to rhythm and arrangements, contributing to the distinctive sound of KONGOS. Here are Jesse's choices…

Keith Jarrett Trio, *The Cure* [1990], "The Cure"
**Drummer** - Jack DeJohnette

If I had to pick one drummer, gun to my head, it would be Jack DeJohnette. I love his work over the different eras, but the Keith Jarrett Trio is arguably the best example of genius + genius + genius = more than 3x genius. The virtuosity of each player, the emotional depth, and the embodiment of universal communication principles through improvised music is a combination that has an ongoing impact on me.

In this track, aside from the wild, snare-off, explosive, tension-filled playing, the melodic use of all the toms, and restrained cymbals, what I get most out of it is what I can only describe as profound presence and intention. The recording has captured an alignment of 3 individuals fusing into an interleaved Trinity-like force. Sounds grandiose, but I mean it.

---

## Bob Marley & The Wailers, *Rastaman Vibration* [1976], "Roots, Rock, Reggae"
### Drummer - Carlton Barrett

This was never my favorite Bob Marley song, but it was in my practice playlist for time and feel. I would play along with records that I thought had A+ pockets. There are very few examples of what I consider God-tier groove/feel/time (however you want to put it), and this is one of those. With in-ears, I would try to get into the physical space of the record; this is possible with good sound isolation, where I'm less concerned with the sound of my drums and more focused on having some sort of body awareness and sense of the physical impact in sync with those players.

---

## Stevie Wonder, *Talking Book* [1972], "Superstition"
### Drummer - Stevie Wonder

Aside from this record's global, timeless popularity, I'm particularly drawn to Stevie Wonder's drumming and hi-hat feel. There's something special about the records where he played most/many of the instruments. He's a rare case of genius who can layer things down himself and make it feel like a live, cohesive band of compatible individuals. His approach has influenced me from a playing standpoint as well as production and mixing. Few people can get away with mixing the hi-hat as loud, present, and dominant as him.

## Led Zeppelin, *Houses of the Holy* [1973], "D'Yer Mak'er"
### **Drummer** - John Bonham

Like 99.9% of drummers, the inescapable influence of John Bonham has had an effect on me. Aside from the iconic sound, feel, tuning, and recording techniques defining his sound, I'm again drawn to the quality of intent I perceive in his playing. This song is an excellent example of putting one's "self" totally into each stroke. His playing seemed to embody a particular type of emotional cocktail, including aggression, humor, cool, nonchalance, and utter commitment.

## Bill Withers, *Still Bill* [1972], "Use Me" (at 2:40)
### **Drummer** - James Gadson

This song was terribly overplayed on the local classic rock station in Phoenix during my teenage years, so it took me a long time to return to it and truly appreciate it. The sheer perfection and underplayed polish of the whole track are legendary. Gadson has a relentless commitment to being an anchor, generously providing a solid foundation and never stepping out to a point of what might be perceived as egoism. This track belongs in the history books, and for me, the crown jewel of the track is around 2:42 when the "baby, baby" clap syncopation happens. There's something so perfect and climactic about it that the choice to be so sparing and almost throw it away as a passing gem makes it that much cooler.

---

### HONORABLE MENTION:

I must give a quick shout-out to Phoenix-based session/touring drummer and long-time family friend Todd Chuba. Growing up, I never officially took lessons from him, but family hangouts, spending time together, talking and watching him at local gigs were highly influential in that I got quality time with a world-class player with impeccable time, taste, and versatility who was very encouraging and supportive to me

---

# Kyle Jeffrey Crane

*"I went and bought a left foot clave after seeing him...working on it alone in the practice room was really fun. Maybe that's why I was single in college."*

Kyle Jeffrey Crane is Los Angeles-based percussionist renowned for his work with producer Daniel Lanois and an array of well-known artists, including Madison Cunningham, Neko Case, Rufus Wainwright, Conor Oberst, and Kurt Vile. In 2019, Kyle released his debut album, *Crane Like the Bird*. Additionally, he showcased his talent as a drum double in the acclaimed film *Whiplash*. Here are Kyle's choices…

Terry Bozzio, *Drawing The Circle* [1998], "Maya"
**Drummer** - Terry Bozzio

My first drum clinic ever was Terry Bozzio. He played a 40-piece drum set with toms tuned to the chromatic scale! I took home his CD, which was solo drums, and from then on, I was really into composing.

Led Zeppelin, *Physical Graffiti* [1975', "The Wanton Song"
**Drummer** - John Bonham

346

"The Wanton Song" was the first thing I had heard that had a lot of double strokes on the kick as part of a beat. Also, I loved how aggressive Bonham's playing was. I later had a drum set made by CC to replicate his kit.

---

### Soilwork, *Stabbing The Drama* [2005], "Blind Eye Halo"
### Drummer - Dirk Verbeuren

I went through a significant metal phase, and Soilwork was my favorite. Dirk was so clean live, and I loved all his parts. He plays with Megadeath now.

---

### Caribbean Jazz Project, *The Gathering* [2002], "Masacoteando (In The Grove)"
### Drummer - Dafnis Prieto

Dafnis was one of the first guys I saw with insane independence. After seeing him, I bought a left foot clave. I can't say I've even played it on a gig, but working on it alone in the practice room was really fun. Maybe that's why I was single in college.

---

### Kurt Rosenwinkel, *The Next Step* [2001], "Zhivago"
### Drummer - Jeff Ballard

Jeff's brush playing on this is so light and fluid. Even though he's filling a lot, the time never gets pulled down—I'm also a big fan of his stuff with Brad Mehldau.

---

# Index

# I

# J

# M

# N

# About The Author

Ben Hilzinger is a professional drummer, podcast host, and creative force in the music industry. Known for his work with bands like Cannons and Eve 6, Ben has performed on some of the world's most renowned stages. As the host of the popular podcast *Drummers on Drumming*, he explores pivotal stories, influential records, and polarizing topics that shape what it means to be a drummer today, bridging the technical and professional aspects of the craft with the pursuit of artistic expression.

With a passion for music, innovation through his work with Big Fat Snare Drum, and fostering community, Ben's contributions resonate far beyond the kit. Whether unpacking the nuances of drumming philosophy or sharing his own journey, his perspective inspires musicians and fans alike to think more deeply about their art.

Printed in Great Britain
by Amazon

57272627R00219